SAS
Action in Africa

Also by Michael Graham
Secret SAS Missions in Africa: C Squadron's Counter-Terrorist
Operations 1968–1980

SAS
Action in Africa

Terrorists, poachers and civil war
C Squadron operations: 1968–1980

Michael Graham

Pen & Sword
MILITARY
AN IMPRINT OF PEN & SWORD BOOKS LTD.
YORKSHIRE – PHILADELPHIA

First published in Great Britain in 2019 by
Pen & Sword Military
An imprint of
Pen & Sword Books Ltd
Yorkshire – Philadelphia

HB ISBN 978 1 52676 084 5
PB ISBN 978 1 52676 228 3

A CIP catalogue record for this book is
available from the British Library.

Printed and bound in the UK by TJ International Ltd, Padstow, Cornwall.

Pen & Sword Books Limited incorporates the imprints of Atlas, Archaeology,
Aviation, Discovery, Family History, Fiction, History, Maritime, Military, Military
Classics, Politics, Select, Transport, True Crime, Air World, Frontline Publishing, Leo
Cooper, Remember When, Seaforth Publishing, The Praetorian Press, Wharncliffe
Local History, Wharncliffe Transport, Wharncliffe True Crime and White Owl.

For a complete list of Pen & Sword titles please contact

PEN & SWORD BOOKS LIMITED
47 Church Street, Barnsley, South Yorkshire, S70 2AS, England
E-mail: enquiries@pen-and-sword.co.uk
Website: www.pen-and-sword.co.uk

Or
PEN AND SWORD BOOKS
1950 Lawrence Rd, Havertown, PA 19083, USA
E-mail: Uspen-and-sword@casematepublishers.com
Website: www.penandswordbooks.com

Contents

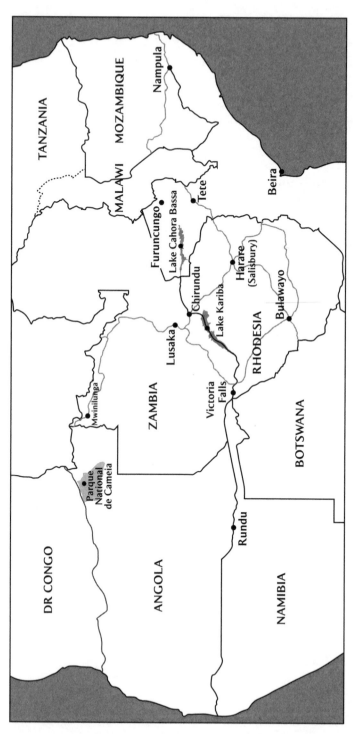

C Squadron SAS operational area.

Author's Notes and Acknowledgements

I walked into the Air New Zealand Koru Club lounge ahead of a flight to Wellington and sitting on his own in a corner was Wilbur Smith. I went over to him to say hello and after introducing myself said I had a question.

'Is it true that my mother used to do your medical prescriptions at Highlands Pharmacy in Salisbury back in the 1950s?' I asked.

'Absolutely true,' he replied without any hesitation. 'And how is Mrs Graham?'

We ended up sitting together on the hour-long flight from Auckland and chatted about Africa. He was especially interested in my time in the SAS.

Before going our separate ways he said, 'Mike, you should write a book. It was an extraordinary time in Africa and the world should know what part the SAS played in shaping history. It will be a great story.'

It took me a few years but after regular prompting by good friend André Louw in Sydney, I eventually got started. Wilbur Smith had said it would be a great story and that's what I wanted to write. I had no wish to write a precise, accurate history.

I needed help to achieve this so joined the New Zealand Society of Authors. Government department Creative New Zealand gives the society funds every year to assist and encourage new writers and they use this to pay for manuscript appraisals.

I applied twice without success, but after the second time the secretary called to say my problem was genre. I'd said my work was fiction but that was firmly rejected by the committee who said it was non-fiction.

I argued that I thought non-fiction was the truth, the whole truth and nothing but the truth, and while most of what I'd written was based on actual events I'd mixed things up and added detail to suit the narrative in each story.

I was told about 'creative non-fiction' or 'faction' as one of the committee put it. I changed my genre and got the grant.

That put me in touch with Caroline Martin. After leaving the *Otago Daily Times*, Caroline now helps new writers like me with professional editing.

Caroline has been wonderful to work with and her contribution has been immense, not just with the writing but also with the critical presentations to get the attention of potential agents and publishers.

Caroline's assistance continued with this second book and has been as professional as ever. I have been blessed with a great editor.

In May 2017, I went to England to meet my publishers, Pen and Sword. I didn't think Barnsley in Yorkshire would ever make my bucket list, but it did and I thoroughly enjoyed myself there. The small town is neat and tidy and Barnsley folk are some of the friendliest you'll ever meet.

Tucked away in the rabbit warren of the old *Barnsley Chronicle* building in Church Street is one of England's leading publishing houses. I was warmly welcomed by everyone at Pen and Sword, but would like to make special mention of publishing editor Henry Wilson and author liaison and marketing coordinator Katie Eaton.

With both of us being ex-army, Henry and I got along well and I am most grateful for the good advice he gave me regarding this second book. He told me to treat it as a completely new entity, pointing out that some readers will find book two before *Secret SAS Missions in Africa* so it made sense just to add to the original introduction and keep our team profiles.

Katie has done a sterling job marketing and promoting my books. I cannot thank her enough. Enthusiastic new authors like me need someone like Katie in our corner.

I left Barnsley and Pen and Sword feeling I was in good hands.

I am very grateful and my sincere thanks to you all.

Mike Graham

C Squadron SAS

Serving in the Long Range Desert Group and with the original SAS during the Second World War, Rhodesians had proved they were good Special Forces material, and it was this background and the offer of 100 trained men that in 1950 persuaded the British government to add C (Rhodesia) Squadron to the newly formed Malayan Scouts – later to become 22 SAS.

A and B squadrons in the new SAS were English-based units, with D Squadron formed in Scotland.

At the same time, both New Zealand and Australia formed SAS regiments and while there was close liaison with 22 SAS they retained control by keeping them as part of their own armed forces.

Three years later, at the end of a campaign to contain the spread of communism into South East Asia, the members of C Squadron were returned to Africa.

Here trouble was brewing, with a Mau Mau uprising in Kenya, with rebels in the Katanga province of the Belgian Congo, and with what was seen as communist-inspired dissent in other regions. The squadron was initially based in Ndola, Northern Rhodesia – now Zambia.

There were ups and downs in the years that followed before C Squadron eventually moved to what was then Southern Rhodesia and that became their permanent base. The Rhodesians had an air force with helicopters and DC3 Dakotas for parachute operations – both critical to SAS operations.

At the height of the Cold War the Russians, the Chinese and to a lesser extent the North Koreans were actively courting dissident political and tribal factions throughout Africa, training and arming them, and backing so-called 'liberation' struggles. Not that liberation interested them in the slightest – their eyes were firmly fixed on the vast mineral riches of the region, and nowhere more so than in central Africa: oil in Angola; copper in Zambia; gold, chrome, asbestos, nickel and coal deposits in Zimbabwe and Mozambique; platinum and diamonds in Botswana.

Ultimately they wanted South Africa but first they had to establish themselves in central Africa, and our job in C Squadron SAS was to make that as difficult as possible for all parties involved.

We operated with the Portuguese forces in Angola and made sorties into Botswana and the Caprivi Strip in Namibia, but predominantly our offensive was in Mozambique and Zambia where the terrorist camps were established for training and infiltration into the southern targets – starting with Zimbabwe.

We had three sets of gear.

Most often used was our NATO-style gear, which in terms of hardware was the Belgian-made 7.62 millimetre Fabrique Nationale (FN), a 'GT' version of the SLR used by the British Army and others. The FN was a beautifully made firearm. It was simple enough and robust enough for servicemen and was exceptionally reliable. Most of all, though, it was high velocity and the round was heavy, so it packed a serious punch. If you hit someone with an FN round they stayed hit and down – which was more than you could say for the AK-47 and its predecessors with the shorter, less powerful round. However, the AKs have undoubtedly killed many more people than the FN ever will.

We contributed significantly to that statistic because we also used Chinese gear, including the basic AK-47, and we also had their 'bamboo bazooka' – the RPG – which, like the AK, has been an absolute icon for any terrorist group – they've all had them.

Thirdly, we had Russian-made gear: the AKM was a more modern version of the AK-47 and used the same ammunition; similarly their RPG7 was way more sophisticated than the bazooka made in China but used the same rockets. We added more Russian gear to our armoury as the campaign progressed and as we captured it, including light anti-aircraft weapons such as the 12.7 millimetre cannon that we mounted on a couple of our Mercedes Unimog combat vehicles.

Having three lots of gear was a premeditated plan we hoped would disguise our identity and perhaps deflect the interest of intelligence agencies. We used the different weaponry and equipment to take advantage of the ideological and often tribal differences between factions caught up in this Cold War struggle. So when we attacked a Russian-sponsored training camp, for example, we would deliberately dress and arm ourselves with Chinese gear and made sure we left some clear sign suggesting the involvement of a rival faction. We'd then wait and watch the newspapers for reports of retaliatory raids instigated by our victims, and they seldom let us down. Raids and counter-raids sometimes went on for weeks and in one case the Zambian government had to intervene to stop the mayhem. Once it settled down we would start planning the next raid, and next time round we would target a Chinese-sponsored camp and use our Russian gear. And so it went on. Several years later, Zimbabwe leader Mugabe was told about it and said that throughout the long campaign they'd had no idea an SAS regiment was operating against them.

C Squadron was disbanded in 1980, but has remained on the organizational spider of 22 SAS. It may again be resurrected but the Rhodesian connection is now history.

It was originally formed on the back of 100 troops offered to the British by the Rhodesian government of the day, but was never truly Rhodesian thereafter. In my time the first two COs were British followed by a South African. The 2 i/c (author) was born in Burnley, England, and the troops were a real international mix. The New Zealand SAS had no operational commitment at this time and several of their team came over to join us and, along with a couple of Australians, made a big impression. We had a few British from our parent regiment 22 SAS who were then busy countering urban terrorism – especially in Northern Ireland – but the best of the Brits came from the Parachute Regiment, which I still rate today as the best bunch of fighting men on the planet. We had a couple of Germans – one with an extraordinary record with the French Foreign Legion – a couple of Poles and a good number of great South Africans who slotted seamlessly into the bush warfare role. We had a few Americans – veterans from Vietnam and 101st Airborne – and they too made a great contribution.

So this international mix of SAS soldiers, using an international mix of equipment, ambushed terrorist infiltration and supply lines and attacked and destroyed training and battle camps. We blew up bridges, roads and railways, boats and ships, fuel dumps and stores to disrupt the logistical effort – often deep inside unfriendly country.

Night parachute drops were a frequently used means of reaching these targets, we sometimes were deployed by French Alouette helicopters, and occasionally we were able to use our very versatile Klepper kayaks which could be carried or air-dropped in kitbags and assembled before taking to the water. The terrain of central Africa did not lend itself to vehicle operations although we did a couple with our Mercedes Unimogs, but generally we moved around in our purpose-built Sabre Land Rovers.

These long-wheel-base 4 x 4 vehicles were open-top; they had a windscreen for the driver while the front passenger seat was a GPMG position with the 7.62 millimetre machine gun mounted over the bonnet. At the back, between roll bars and the rails, to which we could strap our Bergen packs, was a second GPMG mounting with a 360-degree traverse. These modified Land Rovers were highly capable vehicles with an intimidating display of firepower if ever we needed it.

Most of all, though, we walked – a lot of the time at night, concealing ourselves during the day in observation posts or ambush positions. And we did a great deal of this in serious big game country.

Lion, leopard, hyena, wild hunting dogs, elephant, rhino, buffalo, hippo, crocodiles and deadly snakes were regular companions and sometimes dangerous adversaries. Birds, baboons and monkeys could compromise our hiding places.

There were tangled vines with razor-sharp, backward-pointing barbs that would rip your clothing and flesh, bean plants with toxic fine hairs that caused an agonizing burning itch.

There were malaria-carrying mosquitoes; tsetse flies, which caused sleeping sickness; aggressive wild bees; and the dreadful, minute, salt and pepper ticks that crawled into and embedded themselves in the inner ear.

As crazy as it may sound this environment was the big attraction. We mastered it and loved every minute of it. And in doing that we were, without question, the bush warfare elite force.

There were many adventures with the wild creatures of this environment, but if you knew and understood them the risks were minimal.

Keeping out of trouble in this sort of country required a combination of knowledge and concentration – you had to be incredibly alert. A bird call, for example, could signal the imminent arrival of a herd of buffalo and would give you time to get out of the way. You would hear lion not too far in front and instinctively check the wind direction to see if they would get your scent and hopefully retreat. If they didn't and you stumbled across them at close quarters anything could happen. If you had to use a shot to get out of trouble that could give away your position and compromise the entire mission.

Quite simply, I reckoned the very nature of operating in big game country gave us a huge advantage over any human enemy. If we could avoid conflict with lions, buffalo and elephants there was no way we would be caught out by a bunch of people trained in Russia or China. We were the bush warfare specialists – we were playing on our home ground, there was no referee and we never lost a game!

We were the African Cold War killers.

Following on from *Secret SAS Missions in Africa*, the action continues in this second book with more covert operations, and a highly publicized attack on a major terrorist training base in Mozambique that rates as the biggest and most devastating operation in the history of this SAS regiment.

As the conflicts escalate, C Squadron SAS demonstrates the full capability and effectiveness of a highly trained and motivated Special Forces organization. Full-on infantry-style attacks in broad daylight, clandestine night attacks on remote targets, reprisal raids, pseudo gang operations, and ultimately the training of and operating with rebel groups in enemy territory.

The most lingering effect of C Squadron SAS action in Africa must be its association with the Mozambique rebel group, Renamo, which continued the campaign against the communist-backed Frelimo for twelve years after C Squadron was disbanded. The conflict ended when a peace treaty was finally signed in Rome on 4 October 1992.

Renamo became – and remains – a de facto opposition political party in Mozambique. In 2004, it won 29.7 per cent of the vote and took 90 of the 250 parliamentary seats. Frelimo could not defeat it in the field and with such political representation it is an effective opposition. Today there is hope and optimism amongst the people of Mozambique because the influence of Renamo has so far successfully managed to steer the country away from the self-destructive path taken by Mugabe in Zimbabwe.

SAS Africa – the Team

The Brigadier – Peter Tremain

Born in Bury St Edmonds in the south-east of England, Peter was the youngest son in a family that was part of the Tate and Lyle dynasty that owned the local sugar beet refinery. After a public school education he graduated from the Royal Military Academy Sandhurst and was posted to the Argyle and Southern Highlanders.

Peter moved from his training role with 22 SAS in Hereford to take over command of C Squadron in the early days of our bush warfare campaign in Africa. He had seen action in Korea and in Malaysia, and then later on he was one of a small number of covert operators whose job, in the event of war, was to infiltrate behind East German and Russian lines and locate the assembly areas of armoured divisions preparing to advance. Once they had found a target, they would radio back the details and location and then it was 'Goodnight nurse' as he put it, because within minutes a missile with a tactical nuclear warhead would be launched and on its way.

There would be no escape option for the SAS men who delivered the critical information, and they were not expected to make it home – which goes to prove suicide bombers have been around for a while and are not exclusively Muslim.

Peter's immense experience combined with a razor-sharp mind and his laid-back leadership style generated huge respect. He made us proud to be SAS and we'd do anything for him. He was the perfect choice as our SAS leader.

The Major – Mike (Mick) Graham

Mike was born in Burnley, on the Lancashire side of the northern moors in England, but raised in Rhodesia where his father was an instructor at an agricultural college with 350 African students. A life-long interest in birdlife started when he was ten years old and from this early age happiness was wandering across the 6,500 acres of college farm and woodland with his pointer dog companion.

After school Mike went to university in Natal, South Africa, where he studied zoology and botany with a dream of becoming a game ranger.

Called up for national service in Rhodesia, he enjoyed the army environment from the outset. He was commissioned as an officer and served in a commando unit before applying for SAS selection. He was duly awarded his wings and admitted to this elite unit.

After a number of years as a troop commander he was promoted to captain and posted to the position of intelligence officer at an operational brigade headquarters.

It was a turning point in his career. The job required close cooperation with senior officers in all the military branches as well as the air force, police and civil authorities and sometimes politicians. Mike made a mark and was decorated for his contribution.

Military staff college followed and a year later he graduated in the top three of his class.

He returned to the SAS as major and second in command of the regiment.

Vital statistics: height 1.8 metres (5 feet 11 inches); weight 82 kilograms (180 pounds).

Rex – Warrant Officer Rex Pretorius

Born in Pietersburg in the Northern Transvaal, South Africa, but raised on a massive 250,000-acre game ranch in the southern Matabeleland province of Rhodesia, Rex had a traditional Afrikaans family upbringing with a focus on hunting and living off the land. As a result he developed an environmental awareness akin to the animals they farmed and hunted.

He became a proficient mechanic and spent hours working on the open-top, short-wheel-base Land Rover that was the love of his life.

A big, powerful man, Rex worked as a professional hunter on another huge game ranch in the lowveld of the Limpopo province before being called up to do national service in the army. His professional hunting work was seasonal and like the major he too was attracted to the SAS and predictably had no problem with the selection course.

Rex led two lives, the first with the SAS and the second as a professional hunter. R and R for him was being reunited with his beloved Land Rover and going hunting. He was a true bushman.

Vital statistics: height 1.95 metres (6 feet 5 inches); weight 105 kilograms (230 pounds).

Horse – Sergeant Maurice Greenfield

Born in Launceston, Cornwall, England, he was the second of three sons in a farming family that had tilled the land close to Bodmin Moor for centuries.

Mum and Dad and the three boys from the marriage were, without exception, big people: big hearts that gave them stamina, determination and compassion; and big smiles because the Greenfields loved being the clowns. They seemed to have a never-ending repertoire of jokes they recounted with an infectious laughter that got everybody going.

As there were too many of them for the farm in Cornwall, 'Horse' as he became known through his schooldays, decided to join the British Army.

Looking for adventure, Horse ended up in the famous British Parachute Regiment and served in Ireland where the fight was with IRA terrorists. The Paras did well but their no-nonsense approach offended the left-wing politicians of the day. Stagnation and boards of enquiry followed.

Horse had better things to do with his life while this was going on and one night in London's Earl's Court, he met a group of Rhodesians having a good time and enjoying their 'OE' (overseas experience). They spoke of Africa and the wonderful land and wild animals of the bushveld.

'You should come and join us,' one voice piped up. 'We can always use men from the Brit Paras!'

It was Karate, on leave, full of beer, and he brought us one of Britain's best.

Vital statistics: height 1.95 metres (6 feet 5 inches); weight 106 kilograms (233 pounds).

Karate – Sergeant Tony Caruthers Smith

Born in Bulawayo, Rhodesia, Karate, as he later became known, lost his father in a road accident when very young and was brought up by his mother who worked with the education department. He had a good academic record at school and was interested in electronics but had no specific career ambition.

Called up for national service with the army, which he enjoyed, Karate became a skilled radio operator. After joining the SAS, he took this to new levels with his mastery of Morse code and an uncanny knack of knowing just how to set up an aerial to ensure communications.

Karate and the major were on the same advanced demolitions course and the two subsequently worked together on many operations involving the use of explosives. They were especially known for their skill in the tricky business of melting down Pentolite and moulding it into deadly 'bunker bombs' – family sized plastic Coke bottles filled with the high explosive that were used to great effect on many occasions.

Karate had a cool head: relaxed when laying charges, calm under fire, and calculated and proactive during crises.

His slight stature and crooked, toothy grin disguised a hard, sinewy frame and tireless stamina. This physical strength combined with his mental resilience and technical skills made Karate one of Sierra One Seven's vital assets.

Vital statistics: height 1.725 metres (5 feet 8 inches); weight 75 kilograms (165 pounds).

Simmo – Corporal Peter Simmonds

Born in Perth, Western Australia, where his father worked for gold-mining giant Newmont.

A small gold-mining operation at a place called Penhalonga in the eastern highlands of Rhodesia was looking for a mine manager and his father got the job. After years of working in the heat of the Australian outback and in the steamy conditions of Papua New Guinea, the family was looking forward to living in a cooler climate and enjoying the picturesque environment of the eastern highlands. Simmo's mother was a horticulturalist and conditions at Penhalonga were perfect for growing flowers. They bought a smallholding and started growing gladioli.

Simmo had just turned twenty and in Perth had worked as a builder's apprentice. He was able to help with the construction of the sheds and greenhouses and the initial planting of the gladioli corms. The business flourished and soon the flowers were being exported across the world. In Penhalonga, the Simmonds family had found another source of gold. But for Simmo it was all too tame and he decided to join the regular army. After training he was posted to a commando regiment. The major – then a lieutenant – was his troop commander.

When the major announced he was off to try his luck with the SAS, Simmo put up his hand and said he was going too. He'd proved his worth on operations and as an efficient organizer. Together they conquered the rigorous SAS selection course and inevitably he became one of the team.

Vital statistics: height 1.75 metres (5 feet 9 inches); weight 86 kilograms (190 pounds).

Jonny – Corporal Jonasi Koruvakaturanga

Jonny was born in Lambasa, Fiji, the son of a *ratu* (tribal prince) who was general manager of the local sugar mill. He did his initial military training in Fiji and then joined the New Zealand Army, serving in an infantry unit. Jonny heard about C Squadron through Pig Dog and joined him in the adventure to Africa.

Tall and with massive strength and stamina, Jonny was known as the best MAG gunner in the regiment and handled the heavy weapon as if it were an air rifle. Working in small numbers as we usually did, we relied massively on Horse and Jonny who carried the firepower in our group.

Vital statistics: height 1.95 metres (6 feet 5 inches); weight 106 kilograms (233 pounds), but nimble and quick with it.

Pig Dog – Corporal Verne Conchie

He was born in Riverton in Southland, New Zealand, of part-Maori parents. The family owned a deer farm on the narrow wind-blown plain at the southern extremity of the South Island, between the tumultuous seas of the Foveaux Strait and the impassable inland peaks of Fiordland.

By the age of ten Verne was hunting red deer and wild pigs alongside his father. They fished the streams together, put pots out for crayfish and collected shellfish. They would drive feral goats onto their property from neighbouring forests and either milked them to make cheese or slaughtered them for the Halal market.

Vern walked out of school at the age of fourteen and initially worked fulltime with his father before moving on as a deer hunter and seasonal hand at the local meat works. He was good at his job and managed to send a useful monthly contribution back home to his parents.

At the meat works he met Des and Amy Coles – an older man and wife team who had met while serving in the army together, and both saw the potential in Verne as a soldier. Des, who had been a regimental sergeant major, still had plenty of connections in the army and it wasn't long before he had talked Verne into giving it a try. The New Zealand SAS was on a recruiting drive at the time; Verne took up the challenge and thrived in the environment.

Vietnam was over and a chance to serve with an operational SAS regiment was there for the taking: the Kiwi found himself in Africa.

The name 'Pig Dog' has its origin in New Zealand where wild pigs are hunted with insanely tough breeds of dog that can have a gentle side to them. Bull terrier and bull mastiff crosses are popular. Verne looked a bit like a pig dog, he was built like a pig dog, and he had the strength and determination of a pig dog.

Verne Conchie was also incredibly loyal and devoted. We all knew he would put his body on the line for his comrades without any hesitation or consideration for his own safety. And with bush skills that rivalled Rex the two were an invincible lead-scout pairing with an instinct for danger that could not be taught.

Pig Dog was a legend!

Vital statistics: height 1.75 metres (5 feet 9 inches); weight 86 kilograms (190 pounds).

Fish – Corporal Paul Fisher

Paul was born in Ndola, Zambia, where his father was manager of a large copper mine. A combination of falling copper prices and political corruption disrupted the economy and the family moved to Rhodesia.

Paul had a good education and did well at school. Not a great sportsman, and branded an academic for no reason other than he wore glasses, Paul was determined to prove that physically he could hack it with the best of them.

No better place to do that than with the SAS, and Paul was exceptional.

He announced one day that what he particularly liked about the SAS was that in spite of all the heavy physical stuff demanded we were 'Soldiers who used our brains!'

Amen to that.

'Fish', as we called him, used his brains to enrol for every course going, but discovered a special skill as a paramedic and the SAS subsequently channelled his focus on that.

When not on operations, he'd work as a male nurse at the local hospital accident and emergency ward.

Vital statistics: height 1.77 metres (5 feet 10 inches); weight 80 kilograms (175 pounds).

Mack – Corporal Angus McCrimmon

Born in Leith, Scotland, Mack came from a fishing family in this town on the Firth of Forth to the east of Edinburgh.

With the introduction of the smelt (kapenta) into Lake Kariba, some commercial fishing skills were needed in the land-locked country of Rhodesia. Mr McCrimmon senior responded to the international call and the family moved to Africa. Mack was sixteen at the time and already a competent sailor with a good knowledge of boats and fishing learned from working with his father.

Joining the SAS seemed like a good way to continue his interest in boating, and the Zodiac inflatables and the collapsible Klepper kayaks used by the unit duly became his speciality. He was sent on courses in South Africa to become an outboard motor mechanic – the logic being we couldn't call the AA or the coast guard in the places we operated if our usually reliable forty-horse Evinrudes packed up for some reason.

Mack brought mechanical engineering skills to our group that were invaluable and on several occasions saved us from serious trouble, but more than that Mack was supremely confident on the water.

Mack would lead the unit through nights paddling on mirror-smooth inland lakes where there was no horizon, where the lake surface blended seamlessly with the sky, and where flares of methane gas danced across the water ahead of them. He would lead them in missions launching their Kleppers from submarines at sea and paddling through the waves into unfriendly territory 1,000 kilometres away from home.

Mack was yet another star in the call sign Sierra One Seven.

Vital statistics: height 1.77 metres (5 feet 10 inches); weight 80 kilograms (175 pounds).

Nelson – Lance Corporal Nelson Ogadu

Born and educated in Kampala, Uganda, with a degree in economics, Nelson became a victim of the irrational tribal-based violence that enveloped his country. He fled as his family and those he'd grown up with were being slaughtered by rebel gangs that manned roadblocks and invaded villages.

After months on the road he reached Rhodesia where he got a job as a labourer loading containers with sacks of maize to be shipped to countries to the north that were engulfed in civil conflict and could no longer feed themselves. The major visited the site (run by a friend of his) and saw Nelson at work. He saw something different in the man. He pulled up alongside the container being loaded and greeted him. Nelson told his story but at the end he added: 'Perhaps God has guided me here to meet you? I speak many languages. Will that help you?'

'What time do you finish your work, Nelson?' asked the major.

'4pm, Sir.'

'I will be here at that time to pick you up.'

He breezed through the selection course and the parachute training, revelling in the environment of physical and mental challenges. He became a vital part of our Sierra One Seven team and gave us a point of difference: he was African and an amazing linguist.

Vital statistics: height 1.95 metres (6 feet 5 inches); weight 100 kilograms (220 pounds).

Elephantiasis

I loved elephants from the first time I encountered them in the wild, as a young schoolboy camping in the Mana Pools Game Reserve alongside the great Zambezi River. Every afternoon a huge bull lumbered into our campground. Totally unconcerned with our presence he would feed on the nutrient-rich seed pods of the tamarind acacias that shaded the tents. He would extend his trunk high into the air to reach the pods, and sometimes did a circus trick of standing up on his hind legs to get even higher into the branches. If our tents were in the way he carefully moved between them and never did any damage. He was a true gentleman.

Years passed and I had many more close encounters with wild elephants. I got to know them well. My love for this animal increased greatly as I watched and observed – sometimes for hours on end – at remote waterholes we shared for survival. At the same time, I grew to fear them more than any other animal in the African bush. And that remains the case to this day. I do not take chances with elephants: they are big, smart and fast; and on one extraordinary SAS operation they did their best to kill us. As did their enemies – terrorists-turned-poachers armed with AK-47s and RPD machine guns.

After some hair-raising operations in Mozambique, we had been given ten days R and R. For me that meant being back in the office after a week to see what was in the pipeline for the next deployment. There was a message to contact the brigadier as soon as I was back on board.

'Morning, Major, hope you had a decent break,' he said as I joined him in the SAS operations room.

'You'll be relieved to learn your old trick of violating international borders seems to have gone unnoticed. We haven't heard a word from Malawi – nor have the Portuguese.' The brigadier was referring to a night bombing of a Mozambique terrorist training camp that was actually some distance inside Malawi.

'Well, Sir, that's good news. Tricky business map-reading in the dark,' I replied with a laugh, knowing full well that we both knew exactly where I was on that fateful night.

The brigadier pointed to the top of the map that covered a wall of the room and circled some close contours straddling the Zambezi River with his pointer. It was Mupata Gorge, one of the most remote and inhospitable parts of the Zambezi Valley, not far from where the borders of Zambia, Rhodesia and Mozambique all met.

'Mick,' he said. 'We have had three or four reports from game scouts and from police at Kanyemba of automatic gunfire in this area. They don't want to go in there themselves to find out what's going on and have requested our assistance. I thought this was your sort of job, so I'm sending you and Rex in there to check it out. Personally, I think it is highly unlikely any major terrorist incursion would be planned through such difficult terrain, but it's not entirely out of the question and I don't want surprises.

'You will have to go in by vehicle,' he continued, 'and I can't give you any helicopter support except in emergency. If you need a resupply it will have to be done by airdrop. There are no friendly forces or local settlements anywhere near the area so how you deal with anything you encounter will be entirely up to you.'

I acknowledged and thanked the brigadier.

Walking back to my office, I thought of the only other time I'd briefly ventured into this remote part of Africa. I remembered it as being up and down and hard work, but there was plenty of water in the hills and it was about as wild as you could get. Rex would be happy with that.

After the briefing, I called Rex and was pleased to find him back in town. As we were both still officially on leave, I suggested we meet at a Portuguese restaurant for a piri-piri chicken lunch and a *cerveja* or two. It was a good place to start the operation.

Four days later we had packed up the Sabre Land Rovers and were heading north. Karate was driving and I sat next to him behind the front-mounted MAG machine gun pointing over the spare wheel on the bonnet. Jonny had his MAG on the back mounting tied down with a bungee and had made himself comfortable between the packs for the long drive. Pig Dog had squeezed in next to him while Simmo huddled against the roll bar of the open vehicle.

We motored through the day, stopping for a break and to refuel at a rural police station on the edge of the Zambezi escarpment before winding our way down the hills to the valley floor where we made camp for the night.

My plan was to continue next day all the way to the small settlement of Kanyemba on the Zambezi River, where I could get first-hand reports of what had been seen and heard from the police and the game reserve scouts who knew the area well. They could also tell us about water and the animal highways that would lead from one waterhole to another. If there were any bad guys in the area, following the tracks between waterholes was a sure way of finding them.

We reached Kanyemba mid-afternoon next day and drove into the police camp. Superintendent Peter Saunders was member-in-charge and welcomed us warmly. He pointed to an area of lawn underneath some big, shady trees and brightly coloured bougainvillea and suggested we might like to make camp there. Nearby was a swimming pool with changing rooms and toilets and on the opposite side of the pool was a thatched, open-sided shelter with a barbecue, tables and benches. SAS campsites didn't get much better than this.

Rex's eyes lit up when he saw the barbecue. I laughed out loud as I could see exactly what was going through his mind.

'OK, Rex, here's the plan. We'll get the camp sorted out first. I want the two Sabres with the MAGs covering any approach to our position on the open side of the camp. We'll bed down under the trees next to the vehicles so we can quickly man the guns if we need to. No guard duty tonight. Peter told me they have both foot and vehicle night patrols around the settlement. They are armed and he wants to be sure we won't get excited about that.

'Once we are settled in,' I continued, 'you can do dinner.'

After the long drive over dusty roads, we all took to the pool to cool down and relax. I washed the clothes I'd been wearing for the last two days and put them out to dry in the sun. It would be three long weeks before I could do that again.

I dressed in olive green shorts and one of the Portuguese camouflage shirts we had been given on our last operation. They were made from a lighter material than our issue shirts and were very comfortable. Suitably dressed for the occasion and carrying my FN rifle, the maps and a notebook, I made my way to the police station to find out what was going on.

Rex and Nelson, meanwhile, had gone across to the game reserve headquarters to speak to the staff and get their take on things and, even more importantly, to get information on tracks and the water resources that would help us in the steep and difficult terrain. They both carried ten-day army ration packs that would be greatly appreciated by the African game rangers and a fair exchange for the local knowledge they gave us.

The terrorist hostilities in the three countries that met here had so far missed this pleasant part of the Zambezi and there was regular, neighbourly contact between the respective police and internal affairs staff based on opposite sides of the riverbanks.

At the police base, Peter Saunders told me they had spoken to the Zambian authorities about the automatic gunfire heard in the Mupata Gorge area. The Zambians believed it could be connected with problems they were having with poachers further north on the Luangwa River flats where game was abundant. There were rumours that some of the Russian-backed freedom fighters based around Lusaka had defected with their weapons to form bandit gangs and supply ivory to Chinese agents. Because the Chinese had built the Tan-Zam Railway, the Zambian authorities were said to be turning a blind eye and it had been suggested that such activity was sanctioned by a minister who undoubtedly would be receiving something in return.

Peter went on to say that while he didn't expect the Zambians to tell him if a ZANU or ZAPU terrorist cadre turned up in the area, the fact that they were friendly, as usual, made him think we could rule out a terrorist incursion. He added that it didn't make sense for a terrorist group to infiltrate through the incredibly difficult terrain of the gorge when there were far safer and easier options on either side of it.

The brigadier had said the same thing, but it didn't change anything for us. Clearly there were people in the gorge area armed with automatic weapons. We had to find them and, when we did, there'd be no friendly welcome.

Rex and Nelson returned from their visit with a wealth of useful information and an impala leg for the barbecue. The senior ranger had not been in camp, but Nelson had spoken at length with the other African rangers in their own language. They were pleased to see us, he said, and had willingly provided water and trail locations and suggestions as to how best we might search the area.

We all sat round the maps and looked at the tracks and the vital Ws – water points – Rex had marked. There was a rough vehicle track, used by the rangers, which traversed the southern side of the gorge area and eventually led to the Sapi River where the country opened up again. We could take our Sabres along this track to a point where it crossed a small, dry river bed. It was where the rangers usually left their vehicles if they were going into the gorge area and they'd suggested we do the same.

From there they'd recommended we follow a well-defined elephant track that headed west through fairly open country then split into two branches – one branch continuing west before climbing steadily into the hills and winding its way up and down towards the Zambezi, the other turning sharply north up into the steep country of the Mupata Gorge. Both led to the Zambezi River and there were tracks along the cliff edge between them, making it possible to do a loop and eventually end up back at the vehicles.

In other circumstances, I would have split our group and put a patrol on both tracks. However, I opted to keep all ten of us together. It was going to be hard, physical work in this country and, if nothing else – ten of us sharing the guard roster, drawn from Karate's cap – would make for a good night's sleep.

I don't know why, but I also had an inexplicable gut feeling that ten of us together would be a good idea on this operation. Rex and I weren't afraid to share gut feelings like this and I had spoken to him about it before we left Kanyemba.

'Thought I could trust your instinct, Mick,' he had replied with a grin when I raised the subject. 'Talking to the game rangers convinced both Nelson and me that something is going on here. If it was anything to do with the animals they would already have dealt with it. But that's not the problem. This is a people problem – a bad people problem – and they are both powerless and afraid to do anything about it themselves.'

Rex paused. 'Putting this together with what you got from the police, I'd say we are up against one or more gangs who are well armed and who will have had military training. We don't know how many there are and the ground anywhere in this area is not easy, so keeping the patrol together would also be my call.'

We made the decision to take the longer, marginally easier track first and come back down the steeper alternative when our packs would be lighter. Either way it was still going to be hard work. On the positive side there was no shortage of permanent water in the hills and we now knew where to find it.

'There was one strange thing said at our meeting with the rangers that I didn't understand,' Nelson said once we had sorted out the route on the map. 'Mlanga – the older ranger – muttered to one of his mates something about how he hoped we might finally fix the problem of the tuskless cows. I glanced at him when he said it, and I had a feeling his muted comment was deliberately just loud enough for me to hear. He held my glance for a moment then got up and walked away. I'm sure it was a message but I've no idea what it means.'

I looked at Rex who shrugged his shoulders. 'Tuskless cows are not common,' he said, 'but they have a reputation for being irritable and generally much more aggressive. It wouldn't be good to meet one up there in that steep country.'

We left Kanyemba before dawn next morning and found the rough track the rangers had told us about. It wasn't much trouble for the Sabres.

Along the way we saw a few game animals: impala antelope; a family of warthog that rushed away with their tails erect; a solitary hyena with a bloated belly, full of bones no doubt, returning to a lair somewhere to feed a bunch of hungry puppies.

In the *mopane* trees above us were the straw bundles of sparrow-weavers nests, unerringly built on the west side of the trees. We followed that general direction for most of the morning until we reached the stream crossing that was our landmark. We could see the game department Land Rover tracks leading off towards the hills, but I chose not to follow those and instead we crossed the dry river bed and continued on the track.

I found what I was looking for about 500 metres further on: two anthills supported a dense, green thicket of *masau* – the African wild plum tree. We would drive in behind the thicket; it would be a good place to conceal the vehicles from anyone else using the track.

Once we had all our gear off the Sabres, we put the camouflage nets over them and pegged them down, then we added dry grass and dead branches to complete the concealment. While we were adding these final touches, Pig Dog wandered away for a toilet stop. He quickly hurried back, whistled to get our attention and then beckoned us to join him.

About fifty metres away from where we were concealing the vehicles, the ground dropped away into a deep, eroded gully. There, scattered across the bare, red earth were the dried skin and bones of what had been a large elephant.

'We need to check this out,' said Rex and dropped down into the graveyard. We all stood on the edge of the gully watching as Rex stepped through the remains of the body, examining bits of bone but mainly looking at the skin that by now was hard and dry.

He lifted up a large piece of skin we could see had been part of the head and trunk. 'Look at this,' he said and pointed to two V-shaped indentations. 'This is where the tusks would have been, these marks show they were cut out of the animal. No sign of them anywhere here,' he pointed to all the bones scattered along the gully.

'This is the work of poachers. We should have a good look round to see if they left us any clue as to who they are.'

We spread out and walked slowly in a big circle around the dead elephant, eyes scouring the ground at our feet, looking for an old, faded boot print, a cigarette butt, a matchstick – anything.

On the left flank, Jonny suddenly cried out in triumph. The glint of a metallic object, buried in some dry grass, had caught his eye. He leaned forward and picked up the object. It was a cartridge case.

We gathered around where he had made his discovery, searching for more clues, but there was nothing else. Rex took the brass cartridge case and held up the base for all of us to see. 'It's a .303,' he said, fingering the distinctive protruding rim of the casing that was a characteristic of the calibre.

'This elephant was not shot by terrorists or a bandit group,' I said at once. 'And you can rule out safari hunters as they would have used much heavier ammunition. It leaves just two possibilities – the local police or the local game rangers. Both are issued with .303 rifles; we all saw them being carried at Kanyemba.'

There was a murmur of agreement from the boys. But I could also see the questions in their faces.

'This animal was killed well over a month ago. My guess is it has nothing to do with what has been reported more recently: the automatic fire up in the hills that we are here to investigate. We'll check this out further when we get back; it's possible the empty cartridge case Jonny has found will provide the answers. Meanwhile, Rex, put it somewhere safe so we don't lose it. I'll get my camera for you. We should take a few pictures of this.'

We returned to our packs, adjusted the loads and the critical shoulder and back straps of the Norwegian Bergens, and then headed slowly back to where the rangers customarily parked their vehicles and where we would find the elephant track that would take us high into the hills.

It was early afternoon and the hottest part of the day. On top of that we had just come off R and R and had been sitting in vehicles for the last two and a half days. We were carrying a heavy load: seven days' rations, supplemented with extra brew kit and biltong to last ten days or longer; two full water bottles; HF and VHF radios and spare batteries; first-aid kit; our camo jackets to keep us warm at night; parachute nylon sleeping bags; a light-weight plastic shelter in case it rained as well as our plastic ponchos.

My personal gear consisted of a spare pair of thick woollen socks, a toothbrush and powder, a notebook and pencil, a miniature Minox camera about the size of a mouth organ which I kept in a plastic bag with our radio code sheets. As a birdwatcher, I didn't go anywhere without my compact Leica 10 x 24 binoculars that for recce work were invaluable. I carried a Zeiss prismatic compass for serious night navigation, and for routine checks on direction I wore a wrist compass, like a watch, on my right hand. On my left wrist, face pointing inwards so I could see it while holding my rifle, was the Omega Seamaster watch Mum and Dad had given me on my twenty-first birthday. So far it had done 109 parachute jumps and over ten years of SAS operations with me and, while I'd once replaced the scratched watch face, it had never missed a beat.

Having been into the area once before, knowing how steep and difficult it was, I had made the call not to carry the heavy MAG machine guns Horse and Jonny would normally use. We'd taken them off the Sabre mountings and left them with the police in Kanyemba. Instead I'd opted for the lighter, Russian-made RPDs that had a compact drum magazine. They would be a lot easier to manage while struggling uphill in thick bush. Horse and Jonny would have taken the MAGs without hesitation but in the circumstances were not unhappy with the lighter weapon, which we all knew and respected greatly.

The rest of us carried our NATO 7.62 millimetre Belgian-made FN rifles that in the African theatre were unsurpassed and in which we all had unwavering confidence.

We had tried some of the much lighter, high velocity American weapons –
such as the Armalite – and were not blind to the advantages of these amazing
weapons. In later years we did get a supply in our armoury. But they were
not designed for bush operations where close encounters with big game
animals were an hourly hazard in some places.

Experience-based decisions like what weapons to carry made a big
difference and, as we would soon find out, they also saved lives.

I'd made further weight reductions by replacing the fragmentation
and blast grenades we usually carried with the deadly but much lighter
white phosphorous grenades that we could also use as smoke if we needed
to indicate our position – or an enemy target – to the air force.

Adding to our firepower, Fish carried a light-weight, Chinese bamboo
bazooka. He took two rockets and we shared another four amongst us.
He slung the bazooka over his shoulder and in his hands he carried a folding
butt AK, designed for the Russian paratroopers.

With our heavy loads I wouldn't go as far as saying we enjoyed our first
day in the Mupata Gorge area but, on reflection, it was far from unpleasant,
especially as the heat diminished in the late afternoon. By that time our
bodies were once again getting used to the demands we often had to ask of
them and we started to appreciate the unique African environment we were
challenging.

The track was a wide elephant highway which skirted the steep spurs
then tracked inland to cross the riverine tracts that descended in difficult,
deep gullies. It was a well-graded track, steadily rising into the fringes of the
hills with undulations in and out of the watercourses. It was good going but
there was no room for complacency; other animals also took advantage of
these toll-free highways and encounters had the potential to be both difficult
and dangerous.

Rex, Pig Dog and I took turns as lead scout, changing position every
forty-five minutes as it required intense concentration. I'd just started
my second spell when a familiar, *whirring* bird call caught my attention.
No more than thirty metres away, a dozen red-billed oxpeckers had spotted
us and spiralled upwards sounding the alarm. We were crossing a steep spur
at the time so the only safe way off the track was to go up. I shouted to the
boys behind me as I ran off to my right and up onto an open, rocky outcrop
as fast as my heavy pack would allow. Panting, I reached the rocks and looked

back to see the others scrambling to reach safety just as three huge, African buffalo bulls with wide, sweeping horns trotted onto the track where I had just been standing.

The oxpecker birds would feed on ticks and other parasites carried by these big animals, but in addition to this personal hygiene service they were also an alarm system as they would detect danger well ahead of the host animals. When that happened, they would rise vertically into the air and sound the alarm with a loud, strident whirring call. Every animal in Africa knew the call and would either take flight or go into an aggressive, defensive mode, as was the case now with the buffalo.

Jonny and Simmo looked down on the three big, black bulls as they trotted past no more than twenty metres away, noses up sniffing the wind and snorting. One-tonne heavyweights looking for a fight, they suddenly got our human scent and, heads down, blindly charged along the track we had just vacated.

'You guys would do well to remember this incident the next time you feel like taking the piss out of the major when he's birdwatching,' said Rex. 'Stay alert and stay especially close to your buddies. You do that and you'll be fine in this country.'

The rest of the afternoon was uneventful. We steadily gained altitude on the elephant track; there were great views sweeping as far as the Sapi River that cut through the Zambezi Valley to the west of us. By 1700 we had reached a high plateau where the game scouts had told us they'd made a camp next to permanent water. I could see palms and fig trees up ahead and guessed that would be where we'd find the water.

We fanned out in the open woodland behind Rex and Pig Dog who had moved fifty metres forward of us. If there was permanent water there was a good chance at this time of day of finding game animals there – like the three big heavies we had just encountered.

I hoped we would find game – it would mean there were no humans around. But we were not taking chances. As we got closer, I signalled for Jonny and Horse to move forward on the flanks with their RPD machine guns. If we met opposition there would be crossfire cover while those of us in the centre closed in to deal with the problem.

I saw Rex suddenly go into the aim. We tensed and stopped. He looked round and with a sheepish grin pointed to a family group of kudu antelope that galloped off to the right of us. They ran with their heads held high and the long, spiral horns out of the way on either side of their necks.

We approached the green treeline with caution. Some noisy hornbills flew away protesting, but that was all – kudu and hornbills had signalled all was OK here.

The water came from a rock fissure amongst the trees the birds had been feeding in. It trickled into a small pool between the tree roots that was no bigger than a handbasin. From there it overflowed onto a vertical rock face and trickled down into some slightly larger pools before finally reaching the main reservoir at ground level. Here the pool was the size of a bathtub but deeper, and it was where the game animals came to drink. The water was surprisingly clean with very little green algae and the spoor around it suggested it was a popular spot.

We filled our water bottles from one of the higher pools then moved to where we had seen the game rangers' camp about 200 metres away – far enough not to disturb thirsty animals coming there to drink after dark. It was a good campsite and we settled down for the night.

I drew the 2200 guard from Karate's cap and enjoyed a starlit night with a soft wind that rustled the leaves in the trees above us. I listened to the insect-like purring of the tiny scops owl and the ghostly, wavering call of the freckled nightjar that lived amongst the rocks. I heard the yelping of a jackal, and gasped out loud as a brightly burning meteor flashed through the sky above me then split into several fragments before disappearing.

The hour-long guard passed quickly. My relief was Simmo. I woke him up and decided I'd stay with him for half an hour and enjoy the noises of the African night.

We heard the cracking of branches in the distance – elephants feeding and no doubt heading our way for a drink at the pool. Just before I returned to my sleeping bag a loud, guttural, 'sawing' sound came from the direction of the water. It was a leopard. The quiet of the night was dramatically ended with the terrified screams and barks of a nearby roosting baboon troop. Baboons were a favourite prey of the leopard and there would be one less in the troop come morning.

I drifted off to sleep with a contented smile on my face. How good to be there.

Rex got everybody up early and after a quick brew and a biscuit we started on what would be the steepest part of the climb up to the high ridges. The elephant trail was good underfoot and we made steady progress in the cool of the morning. We zigzagged across the bare, rocky ground of the exposed spurs where stunted thorn trees somehow managed to survive. As the path crossed a watercourse there would be long grass – sometimes above our heads – and good-sized evergreen trees: figs, wild plum and the African sausage tree with dangling seed pods the size of a big salami.

There was plenty of evidence of game: piles of sweet-smelling elephant dung covered in clouds of small, colourful butterflies; dust hollows we could see had been recently used by buffalo; as well as the hard hoof prints of antelope and wild pigs.

We took our first break after two hours. By that time the hill tops were getting close, maybe another hour away. Once we were up, we would follow the undulating ridge lines towards the Zambezi River for another two or three days. While the going would be less strenuous than the steep ascent we were now climbing, it would still be far from easy. The map showed deep riverine cuttings and vertical cliff faces ahead of us – up and down, up and down.

By late morning, I was looking out for a place where we could rest through the heat of the day. Ahead of us we could see a green belt in one of the re-entrant watercourses that cut across our path and it looked promising – shade trees and possibly some more water.

I moved in behind Rex as we descended through long grass and tangled shrubbery towards the bigger trees. I was no more than three steps behind him when he suddenly froze and went into the aim. He was aiming high and as I joined him I saw why and immediately went into the aim myself.

Less than ten metres in front of us, a big elephant bull stood at an angle across the path. He turned his head towards us and extended his trunk sniffing the air. He knew we were there and this was just to get our exact location. He dropped his head and shook his trunk, Rex and I backed off a pace.

As we moved he turned to face us again, staring intently at us. He dropped his head and once more shook his trunk. We backed off another pace.

I was now alongside Rex and whispered, 'If he comes, you go high. I'll go low.'

Rex nodded. For the third time we backed off as the animal again looked away.

Just as I was thinking we could safely retreat the massive animal charged us. He trumpeted loud and angry – and he was so fast.

Rex fired first before the animal was fully front-on and managed to get his shot in behind the ear. Elephants have a massive honeycomb of bone in front of the brain and a frontal head shot with our weapons would have done nothing.

I dropped to my knee and fired an instant later. I aimed up between the front legs, hoping for the heart or some of the major blood vessels.

The huge animal staggered as Rex's shot hit home then, with my shot, he stumbled forward towards us. Rex jumped away to his left and I rolled right just as the trunk smashed into the ground where I had been kneeling.

Rex and I stood off on each side of the animal ready to fire again, but we both knew it wouldn't be necessary. The elephant writhed in the grass for a few moments then let out a deep and prolonged sigh. The movements slowed until finally he lay still.

As the adrenalin diluted in my bloodstream, my first feelings were deep remorse and frustration. I'd never in my life wanted to kill an elephant and now I had just done that. But if we had done nothing he would have killed or seriously injured Rex and me; on top of that we also had to consider the safety of the eight men behind us. The shooting was easy to justify, but that didn't make me feel any better.

'Come and look at this.' Rex's voice brought me back to reality.

I moved across to his side of the animal and could see at once the weeping holes of bullet wounds. We counted eleven of them. They were no more than 150 millimetres apart and started in the big muscles of the rump and back leg and progressed in a line across the ribs and up as far as the shoulder. This elephant had been machine-gunned!

I shook my head in disbelief.

'At least we ended his torture,' said Rex. 'You can smell the festering wounds. He must have been in immense pain for at least three or four days. It has to have been an RPD. This is nothing but cruelty. I'm looking forward to meeting up with the people who did this.'

We moved away and into the shade where we rested through the afternoon heat. I sent a report back to the police at Kanyemba with our location. The elephant had medium-sized tusks the game wardens would probably want to recover at some future date.

It wasn't a happy afternoon for me.

On top of killing the elephant, the two shots we'd fired could well have compromised us. The sound of gunfire carried a long way. If the poaching group had heard them they would either beat a hasty retreat out of the area or they would be ready and waiting for us. They would probably think it was a game ranger patrol and would be confident they could deal with that. We would soon shatter such thoughts, but having lost the initiative it would be that much harder for us and would increase the chances of casualties. It wasn't how I liked to operate.

We started moving again at 1545 and by that time the first vultures had arrived to inspect the carcass. I wasn't happy about that either. Anybody watching on top of the hills would see the circling birds and know that was where the shots were fired.

We were all tense for the remainder of the day, in spite of there being no sign of human activity on the tracks or at the small waterholes we encountered along the way.

We cooked our evening meal in another wooded gully, and then afterwards, in the dwindling twilight, moved up to the top of a ridge well away from the track where we would not be disturbed by animals – or humans for that matter. It wasn't the greatest place to spend the night. The ground was hard and we shared our sleeping space with small stones that felt like boulders beneath the thin plastic of our shelters we were using as groundsheets, and there was certainly no padding in our flimsy sleeping bags of brown, parachute nylon.

I could hear everyone scratching and rustling as they tried to get comfortable but eventually it became quiet as we settled down. To get the elephant episode out of my head, I focused again on enjoying the night sounds and marvelling at the magnitude of space and the stars above me.

I was just nodding off when I heard gunfire in the distance.

Pig Dog was on guard and came over. There was a soft sound behind me. It was Rex – he too had heard it.

I sat up and reached into a side pocket of my pack for the Zeiss prismatic compass. 'Get a bearing, Pig Dog,' I directed.

The stocky New Zealand bushman conferred with Rex in whispers and after some arm-waving he raised the compass and took the bearing:

'West–north–west 300 degrees. Best guess about eight kilometres away.' Rex nodded in agreement.

While I was digging around again in my pack to get out the maps, we heard a sustained burst of machine-gun fire.

Rex and Pig Dog took another bearing. 'No change,' said Rex. 'That was an RPD. It'll be the same weapon used on the elephant.'

I gave the map to Rex and Pig Dog to work out where our target might be and went to help the ever-faithful Karate unwind the antenna of the HF radio to report back to base. Better to lose a bit of sleep now doing this than waste time the following day while closing in for the kill. I suddenly felt a whole lot better and knew I'd sleep well – which I did.

We were up before dawn and on the track that undulated across the ridge tops. In two hours I estimated we would cover most of the eight kilometres to where we guessed the gunfire came from. At that early hour I was happy we could move without excessive caution but I put Horse with his machine gun up front with Rex, on the off-chance of a head–on encounter.

About seven kilometres away from our overnight position the maps showed a branch of the hills that spread further to the west. The contour-spacing between the steep ridges suggested there was an undulating plateau and it was there that Rex and Pig Dog thought we would find those responsible for the gunfire.

Our elephant trail skirted the side of this branch and continued in a more northerly direction towards the Zambezi River, so the first part of the plan was to reach the edge of the branch as quickly as possible. Once there we would move off the track and start our search in earnest.

We spooked a covey of noisy francolin partridges having an early feed on the grass seeds along the track, but apart from that we reached our targeted area without incident. We moved off the track and made a brew and some breakfast.

Then, leaving their packs with us, Rex and Pig Dog went back onto the main trail to see if there were any signs of humans coming in from the north or from any side track that led into the area we were interested in.

Moving silently, Rex studied the ground for any tell-tale signs of humans while Pig Dog, with his super-sensitive perception, covered the ground ahead. Pig Dog had grown up in the dense beech forests of the deep south of New Zealand where, from the age of fourteen, he and his father had made a living from shooting deer. If a deer twitched an ear, Pig Dog would notice. He was a true bushman, like Rex who'd had a similar upbringing in Africa. With such skills they were masters of the close-in recce work.

Half an hour later they found a side track and the boot prints of seven or eight men – Rex recognized the prints as a Russian-issue boot we had encountered before in other places – and to the north it was obvious there had been regular recent traffic. Maybe some of the group taking trophies back to the Zambezi? They followed the side track for some distance and, convinced it would lead us to contact, Rex radioed to say they had found what we were looking for and were returning.

Closing in would have to be done with patience and stealth if we were to surprise the gang and give ourselves a chance of getting all of them.

And that's what I wanted. None of them must escape. We have to kill all of them. I'd been brooding about the elephant that had been machine-gunned. People like that had no place on this earth, I said to myself with a hatred that was new to me. We would hunt down these people and they would die. There would be no survivors.

We were all sitting together while Rex and Pig Dog described what they had found. It was up to me now to make a decision on what we were going to do about it.

'We have three options,' I said. 'We could simply follow the track and rip into them when eventually we meet up, or we could set up an ambush on the track and wait for them to come to us. But the problem with both these options is that we may only get one or two of them.

'That leaves us with the third option, which is to find their camp. If we can take them by surprise or, better still, while they are sleeping, we will get the result I'm looking for.

'Rex, I want you to take us back towards the track that branches west. Once we reach the track, we'll move into the bush off to one side and go parallel on the high ground that overlooks it. We'll sit up there and watch the track and the ground ahead of us.

'We'll pick an observation point further on and we'll keep watching, while Rex, your team moves forward to the new position. Once there, you watch while we move up to join you. We'll keep doing that, gradually making our way along but above the track until we find the camp.'

There were nods of approval.

We moved cautiously forward. After an hour we found ourselves on top of a small, rounded knoll overlooking an undulating basin, surrounded by higher hilltops that were too far away to be useful. The basin was well grassed with patches of good-sized trees, but on the higher ground we occupied there wasn't much cover. Rex and I moved up to some boulders behind which we could crouch and observe without being seen.

A kilometre further on there was another elevated mound similar to what we were on now and we could see the game track below it.

'Rex, that's the next stop. I'll stay here and watch the track as you move. We'll warn you if we see any activity. Once you are there and organized, you do the same for us as we come forward to join you.'

I gave Pig Dog my binoculars and he and Jonny took over at the top. Rex briefed his team on the next move and pointed to the route they would take to get there. We tested the whisper mikes on our radios. Rex nodded in acknowledgement and they moved silently away from us.

It took them just under an hour to reach their position. Fifteen minutes after that Rex's muted voice came over the air: 'Good position here and good cover on the route we took. I can see smoke. I think we have found the camp.'

I passed on the news to the others and we got ourselves organized to join up with Rex.

I put Simmo up front with Pig Dog while Karate, Jonny and I tagged along behind. Pig Dog was taking no chances and moved carefully forward, picking his route and then scanning the ground ahead before physically moving. I watched from behind in admiration and enjoyed seeing Simmo getting the gist of it and copying Pig Dog's actions. It took us over an hour but time wasn't important. Staying invisible was what counted now and Pig Dog was making sure of that.

We joined Rex who took me up to their observation point. He pointed to a fold in the ground another kilometre ahead. I could see wisps of blue-grey smoke drifting up through the tree canopy. 'My guess is they are smoking meat,' said Rex. 'They'd make plenty selling that in the villages on the other side or they'd trade for *kachase* – the local liquor distilled from *masau*, the wild plum.

'You see that high ridge to the south of them?' he asked. 'Notice how it drops down to a spur that looks like it would be exactly opposite the camp?'

I trained my binoculars on the area in question and could see what he referred to.

'So what you're thinking,' I replied, 'is for us to move up to the higher point where we would still be a safe 300 metres or more from the camp. From there, if we stay on top of the spur it should take us down almost directly into their camp.

'If we follow that we aren't going to get lost in the dark. Let's do it, Rex.' We both smiled as the excitement suddenly clicked in.

But there was one problem: ten of us had to move another kilometre to this final position. There was cover along the way, but were there eyes watching on the hilltops above us?

I was scanning the ground with my binoculars when suddenly we heard automatic gunfire – one burst, a second, then a prolonged third burst of firing.

'They are out hunting. Let's make the most of it.'

We moved carefully and quickly under the dense, green canopy of a watercourse that led us eventually to the high point on the ridge above the camp. We lay low and waited for dusk.

As the sun bathed the surrounding hilltops in early evening's orange light, and as deep shadows pushed into the lower parts of the basin, we suddenly heard singing. The hunters were returning to camp.

Nelson moved forward and tilted his head, trying to hear the words of the song and what they were singing about. '*Chipambere*,' he said suddenly. 'They have shot a rhino.'

Rex and I shook our heads in disbelief. Ivory would bring them good money as it was greatly valued in Asia for ornaments, but a rhino horn was better than twenty tusks.

We looked down the ridge. The ground below us dropped steeply at first then levelled as the spur reached out towards the foot of the basin, where the smoke from the camp continued to drift up through the trees. We could smell the bitter-sweet scent of smouldering logs and occasional whiffs of raw meat being smoked.

'We'll all go down as far as where the ground levels off,' I said to Rex. 'We'll stay there while you and Pig Dog do a close-in recce. It means we will be no more than 200 metres away from the camp so there will be plenty of time. Take Nelson with you, Rex. He'll understand what they will be talking about and that may be good value for us.'

We moved as soon as it was dark. The terrorist poacher group would be busy and noisy after their day's hunting. They would be organizing the evening meal, maybe drinking some alcohol they had carried in. They would collect water and some would wash. It was the perfect time to close in. We reached the level ground in half an hour.

Rex and Pig Dog fixed the bearing on their Recta compasses that hung around their necks on green nylon cord. They moved away from us, stopping to look back and memorize silhouettes of trees that would indicate where we were on their return.

They were carrying starlight scopes. But as they descended, Rex and Pig Dog preferred to rely on their own night vision and the instinctive feel for the ground that only true bushmen possessed.

Nelson was not in this class, so simply told Rex he'd be three steps behind him all the way – which was exactly what Rex wanted.

They moved slowly down the hill towards the camp, pausing to pick a route, mentally noting features: a big anthill, a tangle of thorn bushes, a mountain acacia tree, a dark wooded gully off to the right.

The noise of the voices became more distinct. There was some subdued laughter. The voices got louder as they closed in, suddenly they could see the glow of the fires. They were now within thirty metres of the camp.

Rex crouched down, touched his ear and pointed at Nelson. Pig Dog silently moved in on one side and took out his scope. Rex did the same. Nelson was the listener, and now he could clearly hear what was being said and how many were speaking. The chatter of men organizing and preparing food waned as they sat together around the fire and ate their meal. Rex touched Pig Dog on the shoulder and indicated he should keep scanning the surrounds while he moved his scope into the target area.

Through the light intensifier the scene was now bright as day. The flickering fire illuminated the camp and the terrorists who sat there gorging themselves on smoked meat and handfuls of maize meal from a communal, round, black pot. A bottle passed between them. Rex guessed it was *kachase*, or something similar, and he could smell the sickly sweet odour of the marihuana they were smoking.

There were six of them. They sat on the ground in a semicircle in front of an open-sided, thatched shelter, in which Rex could see packs and where he guessed they would sleep.

After twenty minutes Rex and Pig Dog turned off the scope power to conserve battery life and to regain their natural night vision. They sat and they listened.

Nelson had already identified the language being spoken as Ndebele, suggesting these were ZAPU terrorists who would have been trained in one of the Russian satellite countries.

He jerked back after listening to one conversation and Rex quickly put a hand on his arm to remind him where they were. Nelson nodded and whispered in his ear, 'Their leader with the RPD has been injured by the rhino they killed. Two of them have stayed with him and will try to carry him back, but they say he will die. They are talking about the rhino horn and the ivory at the river. Guessing how much they will make and how it should be shared.'

Rex nodded. They now had all the information they needed. No point staying this close to the camp any longer.

He signalled to Pig Dog who silently moved back five or six metres then crouched down, rifle in his shoulder aiming at the camp. Rex and Nelson moved quietly past him and the three men melted away into the night. Rex signalled a halt opposite the deep, wooded gully and took out the radio. Using the whisper mike, he let us know they were halfway back and would rendezvous in the next thirty minutes or so.

I saw them in my binoculars when they were no more than twenty metres away and blew softly on my high-frequency dog whistle to home them in. I glanced at my Omega. It was 2326 and I could already see the faint glow of the rising quarter moon in the sky behind the silhouetted hilltops. We had plenty of time before daylight and the later we left it the brighter the moon would be.

'We leave at 0300,' I said after the recce team had reported their findings. 'Rex, you guys get some sleep. We'll wake you when it's time to move.'

I took first watch. I wanted to think things through before the attack, and I knew that until I'd got my head-space sorted out I wouldn't be able to sleep anyway.

I'd been trained to consider all possible options before committing to an action. But that went out of the window because I'd already made up my mind.

There were ten of us up against six: who were all together, side by side, beneath the lean-to shelter they had constructed. They had been drinking and smoking dope. We would walk into their bedroom while they slept and eliminate them from this earth.

My nerves tingled with the hate-lust the thought had generated. The hunters had become the hunted.

When you were young and as physically fit as we were, it was remarkable how much benefit you got from just two or three hours sleep. When at 0300 Simmo – who had drawn the last guard stag – woke us up, we were all immediately fizzing with anticipation.

As good as it would have been we couldn't sensibly make a brew where we were, so a mouthful of water and a biscuit was all we had. Everybody loaded up, then we all checked each other, jumping up and down to see if anything on our webbing or in our packs rattled. A few minor adjustments were made, then we got into single file to follow Rex and Pig Dog down into the target area.

We had any amount of time to get in close, so we used it to check every step of the way. Pig Dog took the starlight scope and stayed on Rex's shoulder. He'd scan the way ahead and give Rex clearance for the next leg of our advance on the terrorists-turned-poachers.

We arrived at the recce point used earlier, dropped our packs, and I took over from Pig Dog. I'd mounted Rex's scope on my FN and powered it up. The light of the quarter moon combined with the smouldering remains of the fire made it like daylight.

Smoking meat hung from lines of wire over the glowing embers; beyond that I could see the thatched-roofed shelter where six bundles of humanity slept under single blankets.

I turned to the others and whispered what I had seen. The plan now was I'd use the scope to lead us right into the camp while the others kept their night vision, which with the moon would be good. We'd move in on the shelter and eliminate the sleeping terrorists in a hail of fire. I moved forward twenty metres then signalled a halt.

We crouched down, watching and listening, fingers nervously caressing the triggers of our weapons.

Another twenty metres forward and again we watched and listened. Through the scope I could now clearly see the shelter and the sleeping forms of our enemy. Without prompting, Rex and the boys moved alongside and spread out. Pig Dog angled off to the left to cover our flank and Fish did the same on our right; the rest of us tiptoed up to the fires and to the edge of the shelter where we could hear snoring.

I looked left and right, giving the signal, and then, putting the FN into my shoulder, I opened fire into the middle of the six blanketed mounds. The others followed suit, and I have a memory of dark shapes bouncing on the ground as we all pumped bullets into them. I emptied my twenty-round magazine, changed in a flash, and irrationally emptied another twenty rounds into the blanketed forms that were still bouncing as our second fusillade ripped into them.

'Stop!' shouted Rex.

We crouched then moved into what cover we could see. Lying flat to the ground, we changed magazines again, ready for a reaction from a guard post or another sleeping area we may not have seen.

We were motionless for five minutes or more, then quietly we retreated ten metres from the camp. Then another ten metres back and there we stayed – watching and listening – until the metallic rasping of the fork-tailed drongo announced the arrival of a new day in Africa.

Five kilometres away up in the hills, the injured Moses Ncube and his two guardians heard the gunfire. Moses recognized the heavier sound of the NATO 7.62-millimetre rounds fired from our FN rifles and immediately knew he was in bigger trouble than that caused by the smashed leg he suffered while machine-gunning the black rhino.

He told his two comrades they should now reaffirm their belief in defeating the colonial enemy as they had been taught. He gave his RPD to the bigger of the two and told them to go up above him and find a concealed position. He would draw in the enemy towards him and keep their attention until they were close. He pointed to a small mound with a blackwood tree growing from it, and told them that when the enemy reached that point they should open fire with the RPD machine gun. The enemy would not survive.

He took an AKM and asked to be moved into a slight hollow that would be more comfortable for his leg, and from where he could initiate fire against the enemy he knew would be coming for them. Once he was settled, they put grass and light branches over him for shade and concealment. They put his water bottle where he could reach it, then, at his request, they rolled a marihuana joint and lit it. He took a deep drag and closed his eyes. It would bring some relief to the increasing pain of his broken leg; he hoped it might also help him when confronting the enemy. He shuddered as a wave of fear swept through him.

Back at the camp, we sat concealed in cover and waited until the sun rose above the surrounding hills. I needed to be as sure as possible that nobody else was waiting for us to break cover, so we didn't move.

Eventually it was light enough to have a clear view of our surrounds. Only then did I signal for Rex and Horse on one side and Pig Dog and Jonny on the other to sweep around behind the camp and clear the area. The rest of us sat still, senses on high alert.

Rex gave us the all clear on the radio and we moved forward into the camp.

Four fires with big logs continued to smoulder and smoke. Above and around these were washing-line wires strung between trees and improvised posts that were festooned with long strips of elephant meat.

The open-fronted, lean-to shelter had a crude roofing frame made from cut branches, and on top of this they had laid palm fronds and long grass to give them shade.

The six bodies lay still on blood-soaked ground beneath their blankets. Behind them were their packs. In a vacant space between the bodies were three additional packs: three terrorist poachers we still had to account for.

We pulled out all the packs and weapons. Then I used the Minox camera to photograph the face of each individual as we searched the packs for any possible identification. There were photographs of the terrorists during training, posing with anti-aircraft guns, grenades hanging from their shirt-fronts. There were some names that Special Branch police might recognize.

The most important information came from a pack that belonged to Moses Ncube. We found his name on several items in the pack, including an interesting notebook with other names and what was clearly some basic accounting.

It was going to take some time to sort through what we had found and we also needed to check the area more carefully. More importantly, there were three more terrorists still at large, including their leader with the RPD machine gun they had used on the animals.

It was by now obvious we were under no immediate threat there, so we made ourselves a brew. I saw Rex and Pig Dog examining some of the smoked meat above the fires. Rex looked across at me and asked if I wanted a strip. I shook my head. On principle, I was not going to eat elephant meat killed by these poachers. Rex shrugged his shoulders and helped himself.

Leaving Jonny with his RPD in charge of security at the campsite while Karate sent a report back to Kanyemba police, I continued to sift through the packs, organizing what we needed to keep and what we would destroy. I told the others to gather firewood and pile it up on top of the bodies. When we returned, I wanted a big fire to burn the camp and bodies; we'd use the smouldering logs beneath the meat lines to get it going.

Rex, Pig Dog, Horse, Fish and I, meanwhile, recharged magazines and got ourselves generally organized to track down the three remaining terrorists.

Judging from where we had heard the firing the previous afternoon, we reckoned they were between two and three kilometres away from us. We had a look at the map and decided we'd start by following the elephant trail behind their camp. Once we were in the zone we'd have another look and refine our plans.

I knew we had lost the 'invisibility' so helpful to our usual operational success. There were three desperate and dangerous men ahead of us who knew we would be coming and one of them was armed with a deadly machine gun. They would be waiting for us and we'd need all our skills and guile to neutralize that advantage.

I shuddered at the thought of us having a casualty, but had to accept it was a strong possibility in these circumstances. I didn't need to explain my misgivings to the boys. They knew as well as I did what we were heading into.

Fish loaded an RPG rocket into his bazooka and gave a little fist-forward gesture that made us smile and boosted our confidence. We moved off along the track.

The ground opened up and we found ourselves on a rocky hill slope with little cover. We were still some distance from where we suspected the three terrorists would be, but crossing this ground would mean dangerous exposure to us, so our first instinct was to go to ground and have a good look ahead.

I moved forward, and my attention was immediately drawn to four or five vultures circling in the distance ahead of us. I called Rex and pointed to the birds. 'They will have found the rhino carcass. The injured man cannot be far from the vultures.'

We scuttled across the exposed slope and dropped back into a lower patch of woodland. We paused again at the edge of it. We were getting close. I took out my binoculars and looked ahead at the circling vultures. There were more of them now. I scanned down to a big mountain acacia tree; its upper branches were filled with the hunched, brown shapes of perching vultures.

Problem was they would fly when they spotted us approaching, and that would effectively announce our arrival to the terrorists. The odds were not in our favour. If they lay low, we ran the risk of walking into their ambush.

Reading my thoughts, as he so often did, Rex looked across and said, 'I think we may have to smoke them out.' He tweaked one of the white phosphorous grenades clipped to his webbing shoulder strap.

I nodded in agreement and passed the binoculars to him. 'Have a look at those vultures and notice which way they are looking. That's where the carcass will be.' As Rex watched, two of them obligingly glided off their perch and dropped to the ground.

'Got it,' said Rex as another group dropped down to join the feast. 'They won't be too far away from there so our best option is to stay high then come down onto the vulture tree. There's plenty of grass around and it will burn once we put the grenades into it.'

I nodded again in agreement. 'Wind direction?' I asked.

He looked again through the binoculars. 'Not much at the moment, but it's easterly so the smoke and flames should travel away from us and towards where we think they are. This is starting to look much better.'

'OK,' I said. 'And while you have the glasses, track back and pick the best possible route for us.'

After a few minutes Rex looked at the map, had another look then handed the glasses back to me.

'You go up front with Horse and Pig Dog. I'll follow with Fish so if you run into trouble we are behind you with his RPG. Just tell us where you want us. If all goes smoothly, we'll stop some distance above the vulture tree, have another look then move in and make things happen.'

There was a twinkle in Rex's eye as he turned to show the others where we were going. Meanwhile I collected the extra RPG rockets they were carrying. I gave Fish another to add to the two he already had and put three into my pack.

With our tactics and weapons sorted out, I felt much more confident. The others clearly felt the same. Rex and I had led and nurtured this team and we had already been through a lot together. We had combined our skills and expertise and had absolute trust in each other. It made us a formidable opposition, especially when we were 'invisible'.

But we were not invisible this time.

Moses Ncube didn't know who we were, but he knew somebody was after him and his gang. The gunfire he had heard from his camp suggested they would be security forces.

He was afraid but, having been gored in the leg by the rhino, he knew he was likely to die anyway. His leg was broken and although the femoral artery was intact he was bleeding internally. They were a long way inland from the river and even if they somehow managed to get him there, it would still be a big distance to any medical facility that could deal with his injuries.

All he had left was his AK, a smouldering joint of marihuana and a desire to kill some of the enemy before they eventually killed him, as he was sure they would. He was in great pain and that would end his suffering.

We moved cautiously up the hill away from the track we had been following and reached the higher ground Rex had chosen for our approach to target. Cover was sparse – a scattering of low thorn trees – but Rex had taken us well above our target area and it was unlikely we would be seen. Nevertheless, we inched forward carefully and it took us an hour to reach the large, rounded boulder Rex had picked out on the hill slope as our final staging point.

Rex and I crouched in the cover of low bushes on one side of the boulder and looked down. We could see the tree with the vultures immediately below us. The cover was good but the birds would see us as we approached, take flight and essentially sound the alarm.

We scanned the area for some time, looking for movement, but could see nothing.

'They know we are coming and are waiting for us,' whispered Rex. 'They are down there and close. We have to flush them out.'

'Agreed,' I replied. 'We will all move down together towards the vulture tree. There we'll start the show with the white phosphorous grenades. While there is smoke and fire we'll split into two groups. Fish and I will stay higher up with the RPG while you and the others go left and drop down into the target area to deal with anything flushed out by the fire.'

'Sounds good,' said Rex and he called the others forward. While I briefed them on the plan, Rex was again picking a route over the final 150 metres that would take us to the vulture tree.

We stayed close together on that final descent: hearts pounding, every sense on high alert; eyes looking for the slightest hostile movement; fingers caressing the triggers of our weapons that were now 'safety catch off'. We were closing in for contact.

Large black vultures had the size, strength and beak to rip through the thickest of skins on a carcass, but the armour-plated rhino was still a challenge and often it took hours of struggle to open up the belly. Once they had done that it allowed access to the carcass by the smaller, much more common white-backed vultures, which would consume the animal from the inside out in a piranha-like feeding frenzy.

These smaller vultures were the ones we had seen sitting in the mountain acacia tree, waiting for their turn. They were so intent on the carcass that we managed to arrive beneath the tree without them taking flight in alarm.

We spread out, each of us clutching the olive green cylinder of a WP grenade. I was in the middle. Looking left and right, I held up my hands and pulled the pin from the grenade, still clutching the spring-loaded handle that would trigger the four-second fuse. When I saw everyone else had done the same, I held up three fingers ... two fingers ... one finger. Then I hurled my grenade as high and as far forward as I could. The others followed suit.

There followed a scene as bizarre as anything I had ever witnessed.

Phosphorous sizzled into the air and dazzling white smoke erupted as if from a rampant volcano. The bush caught fire immediately and through a haze of white and black smoke, flames and the crackle of burning dry grass, there were the vultures. Some were already flying, wheeling erratically through the smoke, others were desperately trying to get airborne ahead of the flames and some were flapping on the ground, injured by our attack.

Two jackals that had also been at the carcass fled yelping as phosphorous splinters burnt through the thick, black hair on their backs and reached the skin.

Ignoring the mayhem Rex, Pig Dog and Horse leapt down the slope and into the smoke.

Fish and I stayed where we were, watching in amazement.

We heard the cries of anguish as the phosphorous and flames reached Moses Ncube. Screaming out in anger and pain, he prised himself up and blindly fired his AK into the smoke. I saw Rex and Horse respond with a sustained burst of fire. Moses danced for the last time as the bullets ripped through his body. The impact threw his AK into the air.

We all sat and watched as the fire we had started spread up through the gully, hoping it would force the other two out of their hiding place. We knew by then they would have the RPD that had done so much damage to the animals they hunted. We could not take chances.

I signalled to Fish that we should move forward and get in closer. We covered each other and took it in turns to advance. We were still above where Rex had made contact; he responded with a nod as he saw us move higher and forward of his position.

We waited again, watching, reluctant to reveal our positions, knowing a terrorist with an RPD was waiting for us to make a mistake and show ourselves.

Signalling to Pig Dog that he was moving, Rex leapt forward, and crouching low he weaved his way towards a shallow depression behind a small mound with a young tree that would give cover. Then the RPD opened up.

Rex dived down and rolled behind the tree. From above I watched in horror as the machine gun bullets stitched the ground on either side of him. I could see the bark spinning away from the tree that sheltered his head. I was sure we had lost Rex: my right-hand man, my team, my friend.

We had to do something and quickly, but I could not see where the firing was coming from. I moved forward but still could see nothing. Then, out of the corner of my eye, I saw Fish kneel and aim the bamboo bazooka on his shoulder.

Whoosh! There was a massive explosion as the rocket exploded into a thicket below us. An AK spiralled through the air, thrown from a body hurled back by the blast. I still couldn't see a target, but as the machine gun continued firing at Rex, I threw my last WP grenade into the general area as Fish reloaded the RPG. It was a long throw and I gave it plenty of height so the grenade detonated in a spectacular airburst and a shower of deadly phosphorous rained down.

I heard a scream. Then there was a *whoosh* as Fish fired again, and this time we saw the bipod of the RPD fly up as the rocket hit the target. It was over.

I jumped up and ran down the slope to where I had seen Rex enveloped in a hail of bullets before Fish had found the target. I have no religion, but as I ran I prayed: *My God, let him be alive.*

I found him sitting with his back against the tree he'd hidden behind, one boot off, examining the damage to the heel that had been hit by the RPD.

He was furious. 'Fuck them, Mick,' he said as I approached. 'These moulded soles cost me a fortune and now that bastard has blown the heel off.'

He'd also lost his cap in the action. With tears of relief welling, I ruffled his curly, black hair and, as gruffly as I could muster, told him to go and find his cap while I sorted out what we had just done.

Rex had been saved by a slight hollow in the ground and the sturdy blackwood tree – also known as ebony – which had not yielded in spite of multiple hits by the RPD. He had somehow compressed his 105 kilograms into the narrow hollow behind the tree as the machine gun raked the ground on either side of him.

I took pictures of the faces with the Minox and searched the bodies without finding anything of interest. Pig Dog collected up all the weapons and ammunition. Apart from the AKM that Ncube had fired, they were too badly damaged to salvage, so we stuffed them down an old antbear hole.

We left the bodies where they were. We hoped the vultures would move in on them once they had finished the rhino carcass. Like the elephant, it too had suffered multiple gunshot wounds. We counted twenty-six bullet holes. The front horn and the stumpy rear horn had been sawn off.

We made our way back to the camp where Karate and Mack had everything organized, including a pile of logs under the shelter and on top of the six bodies. We were all keen to move on, but I was desperately tired and I knew the others would be too. We had done our job and now there was plenty of time for a rest. Apart from the company of six dead bodies, this was as good a place as any. We filled our water bottles, made a brew, and as Jonny watched over us with his machine gun, I slept and dreamed of vultures flying through white clouds of deadly ash from erupting volcanoes.

Next morning, we managed to communicate with Kanyemba police and gave them an update on what had happened. I told them our plans were to follow the trail used by this poaching group to the Zambezi River and that we would make contact again once we got there. We were running short of food and our radio batteries were low, so I hoped they could bring a resupply up the river to us by boat. We could then hand over the poachers' weapons and items of interest we had found in their packs we thought the police would be interested in, and I could brief Peter more fully in person.

Before closing, I told him we had found the two rhino horns in one of the packs and said I wasn't keen to bring them out. They were a heavy, bloody mess I didn't want to carry. More importantly, I was concerned that the illegal value of these items might just be too tempting for some if we handed them over. I didn't expand on the point, but I was thinking about the elephant we had found on the first day that had been shot with a .303 service rifle by somebody based in Kanyemba.

Peter was thinking about the paper trail a find like this would generate, so readily agreed it would be better all round if I just got rid of them. I told Karate to put the horns on top and in the centre of the log pile then I ordered everyone to spread out and find more wood. If the temperature was high enough, the fire would surely destroy the horns.

I was going to take down the washing-line wire with the smoked elephant meat and put that on top of the fire as well, but I changed my mind on seeing two yellow-billed kites sitting in a nearby tree, feeding on strips of meat they had snatched off the line with their talons. The birds were welcome to the meat.

We lit the fire and a little breeze soon fanned it into life. The flames quickly spread and grew higher.

We watched as the flames caught the roof of the shelter, which collapsed on top of the log pile below. By now there was a decent inferno. The kites swooped down through the smoke catching locusts and lizards flushed out by the blaze.

It was time to move on.

We reached the Zambezi late morning the following day. Along the way we saw another flock of vultures circling over the hills to the north of us. I didn't want to see another machine-gunned elephant, so I made a note on the map and left it at that.

We all felt good as we reached the great river and made camp beneath tall, dense trees at the base of a huge sandbank. There were plenty of crocodile signs around; we'd have to be careful collecting water and washing in the river.

The river itself was compressed between the hills of the gorge; while upstream it was over a kilometre wide, here it was no more than 150 metres wide and very deep. The water was crystal clear and we could see shoals of *tilapia* bream feeding below while big, brown catfish hovered just below the surface, waiting for morsels to float down in the current.

We always did a clearance patrol around any area where we were going to camp, and it was in the course of this exercise that Jonny made his second discovery of the trip. Across the sand he noticed two grooves that were too straight to be crocodile markings. He followed them and hidden under low bushes found two kayaks. On the sand next to them lay four elephant tusks.

We'd found the poachers' boats and their haul of ivory.

We pulled the boats out onto the sandbank and saw they were the 'Pouch' brand, made in what was then East Germany. They were an olive green colour and similar in size and shape to the Kleppers we used, and like them were made for two people. The basic design was also much the same as the Kleppers: with timber ribbing that fitted inside an outer waterproof fabric that had a texture almost like elephant skin. We'd keep these for ourselves. They were brand new and would be a good addition to our limited stock of the Kleppers we were starting to use increasingly on operations.

We settled into our camp then called Peter Saunders on the radio, to give him our location and details of what we needed from the stores we'd left with him. He would bring the police boat up the river in the morning and was looking forward to seeing us.

Knowing we had a resupply on the way, that night we enjoyed using up what rations we still had. I'd kept some special coffee and made a dark, strong mix. I called Rex over and told him to bring his billy.

We sat together on the edge of the sandbank, silently watching the river in the fading light of the day and sipped the scalding black coffee.

'That was close, mate,' I eventually said.

'It was,' replied Rex. Then turning and grinning at me he said, 'We've both had close calls but don't let it worry you, Mick. Only the good die young.'

We threw the grounds onto the sand and walked back into camp where Karate was waiting with his cap to draw the night guard roster. I got the midnight shift and was happy because I had a good chance, at that time, of hearing the weird and ghostly calls of the big Pel's fishing owls I knew would be hidden in the dense foliage somewhere close.

First thing in the morning, we set about dismantling the Pouch kayaks. There were some differences, but generally they came apart like our own Kleppers and Mack soon had them in their carry bags and ready for shipment back to base.

We heard the sound of the twin outboard motors that pushed the police boat upstream against the current and welcomed Peter and three of his team to our sandbank. We had moved the kayaks to the edge of the river where Simmo had put the tusks and everything else we had found in a neat row for inspection, before handing it over to the police.

I left Simmo and the others to organize the loading of our booty onto the police launch and to get our supplies while Rex, Nelson and I took Peter and his sergeant off to a quiet, shady corner of the sandbank to record and discuss everything that had happened. I gave Peter the notebook we had found in Moses Ncube's pack and pointed out the names and the elementary accounting that would surely be worthy of further investigation. I also handed over my Minox camera, which would go to Special Branch. They would develop the film and try to identify the victims.

Finally Rex handed over the .303 cartridge case that Jonny had found by the first elephant carcass. He explained the circumstances of finding it and mentioned I'd taken pictures with the Minox.

'Peter,' I said. 'It looks like we have a second poaching problem, unrelated to the one we have just sorted out, and we think it's in your own backyard. I have been thinking about it and have a suggestion for you. Could you issue a police notice advising that defects have been found in some of the older .303 rifles being used throughout the country? Say that as a precautionary measure you have been ordered to fire one round from all .303 rifles in your area and record the weapon number against the cartridge case used in the test, which will be sent away for forensic examination. And that thereby the experts will be able to establish if the problem is the ammunition or a defective part in the ageing .303s.

'Meanwhile,' I continued, 'send this case we found at the scene of the dead elephant to the forensic team in Salisbury. Ask them if the ejector markings match any of the test samples that will follow. The only people in this area with .303s are your own police constables and the game department, so logic says one of their weapons is responsible for the poaching.'

Peter nodded in agreement. I then got Nelson to tell them exactly what he had heard when we went to seek advice about routes and waterholes, particularly the message we felt had been given to us by Mlanga, the old ranger who'd alluded to a problem with 'tuskless cow' elephants.

Nelson asked the African police sergeant his tribe and language then repeated everything we had said in his own language. It was a much longer conversation and the sergeant asked several questions. The sergeant looked at Peter and smiled: 'This is good advice, Sir. We should do this,' he said in English. Then he looked back at Nelson and the rest of us, shaking his head in admiration and wonder.

'Got it,' said Peter with some enthusiasm. 'We've had suspicions ourselves for some time, but so far no evidence, and people are afraid to talk. That suggests somebody senior is involved. We think we know who it is and there are other investigations in progress, but finding this cartridge case and doing what you suggest could well bring us a result.'

He too shook his head in admiration. 'You have done a fantastic job. I have kept the brigadier and police headquarters informed via the radio and they are extremely pleased with what you have done. It more than justifies us asking to get you involved. We could never have handled this situation ourselves.'

Peter left us with some welcome fresh food, new batteries for the radios and enough rations to see us through the next three days as we continued on the eastern loop of the track that would eventually lead us back to our vehicles.

We were in no hurry; I told everyone that we should enjoy and appreciate the walk back through a unique landscape we might never return to.

Two enjoyable days followed. We were always alert because we were in big game country and we did indeed encounter big animals, but the pressure was off in terms of being tactical; we were relaxed and in good humour.

We were well on our way down out of the hills and within a couple of hours of the Land Rovers when we ran into a herd of thirty or more elephants.

It was a matriarch herd, led by cow elephants tending a dozen or so youngsters of varying ages. We had been following their tracks and were upwind and slightly above them when we heard them feeding.

We stopped and grouped together to watch them in the woodland below, oblivious to our presence. There was a big bend in the river line at this point, and the track we were following took the shortest route from one side to the other. The elephants had left the track and were feeding in the lush vegetation between it and the river.

Rex and I surveyed the scene with some apprehension.

'This is dangerous, guys,' I said. 'The females are fiercely protective of their young and they will get our scent as we go past them on the track. There will be a panic we don't want to be involved with. We will be OK if we stick close together and move quickly. Once we are downwind they should go away from us.'

Rex agreed, so we moved in single file and hastily jogged down the track. We were halfway to our vantage point when the area erupted into a screaming madness as the elephants got our scent. With fear, no doubt fuelled by the poaching activities in the area, they took flight. 'Bloody jumbos,' said Pig Dog once we were safely downwind. 'Glad we don't have them in New Zealand.' Then, as an afterthought, he looked around and said, 'Where's Simmo?'

We called out and whistled but there was no reply. My heart sank. I knew at once we had a problem on our hands. We spread out and walked back along the track.

I found his FN rifle first. The safety catch had been pushed between the single shot firing status we usually used and the automatic setting. I made the weapon safe and hurried forward.

We found Simmo on his back on the ground next to a jagged tree stump that had been broken by the elephants. I saw the bloody hole pulsating in his chest and my first thought was that he had tripped and somehow impaled himself on the tree stump.

I kneeled down next to him, his breathing was laboured but he was alive. 'Shit, that thing can kick,' he whispered.

Karate and Fish were alongside and ripped open his shirt to examine the wound. Bits of broken rib were evident around the hole in his chest but there wasn't much blood, which was little comfort as we realized the bleeding would be internal. Karate cleaned up the wound while Fish injected morphine. As they were doing this, I saw the trickle of blood emerge from under his back. We lifted his semi-conscious body forward while Karate cleaned up the wound in his back and put a dressing on that as well.

Rex came over. He had already taken out the map and located our position.

'Rex, this is bloody serious. Simmo is bleeding internally and God knows what damage has been done to internal organs. He'll die if we don't get help quickly. Karate and I will rig up the HF radio, but that's going to take some time, and reception hasn't been great anywhere in this region. Take one of the VHF sets and you and Pig Dog get up on top of one of those ridges as fast as you can. Pray for Simmo's sake that you can pick up Kanyemba, or the army relay station on top of *Chiramba Kadoma*.'

Rex grabbed the radio and he and Pig Dog ran off towards the nearest hill.

Fish and the boys had made him comfortable, and as the morphine took effect Simmo was able to tell us what had happened.

He'd been at the back when we started our dash past the elephants. But instead of staying with us, he stopped and watched in fascination as the big animals and their young fed contentedly on the succulent, new leaves of the woodland.

Then suddenly all hell broke out as the herd got our scent. Simmo sprinted down the track after us but he had left it too late. An elephant cow with a young calf met him head-on. His first thought was to use the rifle, but it was swatted out of his hands by the elephant's trunk and he fell down. The animal straddled him and Simmo was trapped in the middle of four kicking legs. After a prolonged period of kicking, the animal backed off. It then kneeled down, pushed a tusk into his chest and lifted him into the air. Simmo said it had hurt so much that he took hold of the other tusk to ease the pain. He was slammed into the ground and left for dead.

The mother elephant then shepherded her calf away from the scene and they both ran off to catch up with the herd.

I called Fish to one side. 'What do you think, Fish?' I asked. 'He's had a tusk shoved through his ribcage and it's incredible the heart has been missed completely. If it or any of the big arteries had been hit by the tusk, Simmo would be dead by now.'

'Yes,' said Fish. 'I also asked him to cough then spit out what came up. There was a bit of blood but not much, so his lungs also look to be largely intact. He's bloody lucky, but the fact remains he's bleeding internally and we don't know how badly. If we can get him out quickly it looks like he's got a good chance. If not he's history.'

Simmo got lucky.

We heard Rex calling over the radio then pumped our fists in the air as we heard him responding: 'Cloudbase, this is Sierra One Seven. Reading you strength five. We have an urgent casevac request. One of our call sign has been seriously injured by an elephant. Roger so far?'

We couldn't hear the Cloudbase transmission, but we listened as Rex went on to give them our position. There was a pause in the radio traffic and I took the chance to call Rex.

Fish had warned that for Simmo to survive he'd need to be treated in a big base hospital where, apart from everything else, he could get blood: 'O positive' he'd told me, checking Simmo's dog tags, and he'd also need plasma.

I passed all this on to Rex and heard him in turn repeat it to the Cloudbase relay station. He then got back to us, saying they had all the information and had passed it back to headquarters. I was greatly relieved, because I knew the brigadier would move heaven and earth to help us.

Simmo got lucky again.

Earlier in the day a helicopter had been sent into Mukumbura, an inland police base in the Zambezi Valley about thirty-five minutes flying time away. The helicopter would pick up Simmo and Fish and take them to Kanyemba where there was an airstrip, and from there the brigadier had organized an Aermacchi to get them rapidly to the nearest hospital.

We gave Simmo a second shot of morphine and changed his dressings. It wasn't cold but nevertheless we wrapped him up in our sleeping bags and jackets in case the shock reaction was stronger than the tranquilizing effect of the morphine.

Apart from finding and preparing a suitable landing zone for the helicopter, there was nothing left to do except wait and hope. Rex and Pig Dog stayed on top of their hill with the VHF radio in case there were changes to plan. They would guide in the helicopter as soon as it made comms with us.

Simmo drifted in and out of consciousness as we waited anxiously for the familiar sound of the French Alouette helicopter. He was comfortable enough and still had colour in his face, so I was optimistic. 'Looking good,' said Fish reading my thoughts. 'But it will be touch and go towards the end of the journey. Things have gone well for him so far. Let's just hope he can hang in there.'

As the chopper closed in, I knelt down next to Simmo and told him he would be transferred to a light aircraft at Kanyemba and flown to a big hospital. I told him Fish had said he'd need to guts it out during the final stages of the flight, if he did that there was every chance he would be back with us once he had been patched up. 'And Simmo,' I said, 'that's what I want to happen. I want you back here as part of our team as soon as possible.'

I didn't intend it, but the last bit came out like an order.

'Yes, Sir. I'll be back,' Simmo replied weakly, with a sigh that uncomfortably reminded me of the dying elephant we had shot. 'Sorry to have caused all this trouble. You told me to stay close and I fucked up by watching those elephants.'

'You'll be fine, Simmo. Fish will be with you and we'll come and see you when we get back to base.'

The Alouette took them away from us and within twenty minutes they had landed at Kanyemba. Simmo was transferred to the light aircraft, which wasted no time in taking off while Fish rigged up a drip.

The brigadier had called ahead to explain the incoming SAS soldier's injuries, so the hospital's emergency services were already geared up and waiting for him.

The only question remaining was would Simmo reach these services in time? Could he somehow cling onto life and give them enough time to repair the damage? If indeed it was possible to do that.

As the aircraft descended onto the airbase runway, Simmo's lungs collapsed. Fish hooked up the oxygen bottle in the aircraft and asked the pilot to get the waiting ambulance to meet them on the runway. The police knew about this by now and had a patrol car escort waiting with the ambulance.

Simmo was rushed unconscious to the emergency ward of the general hospital. There was no time for finesse; the surgeon immediately cut open the ribcage to examine the damage caused by the tusk. He was as astonished at Simmo's luck as we had been. He said he thought it must have been a young elephant cow with short, thin tusks because the impalement had missed everything important – although it had done some damage to the left lung.

The surgeon cleaned everything up then pulled the ribcage back into place. It took seventy-six stitches to keep it there and while all this was going on, blood was being fed continuously into Simmo's body via transfusion.

Six weeks later, Simmo was at the Outward Bound School in the high Chimanimani Mountains on the eastern border, where we had sent him to recover and get his strength back. They insisted he stay longer than we wanted because he proved to be the best abseiling instructor they had ever had. He apparently encouraged the youngsters there to stay close to each other and develop a team culture, like his team – call sign Sierra One Seven in the SAS.

That's how the operation ended for Simmo. Eventually, we duly welcomed him back into the fold.

Once the helicopter had gone, the rest of us walked silently down from the foothills to our Sabres. It was a depressing end to the operation and there was none of the usual humorous banter or excitement at the prospect of going home.

We spent a quiet night with the vehicles, and before packing up camp next morning Karate fired up the radio and called Kanyemba. Peter's familiar voice answered the call. 'You'll be happy to learn that Simmo is OK,' he said and went on to give us the details. We all breathed a sigh of relief and the mood of the team immediately picked up.

Peter added that when the Aermacchi had come in, he'd taken the opportunity of giving the pilot the .303 cartridge cases he had collected from the test-firing ruse, as well as the one we'd found by the first dead elephant. They had since been handed over to the police, and the forensic team would waste no time in trying to match our cartridge with the test rounds. He said it wouldn't take long and by the time we got back to camp later that day he hoped to have more good news for us.

We reached the police base early afternoon and again set up camp on the lawn by the swimming pool. The priority for us was a good wash and clean clothes, but we decided first to check in with Peter. We were told he was out but had left a message inviting us to make ourselves comfortable and saying he would catch up later.

We were relaxing in the sun, cleaning our weapons and sorting out our packs when two grey police Land Rovers roared into camp. We watched as the police sergeant we had met at the river opened the back door of the lead vehicle and took two men in handcuffs away to the cells. From the second vehicle, four constables each pulled out an elephant tusk and took it away into the base. Peter looked on and, after giving a few instructions, came over to see us – a broad smile on his face.

'We got them,' he said and pumped my hand, then did the same to Rex, Nelson and the rest of the team. 'Thank you all. It's been a remarkable operation. Not only did you sort out the terrorist-turned-poacher problem, but you gave us the evidence we needed to terminate another poaching operation in our own backyard – as you put it to me, Mick.

'The cartridge case you found matched the one we later fired from the rifle of David Changamire, head of the game department operation in this north-east corner of the Zambezi Valley. We confronted him this afternoon with a warrant for his arrest and a search warrant for his home and the game department buildings. He admitted to killing two elephants and we have recovered the ivory.

'He was working with his senior ranger, who we have also arrested, but of more interest is the fact that they were doing this in cahoots with one of the game department managers based in Salisbury. The police moved in on him as soon as we sent word and guess what? He – like the Zambian-based terrorists you eliminated – was also working for a Chinese agent. I guess the problem for the world is convincing the Chinese they don't need ivory, and that powdered rhino horn doesn't help anybody's sex life.'

Later that night, as we sat round a campfire with the police team and the local game rangers, Nelson turned to Mlanga – the old tracker who'd given him the message – and said that he still couldn't understand the significance of the 'tuskless cow' he'd referred to.

Mlanga only had three or four teeth left and, grinning, he pointed at his mouth: 'It is like this,' he said. 'The elephant has tusks but if you cut them out then it becomes toothless – a tuskless cow – and that is how the two animals killed by David Changamire were reported. One of the rangers saw the reports and told us about it. We have been living here since small boys and know this country and the animals. We have never seen a tuskless cow elephant and so it was a mystery to us.'

Nelson shook his head in disbelief while he interpreted for us.

'A mystery, Mlanga? I don't think so. You are too clever for that to be a mystery,' he laughingly replied.

That in turn brought on laughter from Mlanga and the rest of the game rangers.

'It is true,' Mlanga said eventually. 'But we could do nothing. We too found the carcass where you took your Land Rovers and we reported it to our boss. He said it would be investigated. Although nothing happened, the gods were clearly on our side because if we had found the bullet you picked up, we would have given it to him and still nothing would have happened. You were sent here to fix the problem of the tuskless cow.'

He rummaged in a small cloth bundle and produced a bangle made from the hairs of an elephant's tail that had been tied together beautifully with thin strips of brown bark. He handed it to Rex.

'This came from the tuskless cow,' he said. 'Please give it to the young soldier who was injured. Tell him it was not the elephant who caused his injuries, but the evil people who hunt and kill them with guns.'

And with those words, Mlanga brought an end to our operation with the elephants.

Pig Dog does the Haka

After a period of prolonged operations, we were finally due for a break. I tagged on four days leave to the usual ten days R and R and was looking forward to two full weeks away from it all. I would definitely go birdwatching somewhere but didn't have any firm plans.

It was early November in Rhodesia and the country already had had good rain. The *msasa* trees on the highveld were ablaze with the red, brown and amber of new leaves. In the dry low country the *mopane* trees had come back to life, their bare branches now covered with bright green leaves shaped like big butterflies.

For a birdwatcher, it was the best time of year. The new growth and humidity increased the insect population and, to take advantage of this, dozens of migrant bird species arrived in the country – many of them to breed.

I was mulling over where I might go when I got a call from my closest friend, Professor John Hargrove. We had been buddies since the age of fourteen. We shared a love of birdlife and the African bush and had had many adventures together.

John was a seriously good mathematician. After graduating from Oxford University with a PhD, he found himself a job doing research into the tsetse fly that caused sleeping sickness in humans and death to domestic stock. Essentially he was a data analyst, but John being John it was just a matter of time before he immersed himself in the complete science and inevitably ended up running the show.

John's fieldwork was done at a research station on the Rekometjie River at the base of the Zambezi Escarpment, the southernmost part of the Great Rift Valley. With perennial waterholes and lush, riverine vegetation it was an ideal location: there was a lot of big game around and travelling with it were swarms of tsetse flies. While the flies killed domestic stock, they didn't seem to affect the animals they travelled with – buffalo particularly – and John's mission was to find out why.

He was about to leave on a ten-day field trip and invited me along. I had no hesitation in accepting. I knew the bird and animal life would be outstanding, the camp was comfortable and John and his team were great company.

While we were organizing a few of the details, I had a sudden thought: 'John,' I asked, 'is there room on this trip for one more person? One of my SAS team comes from New Zealand. He's a long way from home, but he's a real bushman and I know he'd really enjoy Rekometjie. Is it possible we could bring him along?'

There was plenty of room at the research station and John said they could use another strong man. They planned to do some work on four wild warthogs they had in captivity and it promised to be a boisterous exercise.

'Couldn't be better,' I laughed. 'We call him Pig Dog and he'll be in his element.'

I told Pig Dog where I was going and asked if he'd like to come along. His eyes lit up at once in appreciation, and then with the excitement of going to a new place he could sense, from my own enthusiasm, would be somewhere special.

Pig Dog and John hit it off from the start. During the long drive, the Kiwi bushman entertained us with stories of him and his father poaching deer or rustling goats from conservation land in the deep south of New Zealand.

'Those animals shouldn't have been in our forests in the first place!' he'd exclaim. 'Nobody was going to do anything about it, so we decided to take control. We culled the deer and made good money from the antler velvet. Having been at the meat works, we knew how to make venison sausages, which sold as fast as we could make them.

'The goats were different and easy. We'd round them up with our dogs and they soon became quite docile as we herded them out of the forest. We'd make temporary holding pens and then bring up the truck to add them to our home stock, which we either milked to make feta cheese or killed, halal-style, to sell to the Muslims up in Auckland.'

John shook his head. 'And you did all this in a national park?' he laughed in amazement.

'Well, stuff it, John! Somebody had to do something. If we didn't our forests would be well and truly screwed. What people don't realize is that New Zealand has only two native mammals – two bloody small bats. The introduced animals that do so much damage are – to me – no different from the terrorists Mick and our team hunt down over here in Africa.'

'Pig Dog, you're a bloody hero,' said John, recognizing an environmentalist as passionate in his own way, in his own country, as John was here in Africa.

A few days later, John would have reason to repeat what he had just said, but for very different reasons the second time round.

The narrow, bush road leading to the station had grass in the middle and elephant pats, in big lumps, that splattered the underside of the Land Cruiser. On the fresher mounds clouds of small, yellow butterflies flew up and scattered as we approached. There was a sweet smell in the air like boiled potatoes – a combination of elephant dung and the scent of crushed roadside weeds.

A massive baobab tree stood guard at the entrance to the station, where a sign with a couple of bullet holes in it welcomed visitors to Rekometjie.

The complex was built about 100 metres away from the river line in amongst other big baobabs and tall, thorny acacias. On one side was the living accommodation consisting of several individual rondavels: the rounded African hut made from mud-plastered brick, painted white with a thick overhanging thatched roof supported by black, creosoted timber beams. There was a single door and wide, frameless windows with no glass – just insect screens – on each side.

The rondavels were well spread out, most of them shaded by thorn trees. Some, like the one I habitually used when visiting the camp, had a small patch of lawn and a bed of straggly Star-of-Bethlehem flowers in pink and red. On a previous trip, I had taken a bird bath made from a plough disc and had mounted it on a rock base. I was pleased to see it full of water and a pair of blue waxbills and a small squirrel making good use of the facility.

The centre of the station was marked by a steel-panelled water tank, perched high in the air on top of vertical steel beams bedded in deep concrete. On one side of the tank were the showers and toilets, and on the opposite side – some distance away – were the open-sided shelters that were the kitchen and dining room, the latter with a large table that could seat twenty or more. An owl they named Wal had made one corner of the dining room his home and perched on the roof beams throughout the day, quite unperturbed by the routine comings and goings of the human occupants.

Outside the dining area, a stone ring contained an open fireplace and surrounding it in a triangle were three big logs used as fireside seating during the winter months.

On the far side of the complex were the workshops and timber enclosures that housed livestock being used in the various tests and experiments. In addition to the warthogs, there were several cattle – a local breed that showed resistance to tsetse fly bites – and it was hoped they might help unravel the secret to combating the fly. These enclosures were surrounded by a three-metre high chain mesh fence topped with barbed wire to keep out lions, leopards and hyenas attracted to this captive food supply.

Pig Dog shared the rondavel with me. On that first night he woke me twice.

The first time was around midnight when he gently shook me awake and signalled silence. He pointed to one of the open windows with the thin insect screen. Having just woken up, I wondered why I couldn't see any starlight, then immediately recognized the movement and rasping sound. The window frame was obscured by the body of an elephant, scratching its side on the edge of the roof thatching.

We silently walked over to the window and stood within centimetres of the elephant, separated only by the screen. It scratched itself for two or three minutes then, stomach gurgling, it moved away and the starlight came back.

We heard that slurping sound the straw makes at the end of a milkshake and realized the thirsty elephant had just drained the bird bath. There was a belch as the animal wombled contentedly away towards the river.

The bird bath was popular, and after a couple of hornbills and glossy starlings had done their business there wouldn't be much water left, so I kept a bucketful inside for topping it up.

I was dreaming about the elephant draining my bird bath, when I felt a touch and found Pig Dog next to me once more. He again signalled silence and pointed towards the window. I sat up listening and heard a quiet lap-lapping at the water. And there, no more than three metres away from us was the dark, spotted form of a leopard.

Next morning we were assembled around the breakfast table, talking about the animal experiences overnight and listening to John plot out the day's activities. Wal, the owl, looked on indifferently through half-closed eyelids. Suddenly, there was a shout from the kitchen. We turned to see the cook reaching for an empty pan and the soup ladle, which he clattered with vigour while delivering loud, verbal abuse in the direction of the water tank.

We turned again, expecting to see elephants, but there was nothing.

Pig Dog pointed, he'd seen movement: 'Behind that thorn tree. My God, it's a lion!' he exclaimed. Into view came a lioness walking slowly towards the rondavels. She paused and looked across at us, not showing any concern at the outburst from the cook.

'She's going for a drink,' I said. 'I'll be topping up the bird bath again after breakfast.'

'That's really interesting,' said John. 'A lone female means she's left the pride to have cubs, seeing her here like this means they can't be too far away.

'Lameck,' he said to his leading hand. 'We should get out the electric fence wire and put that around the animal enclosure. She will need to kill to survive and bring up her cubs. She will already know about our cattle and you can guarantee she'll have a crack at them.'

As the lioness disappeared behind the rondavel, Pig Dog turned to me. 'Suddenly I feel very naked,' he said. 'This is my first time in the African bush without a rifle, and here I am with a lioness at my bedroom door.'

I was having exactly those thoughts myself. We could easily have brought our FN rifles with us, but I knew John was not in favour of firearms at his station and I went along with that. But my mind was now questioning whether principle should, in fact, have taken precedent over precaution.

John explained to Pig Dog that over the many years the station had existed, the few troubles they'd had with wild animal attacks had all been due to the involvement of firearms. We listened with interest to the examples he gave us. There were two cases involving buffalo and one with elephant. In all three cases, the humans involved were visiting academics or dignitaries and therein lay the problem, because none of them had any fieldcraft or firearms training worth mentioning. Their inexperience had created panic amongst the animals and shots ended up being fired. The national parks authorities were not amused by such actions, even less at the prospect of having to go after the wounded animals to stop their suffering.

John's logic was good. In the circumstances, I too would have made the call to leave the rifles locked in the cupboard.

Pig Dog nodded. 'We'll have to stay wide awake with her around,' he said. 'But I guess we are used to that.'

We exchanged glances again, both of us still wishing we'd brought our SAS 'comfort blanket' – the Fabrique Nationale 7.62 millimetre self-loading semi–automatic rifle with a twenty-round magazine.

Later that morning, Pig Dog amazed everybody with his skill at handling the warthogs. There were four in the pen, the largest a good-sized boar with big tusks on either side of its jaw. John wanted them taken individually into a crush pen, where he could take blood and DNA samples and implant a microchip and tracking device before letting them go back into the wild.

Once John had explained what he wanted, Pig Dog assumed command and issued instructions to the staff. He wanted a strong pole about three metres long and a length of rope.

They returned with a cut *mopane* branch Pig Dog bent and flexed and eventually declared suitable. He knotted one end of the rope to the top of the pole and after measuring out the length he wanted, he cut the rope and made a large loop like a hangman's noose that dangled below.

'Now we go fishing.' He grinned and jumped over the railings into the pen with the four warthogs.

The pigs immediately panicked and ran around the pen trying to escape. Pig Dog prodded the biggest with the tusks and it turned to face him – confrontation was imminent.

It was exactly what Pig Dog had been waiting for. With the big warthog now head-on, he lunged forward with the pole and deftly got the rope loop around its neck. He lifted the pole sharply – striking as in fishing.

The startled hog launched itself at Pig Dog, only to have its head and neck squeezed tight by the rope and its front legs lifted off the ground by the pole. It danced around for a while on its back legs trying to reach Pig Dog, but he kept it at bay. The pole bent over with the weight and strain but held firm.

'Let the rod do the work, my father used to say when I'd hooked a big one. Pigs, fish, violent dogs – no difference – it works every time,' he said triumphantly as the big warthog tired.

Pig Dog kept it under pressure, holding it on its back legs, forcing the animal to stay upright to ease the tension on its neck and breathing. As the pig weakened, Pig Dog eased the pressure and gradually lowered it down until it could once again stand on its front legs, but he kept the head held high and gave the odd little jerk on the rope just to let the animal know he could take it back up if he wanted to.

He called Lameck into the pen and handed over the pole to him. Once Lameck had the rope tension to his satisfaction, Pig Dog moved away to the side and came in behind the captured animal. The other pigs bolted to the opposite side of the enclosure, watching in fear and fascination.

'Lift him up, Lameck,' he ordered, and as the head and front end again lifted into the air he darted in, straddled its back to get the animal between his legs then grabbed an ear in each hand. He lifted the pig's head higher into the air by the ears and the rope tension lessened. The pig responded with its first squeal of pain and panic.

Pig Dog frogmarched the warthog on its back legs into the crush pen, where it was secured and could be worked on. We all applauded, but Pig Dog would have none of it. 'There's another three to go,' he growled as he moved in to snare the next pig.

Over the next three days, Pig Dog and I worked with John and his team and greatly enjoyed our involvement in the fieldwork. John got us to hang pheromone traps in trees along the river line and explained how the bait emitted a scent that was a sexual attractant to male tsetse flies. It was one of many different control measures he was investigating. We could see what he was aiming at and couldn't help but get caught up in his infectious enthusiasm.

'Never thought I'd get excited about checking a mozzie net full of flies,' said Pig Dog with a grin as we went out to check the traps next morning.

During the course of those three days, we saw the lioness twice. She got stung by the electric fence around the animal stockade and fled wondering what had hit her; a night later she came back to drink at the bird bath.

She was no trouble. We all hoped her cubs were doing well and Pig Dog and I had started to relax about having her around. Maybe this was normal for a place like Rekometjie and we just had to get used to it.

Well, maybe.

John had reached a stage where he needed a break from the practical work to document the recordings they had accumulated, update the databases and make reports for government and donor agencies on activity and results.

'We're well ahead of schedule with my plans, thanks in no small way to you two,' John said to Pig Dog and me during breakfast. 'So before I bury myself in my laptop, there is a special place on the river I discovered last year that I know both of you will enjoy. It's about an hour's walk downstream from here. I suggest we leave as soon as you are ready.'

We followed John along a wide elephant trail that gently climbed up to a low, stony ridge where, 600 metres away to our right, we could see the green fringe of the river line. Following it downstream, we could see it cut back inland in a wide bend we were heading for. There would be water there the elephants knew about and our track would take us directly to it.

We moved off the track and waited quietly behind an anthill as a herd of cow elephants with several young passed by, trunks swinging and deep, contented, gurgling sounds coming from their stomachs. The wind was in our favour so the elephants didn't get our scent and continued peacefully on their way.

'That was great,' enthused Pig Dog. 'But sometimes it's better to be upwind.'

In these conditions, we could easily get close to animals without them getting our scent and without us seeing them. Being too close to a startled elephant or buffalo could be dangerous; coming face to face with a lioness with cubs could be even worse.

Without our rifles, and with such thoughts in mind, Pig Dog moved in front of John and silently led us through the thick tangle of creepers and shrubs towards the river. He stopped frequently to look, smell and listen. He got us close to a beautiful bushbuck ram, chestnut brown with thin, white stripes and spots dotted over its body. These antelope could be aggressive and were unafraid of humans, so we didn't move until it eventually sensed our presence and, with a bark of alarm, darted off into the thick undergrowth.

We broke cover on the edge of the wide, dry, sandy river.

Lifting my binoculars, I could see at once why John had wanted to bring us here. The opposite bank was a mass of nest burrows, hollowed out by one of the most colourful birds in Africa – the carmine bee-eater. More than a hundred of these dazzling, red and blue birds called noisily from perches or darted into the air after bees or dragonflies.

'Scan right, Mick.' I heard Pig Dog say over my shoulder as I watched the birds. 'There is something unusual in the middle of the river about 200 metres away.'

I moved the glasses towards what, at first, looked like a dark rock and then adjusting focus I recognized the shape. It was a dead baby elephant, lying in the sand in the middle of the river bed.

A few vultures sat in the trees on the opposite bank and two ugly marabou storks stood watching about fifty paces away from the carcass.

'Why are those birds keeping clear?' I wondered out loud. 'Usually they'd be all over the dead animal. Maybe mum is still around?' I scanned both sides of the river looking for clues, but saw nothing.

'I'm going down to have a look,' said John. 'The little jumbo must have had an accident of some sort. Normally the cows keep them well clear of any danger.'

John and Pig Dog dropped down onto the sandy river bed while I stayed on top of the bank and moved a bit closer to get a better view of the bird colony. I watched the two of them walking in the sand in the middle of the river. Suddenly, Pig Dog jumped off to one side and grabbed hold of something. He held it up and turned to face me, knowing I'd be watching with my binoculars. He'd caught a small python.

Pig Dog examined the docile snake for some time then walked to the tangle of a tree, brought down in a flood, and let the snake go into the cover of the debris collected on the root bole.

Meanwhile, John had gone ahead towards the dead baby elephant.

He had not seen the lioness, crouched in the deep shade of a bush on the opposite bank of the river, overlooking the carcass. She had seen us appear on the riverbank. Her ears pricked up and her tail began to twitch nervously.

She'd found the elephant early that morning. It had probably been accidentally trampled by juvenile bulls still with the herd.

For the elephant cow, it was a tragedy.

For a lioness with two cubs, it was food for a week and she'd already been busy chasing off a jackal and the nagging vultures.

Her tail twitched with increasing agitation as John and Pig Dog dropped down off the bank onto the deep sand of the dry river bed. Her ears flattened onto her crown and her brow wrinkled as John approached the carcass.

She ran out of patience when John kneeled down next to the dead elephant. She snarled, jumped down the bank, and in great, angry leaps, grunting each time her front paws hit the ground, she charged towards John. She would not let him eat her food!

John saw her soon enough, hesitated a moment in fearful indecision, then turned and ran back towards the riverbank.

It was no contest. John had no chance in the deep sand against a mighty animal that could cover 100 metres in about five seconds. But still he ran as fast as he could.

The lioness was getting closer all the time. With each stride she took, John could hear the grunt getting noticeably louder. Soon he also heard her breathing. Fear and panic flooded his mind. She was going to catch and kill him.

John didn't know why he did it. But just before it was too late, he suddenly stopped running and swung around to face the lioness. She was only a few paces away from making the final, fatal lunge. She would have snapped John's neck like a twig and he would have been dead before hitting the ground.

But now he had turned to face her. This was not scripted. Never before had she been this close to humans. And, in that instant, the tables turned as uncertainty and the inherent fear of man were suddenly stronger than the urge to chase and kill.

The lioness screeched to a halt in the sand, no more than three paces away from John. She crouched down looking at him, spitting and snarling.

John was too afraid to move, say or do anything. He just stared at the animal, paralyzed with fear.

From sixty metres away, Pig Dog heard the lioness and watched what he was sure would be the death of his friend.

He turned and sprinted towards the snarling animal and a fearful John facing each other on the river bed. He ran and ran. He cursed the sand and the difficulty of going forward but still he ran, eyes fixed on the crouching lioness.

He ran past John and kicked sand in the face of the lioness, which was baffled by this sudden turn of events.

She snarled, jumped back and swiped the air with a huge paw, the massive, razor-sharp claws flashing in the light as they ripped through the air. She crouched again – menacingly, ready to strike and kill – this time focused on Pig Dog.

The tension left Pig Dog. He was now in control.

He stretched to his full height, lifted his arms high above his head and looked down at the animal intimidatingly.

He strutted a half pace to one side then, in a curious movement, he suddenly dropped into a partial crouch and extended his arms at full length in front of him, pointing towards the lioness. He wriggled his wrists and fingers, put out his tongue and rotated his head from side to side. He slowly lifted his right leg in the air then explosively brought it crashing down into the sand.

'*KOMATEE!*' he shouted with all his might and power.

Then the left leg. '*KOMATEE!*' And he took a pace nearer the lioness.

Bouncing up and down, glaring aggressively at the lioness, he chanted as loud as he could: '*KOMATEE-KOMATEE! KOORRA-KOORRA!*'

He smacked his forearms and again lunged menacingly towards the lioness: '*AH-OOPAH!*' he challenged.

The lioness backed off. She had never seen anything like this before.

'*KOMATEE-KOMATEE! AH-OOPAH!*' Pig Dog repeated, and advanced again, sensing victory. He slapped his thighs and star-jumped into the air.

It was too much for the lioness. She turned tail and scampered back to cover on the opposite side of the river.

Pig Dog did a couple more '*KOMATEES*' – just to make sure – then he took John's arm. 'Let's get out of here, John, before she changes her mind,' he said to his now doubly dazed friend.

Sitting on the bank 200 metres away, I watched all this unfold through the crystal clear vision of my Leica binoculars. I couldn't breathe in those final milliseconds as the lioness closed in on John. I clutched the glasses with white knuckles as I watched Pig Dog intervene. If only we had a rifle, I thought. We could have put a shot in the ground in front of the lioness and that would have been enough to scare her off.

I started to grin when I saw Pig Dog lead into the haka: the famous Maori war dance immortalized by the amazing New Zealand All Blacks rugby team. I pumped my fist in the air as I saw the lioness retreat, and had a lump in my throat at the poignant moment when Pig Dog put his arm around John and led him away to safety.

I joined them in the shade of the riverbank. Pig Dog gave a shaking John a drink from his water bottle. He had escaped unharmed but understandably was still in a state of shock.

We sat down on either side of him and made a brew. 'Nothing like a brew to settle things down,' I said soothingly.

John took a few sips from his mug and eventually got his voice back.

He looked at Pig Dog in amazement. 'Where on earth did you learn to do that?'

Pig Dog chuckled. 'The lioness meant no harm,' he said. 'She just didn't want you around her dinner, John.'

We got up and walked slowly back towards the station.

Halfway there, a recovered John caught up with Pig Dog and put his arm around his shoulder. 'Thank you, Pig Dog,' he said. 'You're a bloody hero!'

Operation Dingo

The story about the biggest and most devastating operation in the history of C Squadron SAS starts on a golf course in the town of Umtali, on the eastern border between Rhodesia and Mozambique. 'Welcome to beautiful Umtali,' said the road sign, as one drove over Christmas Pass and into the picturesque town, nestled in a hollow between the mountain pass and the granite massif of the Vumba Mountains immediately to the south. Lush rainforest covered the hill slopes where the high rainfall and cool temperatures had seen the development of tea estates and coffee plantations.

It was a pleasant and prosperous place with a relaxed, unpretentious feel about it.

That was until the Chinese-backed ZANU terrorists arrived.

We had been on a prolonged period of operations, and that combined with international diplomatic efforts to resolve the conflicts in this part of Africa made it a good time for some R and R.

Pig Dog and I took the opportunity to return to the research station in the Zambezi Valley and John Hargrove's tsetse fly project, while the brigadier headed east to Umtali where he too joined an old school friend from Harwich in England.

David Townsend had moved to Rhodesia in the early 1950s and was now an Umtali town councillor with responsibility for recreation, parks and gardens. David had an office in the municipal buildings but spent most of his time at the depot where the vehicles and equipment were stored and serviced: there was a large plant nursery and a control room with maps and RT communications, with the work parties deployed around the town.

David was an affable character with an infectious enthusiasm for his job of keeping Umtali beautiful. His staff members were well paid and motivated and they worshipped him.

'Good morning, Peter,' he said as the brigadier was shown into the control room. 'I hope you have come well prepared, because the agenda this morning is to conduct a thorough inspection of the Hillside municipal golf course.'

Then, after a joke about their bad golfing skills, they got into David's Isuzu diesel pickup truck.

It was early June 1977 – winter in Rhodesia. Overnight the temperature would drop towards zero; there would be crisp, white frost on the grass first thing in the morning, but an hour or two later it would be gone. There was no wind and no humidity, just a cloudless blue sky with warm sunshine. Perfect weather.

The two men were enjoying their reunion and the golf when the tranquillity of a beautiful morning was suddenly shattered.

They were playing the seventh hole: a long uphill par five with the green in the distance surrounded by protective bunkers. The densely forested foothills beyond the golf course rose steeply to a bare granite feature known as 'Cecil Kop'. It was a popular tourist spot with great views over the town.

A low, muted *boom* stopped the brigadier in his tracks and he called out to his friend. He too stopped as a second, third and fourth *boom* followed. Looking up, the brigadier's sharp eyes spotted a wisp of smoke that quickly dissipated. He immediately realized what was happening.

This was a mortar attack from terrorists firing from the top of Cecil Kop.

They summoned the two caddies forward and the four of them crouched down behind the grass bank of a nearby sand bunker.

'We'll soon find out who they are firing at,' said the brigadier. No sooner had he got the words out when, some distance to the north of them, they heard the *crump! crump! crump!* of the mortar bombs exploding.

Twelve mortars were fired at Umtali. There was no concentration of fire at a particular target, the terrorists preferring to scatter their shots across the residential area, the golf course and the grounds of the nearby high school. There were no casualties and very little material damage – a single power pole was blown over – but psychologically the terrorists had scored heavily. Umtali would now be living in fear.

The brigadier hurried down to the drill hall, headquarters of the local territorial battalion, 4 Rhodesian Rifles. A regular army major with a couple of NCOs were posted there to act as training instructors and manage the day-to-day business of the battalion. The brigadier explained what he had seen from the golf course and made suggestions about patrol activity – particularly around the high school area. It was important for the public to see action being taken in response to the attack.

With things underway in the army camp, he then went down to the local police station where he reported what he'd seen to Superintendent Bill Wallace and gave him a rundown of what the army was organizing by way of response.

The superintendent immediately dispatched an armed police patrol to Cecil Kop.

'I doubt if we'll find much more than tracks heading back into Mozambique,' he said to the brigadier. 'The border is less than a kilometre away; with Frelimo now in control of the country, ZANU can move around with impunity. There have been a few whispers about a big camp somewhere close, but I have no hard intelligence.

'Sorry your golf was interrupted,' he added. 'David and I play most weeks and I usually come second.'

'Maybe just as well,' replied the brigadier. 'It was looking likely I would be paying for drinks after the game. Interesting round, though, there wouldn't be many golf clubs in the world that throw in a mortar hazard on the seventh hole.'

They both laughed and Bill said he'd get David to put up a warning sign on the tee.

The weeks passed and while the army and police stepped up routine patrols along the border and through the town, ZANU lay low. Instead of attacking again, it went on a recruiting drive.

Jameson Makonde worked for David Townsend. He was a tractor driver, one of a small team that kept the Umtali roadside verges neat and tidy. He and his wife, Mary, owned a small house in the suburb of Sakubva on the south side of town. They had been to the local TM supermarket to buy some tomatoes and were walking home when they were approached by two men.

The men opened their jackets. Both were carrying AK-47s.

'Do you have children?' the taller of the two asked Mary.

She shook her head.

'That's good. Come with us,' he ordered.

They led Jameson and Mary to a truck parked in a side street, guarded by another two armed men. There were six men and two women already sitting in the back, they were told to join them.

The two men went away and returned half an hour later with another two recruits. They too were put in the back and were joined by the armed guards as the truck started up and drove off into the night.

In the Western world, there were enlistment drafts, compulsory national service and regular call-ups for military training and service. The ZANU enlistment system was much simpler.

Jameson and Mary were desperately unhappy, but decided to keep a low profile and try to avoid trouble. It was a sensible approach, especially after witnessing several brutal beatings and the shooting of a middle-aged man when he protested about his treatment.

They were kept apart for much of the day but were allowed to be together at night.

One afternoon after training, Jameson found his wife crouching on the ground, sobbing. She had been taken away from the camp by three young, armed activists. She tried fighting them but to no avail. Beaten and gang-raped by the three young thugs, Mary had been left whimpering on the ground.

'We are leaving here tonight,' said Jameson.

The extent of the training camp complex and the number of people there was such that they had no difficulty in slipping away unnoticed. They started the long walk back to the Rhodesian border.

Four nights later, David Townsend was woken by knocking on his back door.

It was Jameson and Mary.

The brigadier's phone was ringing as he walked into his office at 07:30 hours the following morning.

'Peter, you need to come to Umtali as soon as you can. This is big. There is much detail I can't give you over the phone,' said David after a brief general explanation.

The brigadier called me into his office and gave me the keys to his green Peugeot 404.

'Fill her up please, Mick, we're going to Umtali,' he said. 'There's a big camp at a place called Chimoio, about sixty-five kilometres inside Mozambique. Apparently, there are thousands of terrorists undergoing training with Frelimo and Chinese instructors. We are going to talk to someone who has just got back from the place.'

I refuelled the Peugeot at the vehicle workshops, while Karate got me two 9-millimetre Uzi sub-machine guns from the armoury and a couple of spare magazines. As I put them on the back seat with the maps from our intelligence section, I had a sudden thought.

'Sir, it might be a good idea to take Nelson with us,' I suggested. 'Whoever we are meeting may have limited English, but with Nelson along that won't matter.'

The brigadier agreed at once, and we picked up Nelson at the armoury as he signed out a third Uzi.

It would take us about three and a half hours to get there.

'It's good to have you along, Nelson,' said the brigadier as we left the outskirts of town. 'The major has told me a lot about you, but I'd enjoy hearing more about Uganda and your story.

'We've got three hours ahead of us,' he said with a smile. 'You should just manage it in that time.'

Nelson was articulate and confident. He'd been well educated and had graduated from the Makerere University in Kampala with a degree in economics. His future had been looking bright until 1971 when Idi Amin turned the country upside down.

'You are right, Sir. Uganda is a long story and a happy ending still looks to be many years away, but I live in hope,' Nelson began.

'The country is the same size as Great Britain. It has many different clans and tribes, just as your home country did in ancient times. And that is one of the big problems for Uganda. To the north of the country, the people come from the Sudan and Nile regions. The central and south populations are Bantu from East Africa. The official languages are English and Swahili. Neither is Ugandan, but with seven or eight different languages spoken across the country, we had to come up with something everyone could speak.'

'So as a child you learned to speak English, Swahili and presumably your own native tongue?' asked the brigadier.

'Yes, Sir. Then at university, I learned from other students and could speak most of the Ugandan languages by the time I had graduated. Later, as I worked my way south, it was not difficult picking up the local tongue because most derive from Swahili.

'My father owned a supermarket in the suburb of Rubaga, on the south-west side of Kampala, close to where King Kabaka had his palace. You won't have heard of Kabaka, but after independence from Britain in 1962, Milton Obote and Kabaka formed a coalition government. Obote controlled the military and the country while Kabaka was our "king". That wasn't unusual because there were several kings in Uganda at that time.

'It was a good time for my father's business, which prospered because Kabaka and his followers were our customers, but it wasn't a good arrangement for the country. The central and south groups believed they were superior to the northern tribes, and this political alliance increased an already simmering resentment.

'The trouble began when Kabaka got greedy and wanted more of the pie. Obote was unimpressed and he controlled the military. Kabaka was eliminated.

'But Obote didn't have complete control over the military, whose make-up was as diverse as the country as a whole. Idi Amin represented the northern population and had the numbers to oust Obote in a coup.

'After seizing power, Amin's first priority was to purge the military and police of all Obote supporters. Thousands were slaughtered. His second priority was to expel the Indian population and all Jews whom he accused of controlling the economy of the country for their own ends.

'Many successful Ugandans were caught up in this purge, including my own family who were accused of being "black Jews". My mother and father and several of the staff at the shop were shot. Our store was looted then burned to the ground.

'Looking back, I was very lucky that afternoon.

'I was lucky not to have been there – firstly, because I didn't have to watch my family being killed and secondly, because I didn't lose my own life.

'My father had asked me to take our pickup truck to Entebbe, where several sacks of groundnuts he had ordered from Tanzania were ready for collection at the ferry terminal. One of our staff, who escaped the butchery, called the agent and told him what happened. He warned that if I went back I too would be killed.

'I had a chequebook with me so I paid the agent and loaded the groundnuts. I then went into Entebbe and withdrew $US2,000 from the bank. We used US dollars frequently to pay for imported products so my father always had some on hand. With local currency I bought a warm jacket, a blanket and a ferry ticket to Mwanza in Tanzania, at the other end of Lake Victoria.

'I sat on the edge of the lake and wept for my family, while waiting for the overnight ferry.'

Nelson paused.

I could feel the silent struggle with emotion as he recalled that horrific day in his life.

The brigadier and I stared at the road ahead and said nothing.

He took a deep breath and continued.

'I had no travel documents, but I had US dollars so moving through Tanzania and Zambia was no problem. Along the way, I'd stop at a roadside store and sell a couple of sacks of groundnuts so I could buy diesel and food.

'From Lusaka, the shortest route to Rhodesia was via Chirundu. At the customs post, I told them my story and how I had bribed my way across Africa. I told them I knew I couldn't bribe them, but could I apply for political asylum and refugee status? I was driving a pickup with Ugandan number plates, so I guess they thought my story stacked up and I was eventually allowed into the country.

'The rest you know. But there is one other thing about Uganda that I now understand. While our ethnic divisions are the underlying cause of the disaster, I now realize there were other interests involved. The Russians supplied Idi Amin with arms, vehicles and MIG fighters. He could not have pulled off that coup without them. The Russians have a lot to answer for. Since being in the SAS, I have enjoyed what we have done to them.

'My dream is one day to return to Uganda and rebuild the supermarket my family owned. But first the world has to put these communists in their graves. I am happy and grateful to be here and helping with that process.'

'That's a good dream, Nelson, don't ever lose it,' said the brigadier. 'I'm sorry to have opened old wounds, but thank you for telling us.'

We sat silently reflecting on Nelson's story.

Africa was a continent of tragedy and there seemed to be no end to it.

We met in the superintendent's office and were introduced to Jameson. Nelson used the common Shona language to ask him about his tribe and language. They spoke for a few minutes then Nelson turned to us and apologized.

'I am sorry,' he said. 'I know there are pressing matters, but first I needed to find out about Jameson. He is Manyika, from the Penhalonga district to the north of Umtali. All Manyika speak a version of Shona and they have several different dialects. Jameson's dialect is distinctive; it's the same I have heard spoken in Mozambique. We will have no difficulty communicating with him.'

'Thank you, Nelson,' said the brigadier. 'Now let's get started.'

For the next hour we listened as Jameson told us how he and his wife had been abducted and taken to the ZANU terrorist camp of Chimoio. He described in detail the camp activity and how they had been addressed by two leaders, Josiah Tongogara and Rex Nyongo who were based there.

'What intrigues me about all this,' said the brigadier as Jameson reached the end, 'is why ZANU would build such a large and obviously important complex so close to the Rhodesian border?'

Nelson asked Jameson, in his language, if he knew the answer.

'They think they are too far away to be attacked and that Rhodesian forces wouldn't attack targets in Mozambique, especially if they are close to a Frelimo base like the one in the nearby Chimoio town,' he replied.

We shook our heads in amazement.

This was a serious tactical blunder by ZANU and they would pay heavily for it.

'Nelson, I want you to sit here with Jameson and get him to describe the camp complex in detail, and as he does that make a diagram so we can see the extent of it all. Start at the town of Chimoio and work your way forward from that. Get Jameson to give you approximate distances wherever he can,' said the brigadier.

We left them to it and moved into another office.

'Brigadier, our first priority, from a police perspective, is to get some plain-clothes officers into the suburbs and squash the ZANU recruitment campaign. We have the resources to do that immediately but, before I push the start button, will that in any way hinder or compromise what the army may want to do about all this?' asked the superintendent.

'I don't believe so, Bill, and I agree it's the top priority – we have to stop it. A lot of people are going to die in this camp so being abducted by ZANU has just become a likely death sentence.'

While the police prepared for their operation in the suburbs, the brigadier called the air force on a secure line to organize a Canberra photo-recce run over Chimoio.

Meanwhile, I joined Nelson and Jameson to see how they were progressing.

Nelson had plotted eighteen different base complexes that made up the camp and he'd done a table with the names and function of them all. Jameson guessed there were around 3,000 terrorists in the camp and every morning at 0800 they assembled on the parade ground.

Groups came in and went out on a regular basis. He mentioned that one group of 300 terrorists had recently been sent to a camp in Mozambique called 'Tembue' for advanced training by Frelimo and Chinese instructors.

We had never been to Tembue, but we knew it wasn't far from Furuncungo where, some years earlier, we'd been in action against a Frelimo gang that had inflicted serious casualties on Portuguese national service conscripts.

The information given to us by Jameson, combined with the subsequent high altitude photo-recce runs by the Canberras, was invaluable and gave us all we needed to know about Chimoio.

With Russian-backed ZAPU already on the ropes, taking out this ZANU concentration at Chimoio could be the game-breaker in the Rhodesian war.

ZANU would struggle to recover and the momentum could switch back to the Rhodesian security forces who were already dangerously extended.

So now we knew all about Chimoio.

Next we had to work out how we were going to destroy it.

Our SAS intelligence section had a team whose speciality was making models. Nobody – staff college included – came remotely close to them in terms of creativity, detail and accuracy of scale.

They'd dissect the vertical and horizontal detail of an air photograph and take measurements in order to recreate the ground form in the centre of our large operations room. The features would be chalked out on the floor then lumps of cotton wool and other soft material pressed into the shapes of hills, valleys and river lines and held in place with tape.

Over the top of the artificial features, a light green-coloured cloth the size of a double king-size bed sheet would be laid. Once satisfied with the contouring effect, the team would frame the model with lengths of dressed timber.

They would then meticulously add the surface detail. Dyed cotton wool lumps formed woodland copses or boulder-strewn banks, blue-coloured sawdust marked the river lines, brown the roads and tracks. They used matchboxes to make buildings and bridges then painted them to resemble the real thing. They had a chest full of miniature vehicles, weaponry and plastic soldiers and finally they would add signs giving the distance between critical points on the model.

These marvellous, three-dimensional models were works of art and the one they made of the Chimoio camp complex was a masterpiece.

On our return from Umtali, the brigadier lost no time in letting the ComOps chiefs know about Chimoio. He asked for four days to prepare a detailed operational plan.

He told the general and air marshal the assault was too big for the SAS to carry out on its own. Our squadron then had just ninety-six operational troops – me included – too few to successfully attack a camp complex covering some sixteen square kilometres and holding an estimated 3,000 terrorists.

We would need more troops and a lot of air power.

The brigadier requested the two commando companies from the Rhodesian Light Infantry that had been parachute trained, and asked if the RLI commanding officer and a senior air force representative could join the planning team.

His requests were granted. Two days later, the RLI colonel and an air force wing commander were sitting with us around the model working out the attack plan.

Our usual tactic was called 'vertical envelopment' by the academics.

It consisted of encircling stop groups and an assault group that would sweep through the target area, driving the terrorists out of the camp and into the ambushing stop groups. The RLI commandos were just as good at it as we were, so it was decided we'd stick to the tried-and-tested concept.

Getting both stop and assault groups around the target would have to be done by air. The air force had six DC3 Dakotas rigged up for parachute operations. We'd put the ninety-six SAS men into four of them, with forty-eight RLI commandos in the other two. The balance of the RLI force would be taken in by Alouette helicopter. Ten would be needed for this.

We looked at the map and model to work out where everyone would be dropped.

The next consideration was how to initiate the attack. We could initiate using mortar or artillery fire, for example, but most often we used air strikes from helicopter gunships or fixed-wing ground attack fighters.

We knew most of the terrorists would be assembled on their parade ground at 0800 so that was the obvious time and place to start proceedings.

The Hawker Hunter was the most deadly aircraft in the Rhodesian Air Force. They could come in fast and low and use their lethal front guns to strafe the parade ground. The four rapid-firing Aden guns on each aircraft spat out 30-millimetre shells with high-explosive heads that exploded like hand grenades on impact. Against a concentrated crowd they would be devastating.

And that's exactly what we wanted.

Because of the extent of the camp complex, the wing commander decided the Canberra bombers should closely follow the initial Hunter strikes with their targets being the peripheral camp areas. Four Canberras could carry a total of 1,200 Alpha bombs that would saturate an area 1,200 metres long and 500 metres wide.

Finally, a squadron of ten helicopter gunships would accompany the RLI troop carriers and engage any targets in their allocated air segment.

To gain the maximum effect from the initial strike, surprise was essential. The wing commander came up with an innovative deception plan. For two days before the raid, he would get a four-engine DC8 cargo plane to fly close to the camp area at exactly 0750 hours. It would look like a normal commercial flight; the hope was that after the first day the terrorists would assume that was the case and ignore it.

On the morning of the attack, the plane would again fly over the camp area, but this time masking the sound of the approaching air armada.

The following morning, I stood up as soon as we were all assembled and asked to be heard.

'Brigadier sir, Wing Commander, Colonel,' I began. 'I have had a couple of thoughts about this operation. They are a bit left field, but with so much at stake I thought it would be worth raising them with you.

'Last night I went to the movies to see *Victory at Entebbe* – the Israeli Special Forces attack to free their hostages on board a hijacked airliner that was flown to Uganda.

'It was an excellent movie. But what jumped out at me was how the Israeli military converted a Boeing 707 into an airborne control centre. It acted as a communications relay station and from the aircraft the commanders were able to follow every move of the action. If something suddenly turned pear-shaped, they knew immediately and could make the calls needed to keep things on track. It was impressive.

'With the commitment and scale of our operation, it occurred to me that we should do the same thing. Wing Commander, I'm sorry if this offends you, but the air force has a VIP Dakota that doesn't appear to get used much these days. How would the air force feel about converting that for the same purpose?'

'No offence at all, Mick,' he replied immediately. 'It's a bloody great idea.' Turning to the brigadier, he said, 'Command and control aside, the other value in this suggestion is that I'm sure it will appeal to the ComOps chiefs. They will be personally involved and they'll love it. We are going to be asking a lot of them when we make our presentation. This will definitely help us get over the line.'

'Very good point,' replied the brigadier. 'Massaging their egos will certainly help with getting what we want. So what's the next left-field suggestion, Mick?' he asked.

'During the discussions with Jameson, he mentioned that a group of 300 terrorists had been sent to Tembue for special training by Frelimo and Chinese instructors.'

I hesitated. Nervous of the reaction to what I was about to suggest.

'Since we are going to all this trouble to put together a massive attacking force, why don't we make more use of it while we have it? Why don't we attack Tembue with the same team forty-eight hours after destroying Chimoio? It will be a double blow to ZANU and the last thing they will be expecting.'

There was a stunned silence at the magnitude of what I'd just suggested, then slowly they all started to smile.

'Mick, you should go to the movies more often,' said the brigadier.

On 23 November 1977, I boarded the Dakota along with my Sierra One Seven team and another fourteen SAS men from B Troop. We took off from the Grand Reef aerodrome, conveniently located well away from the town of

Umtali on the western side of Christmas Pass. We passed over Cecil Kop –
where all this started – and headed towards Chimoio.

We were soon on our feet and hooking up the T10 static line parachutes.
Ours was the first Dakota in a line of six that would drop us on the south
side of the camp. We were 'stop one' in the order of things and I'd be the
first out over Chimoio.

Standing in the door on the final approach, I marvelled at the Hunter
strike and the skill of the air force in coordinating the timings to perfection.
No easy task given there were five different types of aircraft all with different
airspeeds.

My thoughts were rudely interrupted by a loud *thwack* as a bullet hit the
tail of the Dakota.

'Time to get out of here, Mick. Go! Go! Go!' yelled the dispatcher as the
green light came on.

I leapt into space and had a quick look round. We were jumping from
just 400 feet above the ground so we wouldn't be in the air long. I could see
terrorists running everywhere and could hear gunfire.

I managed to dodge some tall thorn trees and landed comfortably.
The last thing you'd need on a job like this would be to end up stuck in a
tree. I looked around to watch the others land while I unstrapped and loaded
my FN.

A woman in a bright turquoise dress ran towards me screaming
something, spraying the area around me with her AK on automatic fire.
She was the first of three terrorists I killed in my first minute on the
ground.

With the immediate action over, I grabbed my pack and ran to join
Mack, who was about forty metres away in a good place with cover and view
from an anthill mound. We got down and waited for more action.

It didn't take long to arrive.

A group of around twenty terrorists suddenly appeared. They advanced
tactically and were clearly looking for us. Mack and I opened fire and two
dropped. A fierce exchange of fire followed and I was glad of our cover.

I heard the unmistakeable sound of an MAG machine gun – several
terrorists dropped. It would be Jonny, who'd been two or three spaces
behind me in the aircraft. Then *whoosh!* Fish put a bazooka into the
middle of them. We continued firing until all movement stopped.

With a lull in the action, I took the VHF radio out of my pack and called the brigadier. I immediately recognized the voice that answered my call. It was the general speaking from the command Dakota.

The general explained that the brigadier and wing commander, who were in a helicopter coordinating the attack, had been hit by heavy ground fire. They were unhurt and had managed to get back to Grand Reef, but were now out of the game.

I was the next senior officer on the attack but, immersed in it all as I was, there was no way I could control anything except my immediate surroundings.

'Sir, we are still busy in the stop lines and there seems to be a lot of gunfire from the north side of the camp where the RLI were dropped by helicopter. I'd recommend we hold our current positions while there are groups still trying to break out. Once it has quietened down a bit, we'll get the six stop groups to start a tactical advance through the camp. That may well flush out more terrorists in the direction of the RLI, who should hold their positions.

'We'll wait for your orders on that and I'll need your help. I don't have comms at the moment with stops five and six.'

'Roger that, Mick,' replied the general. I heard him then make contact with stops five and six at the opposite end of the parachute line.

I had a little chuckle to myself. My God, that movie ticket had been good value.

As we sat waiting for more action, the helicopter gunships circled the area and used their 20 millimetre cannons without mercy. They fired into the buildings and into the vehicles parked around the garage. As groups of terrorists fled from their hiding places and cover they had no chance.

After about half an hour, we got the order to advance.

I still didn't have comms with stops five and six, so I asked the general to tell everyone I wanted them to connect with the stops on either side of them. I didn't want any holes in our sweep line; more importantly I wanted to be as sure as possible there could be no misidentification. I asked them to check in once they had done that.

We got the OK and our advance commenced.

No orders were needed for this because we all knew what to do. We got into pairs – my buddy was Mack – and we 'pepper-potted' forward with one watching from cover while the other moved forward ten to twenty metres.

We'd been dropped in low woodland and scrub. There was cover and concealment as we waited in ambush, but as we closed in on the main camp complex the ground became more and more open. Suddenly we were exposed.

Off to my right in the direction of stop two there was a loud explosion and gunfire.

'One man down.' Came the urgent call over the radio. 'Recoilless rifle position under a thatched shelter. Looks like they are in trenches.'

'Stay where you are, stop two, and give us covering fire,' I ordered. 'We'll go ahead and get in behind them.'

I shouted to the others and we ran forward across open ground and there – 100 metres or so away from us on the right – was the terrorist position.

Boom! Another shell from the anti-tank gun was fired at stop two.

We opened fire at once, the attention of the terrorists turned to us. They had a couple of RPD machine guns but they were no match for Horse and Jonny, who kept them down under cover with their MAG fire. And that tipped the scales in our favour, because it allowed Fish to get a well-aimed bazooka shot away that blew apart their gun.

We kept firing from cover. No need to risk anything more because I'd called in a gunship.

I dropped an orange smoke grenade behind us, so the helicopter would know where we were, then directed it onto the target over the radio. The aircraft angled to one side and the 20 millimetre cannon spewed out death and destruction over the gun position.

We counted fifteen dead terrorists next to the broken gun as we continued our advance. Stop two had lost one man. I called in a helicopter to recover the body. It was our only casualty.

We put one of the SAS stop groups astride the road that ran through the centre of the camp. We knew there was a Frelimo garrison at Chimoio town just twenty kilometres away to the south. They must have seen and heard all the action, so we were hoping they might come to investigate. Sensibly they stayed at home.

The mop up of the camp took several hours. We brought in a police team to go through the mass of records and correspondence found. One of our SAS groups was sent to destroy the armoury located two kilometres away to the north. We asked them to bring some explosives back to the central camp area; we had collected literally thousands of AK-47s and other weapons, we couldn't take them home so we piled them up inside a brick building, put boxes of explosives on top of the pile and blew them up. We set about burning the camp, as the helicopters began the shuttle to get us back to Grand Reef.

The SAS were the first to be pulled out. Once back at Grand Reef aerodrome, we transferred to one of the waiting Dakotas without delay and headed back to our barracks in Salisbury. We had just twenty-four hours to prepare for the second phase of this operation they had code-named 'Dingo'.

We'd never know exactly how many ZANU terrorists perished in the attack, but swapping notes with other ground commanders we could account for 1,200 kills. There were probably more and a good number of wounded.

This would undoubtedly be a major setback for ZANU. Apart from the terrible death toll and the destruction of their camp, they had also lost the administration and headquarters element of their campaign. But would it bring them to their knees?

In the SAS we had doubts about that.

Meanwhile, Tembue was next.

Early afternoon the following day, two Dakotas ferried fifty-six of us up to a forward army and police base in the northern farming district of Mount Darwin. We'd spend the night there ahead of our attack early next morning.

With a much smaller target the plan was simpler. Because there would be no parade-ground concentration, it was decided to initiate the attack with four Canberras each armed with 300 Alpha bombs. Moments after the bomb blasts, fifty of our SAS men would be dropped around the camp by troop-carrying helicopters escorted by gunships.

While the terrorists were still in a state of shock from the bombing, we would ambush them from our positions on the ground, while the gunships flushed out any survivors in the camp itself or helped us with opposition from heavy weapons.

Tembue was over 220 kilometres north of the Rhodesian border, inside Mozambique. The Alouette helicopters could reach it OK but they didn't have the range to make it back again, so the day before the attack was spent creating refuelling stations for the return journeys.

We put one station on an island in the upper reaches of Lake Cahora-Bassa we knew from earlier kayak operations and another on a high, flat-top mountain we called 'The Train'. Forty-four-gallon drums of fuel were carried in cargo nets slung beneath the choppers. We put three of our SAS men on the ground in each place to look after them and to assist with the refuelling.

Because of the distance involved, command and control couldn't be from a helicopter so the air force organized two of their fixed-wing 'Lynx' aircraft. The brigadier and wing commander would go up in the first aircraft to coordinate the attack. Once their Lynx started getting low on fuel, the second aircraft would be called in and the pilot and I would take over the airborne control function.

The Lynx was, in fact, a Cessna 337. It was an interesting twin-engine aircraft with one engine 'pulling' in the usual nose-cone position in the front while the other 'pushed' from behind and between twin-tail booms.

It cruised at around 230 kilometres an hour and could stay airborne for five or six hours. The air force had mounted twin 7.62 millimetre GPMGs on the wing above the cockpit and they were used to good effect on many occasions.

At 0700 hours on 25 November 1977, I watched in awe as the helicopter armada powered up and headed north from Mount Darwin airfield. The Lynx with the brigadier followed shortly after. I went to the radio room to monitor progress.

The brigadier and Rex both commented later on how precise the air force had been once again with their timings. Rex said he saw the Canberras fly over the advancing helicopter fleet, he watched their bomb bays open and the Alpha bombs drop.

'The earth erupted,' he said, 'as the bombs exploded in a wide pattern across the camp area. The dust was still in the air as we jumped out of the choppers and into an overpowering smell of high explosives.'

It was a lot like Chimoio but on a much smaller scale.

Immediately after landing, twelve terrorists were killed as they tried to flee the horror that had suddenly engulfed them. There were pockets of resistance but the troops, with help from the gunships, soon eliminated them.

After dropping off the troops, all but one of the helicopters went to the island on Lake Cahora-Bassa to refuel and await orders to commence the evacuation. The wing commander got one to remain in orbit close to the camp in case we had a casualty to deal with.

The two gunships took turns in refuelling, ensuring one was always over the target area while the attack was in progress.

Minor skirmishes took place during the next hour as the SAS closed in on the camp. But the terrorists had no answer to our camp-clearing tactics.

As one of our groups doubled forward in the pepper-pot action we used, the terrorists would respond by jumping up and opening fire at us, sometimes with long sustained bursts from their deadly RPDs. But in doing so they exposed themselves to the other fifty per cent of us who were poised and waiting for just such a reaction.

The response would be swift and deadly. In an instant they would be engulfed in a hail of fire from our FNs and MAG machine guns, with RPG bazookas thrown in for good measure. With the numbers we had on the ground there was no way the SAS would ever lose a firefight.

I took over from the brigadier in the air when the show was pretty well over. My role was to ensure the final mop up was done in an orderly fashion and without the risk of us shooting at each other. We managed that OK and while parts of the team did a detailed search of the camp area and a count of casualties, we got the helicopters on the island to start the recovery of the troops.

We stayed overhead while they roared in and picked up the five-man sticks they could carry. Full of fuel they could reach Mount Darwin comfortably.

One of the gunships refuelled then picked up the three SAS men on top of The Train and headed home. In the Lynx, we followed the second gunship to the island on the lake, where after refuelling it took off with our remaining three SAS men.

It was a remarkable operation and we rated it a big success. Our estimate was sixty terrorists killed in the raid and once again we had destroyed their camp and a lot of weapons.

We had hoped for a bigger kill, given we expected 300 terrorists or more to be at the camp. We later learned a big group had moved to Mgagao in Tanzania, a week before the attack and that we had killed most of the camp occupants there at the time.

That's the way it goes in guerrilla warfare.

Better to keep moving. Better to stay in small groups and disperse far and wide. Stretch the resources of the enemy to breaking point.

The establishment of Chimoio went against all these principles set out by Mao Tse-tung, and ZANU had paid for it.

We learned later that ZANU leader Robert Mugabe was in despair after the attacks and close to calling for an end to hostilities.

But his Chinese advisors reminded him of Mao's principles and pointed out he still had many small terrorist groups operating inside the country and that his two military leaders, Tongogara and Nyongo, had managed to escape the carnage at Chimoio. They reminded him that his Russian-backed rivals ZAPU had so far achieved nothing.

Mugabe may have been ready to throw in the towel, but there was no way the Chinese would allow that. They were, after all, in their own race with the Russians. A race we called the second scramble for Africa.

The night after the Tembue attack, we enjoyed a few beers in Mount Darwin with the air force pilots and technicians who'd helped us pull it off. In many ways, Chimoio and Tembue were more air force operations than SAS, but it was our initiative and we were all in this together.

'*Reasonable men working reasonably together*' was what I'd learned at staff college about joint operations. The air force helped with that significantly by running 'air orientation' training courses to give ground commanders, like myself, an understanding of what it was like to be in the aircraft when we called for help. I had been in the front seat of an elderly Vampire jet on a live air strike, dealing with the real-life problems of trying to positively identify a target being described by a seriously stressed ground commander, all while flying at around 400 kilometres an hour.

My father had been Royal Air Force.

Parachuting aside, I was glad I'd kept my own feet firmly on the ground.

The Chimoio and Tembue raids were extraordinary in that they took place within forty-eight hours of each other and were more than 600 kilometres apart.

It was a triumph of the unconventional thinking that was typical SAS, combined with meticulous planning and superb execution by the air force and the RLI commandos that joined us. There would be many more battles as the communist struggle to control Africa continued, but none would ever compare with Operation Dingo.

Snakes Alive!

S nakes are common in Africa, but they are not often seen, as most try to get out of the way of humans. Maybe it was the good rainy season or maybe it was pure coincidence, but for whatever reason we had one exceptional year involving snakes.

It all started pleasantly at Christmas time.

Elizabeth and I had been schooldays' lovers. Together we had experienced the longing of young love that led finally to the discovery and the excitement of sex.

Following school, Elizabeth went to a secretarial college in Cape Town while I too headed south to university in Natal. Inevitably we grew apart and led our own lives, but neither of us ever really lost the affection we had for one another.

The years passed. I joined the SAS and while the ever-increasing operational commitments ruled out any regular social life, Elizabeth and I managed to meet now and then and enjoy each other's company.

She had sent me an early Christmas card from Cape Town, saying she was coming up to the family farm for Christmas and invited me to stay should I be in town. Luckily for me, it was one of the few times in many years I was able to get some leave over the Christmas period. My family was living in the hills of the eastern districts at the time and to get there I would drive past Elizabeth's farm, so I readily accepted the invitation and was greatly looking forward to being with the lovely young lady again.

As a Christmas present, I had found a skimpy blue-grey bikini with white polka dots and knew Elizabeth would look stunning in it.

On arrival, I insisted she open the present immediately and said I'd meet her at the swimming pool.

The bikini fitted her perfectly; it showed off her beautiful body and, tantalizingly, just managed to hide her special places.

'You look sensational,' I said and laughed. 'I've been so eagerly waiting to see you wearing the bikini and, now that it's happened, all I want to do is take it off you.'

Elizabeth smiled, got into the swimming pool next to me and put her arms around my neck and her legs around my middle.

'There is a little path behind the pump house that goes to a grassy clearing in the middle of those gum trees,' she whispered. 'I think we should go there.'

She took my hand and led me along the path. The air hummed as bees busily collected nectar from the flowering eucalypts and on the short, fine grass of what had been an old anthill there was a covering of delicate, white petals that had fallen from the branches. It was perfect.

We put the towels on the ground and sat down. I knelt behind Elizabeth and put my arms around her, holding her breasts and nuzzling the back of her neck. I undid the bikini top and took it off.

I had the bikini top in one hand and a breast in the other, when suddenly I froze.

Elizabeth looked at me, startled by my sudden change.

'*Shh!*' I whispered and pointed back down the path we had just come along.

The rustling I had heard came closer and then stopped.

Silence.

We sat not daring to move, both of us wondering what creature had come to interrupt us at our love nest.

The rustling started again, moving towards us and then, seven or eight paces away, the hooded head of a big Egyptian cobra appeared above the grass. The snake was watching us. We didn't move. I slowly put my arms under Elizabeth ready to pick her up and escape if the snake came closer.

We watched in fascination and fright as the snake's head moved gently from side to side and then it lowered its head and slid forward.

I had planned on picking up Elizabeth the moment the snake reached the edge of the grassy clearing. I waited, muscles tensed, but nothing happened. It had suddenly gone quiet and the snake seemed to have disappeared.

I was about to stand up when I again heard a rustling in the grass along the path. We waited.

A second cobra appeared; it too raised its head and stared intently at us before silently disappearing as the first snake had done.

Elizabeth and I stood up, and while she got back into her bikini top I went forward to where the snakes had disappeared. Beneath a tuft of grass was a hole that led into the old anthill. We'd been about to make love on top of a cobras' love nest.

The close encounter with two big and dangerous snakes killed off the passion for the rest of the afternoon. But in the dead of night while the farmhouse slept, the door of my guest room quietly opened. Elizabeth came over to the bedside and took off her nightgown. She got in alongside me and as her hand slid down over my belly, she whispered, 'I wonder if there are any more snakes around here?'

Four months later, I was back in the familiar territory of the Zambezi Valley. There had been an incursion of thirty-two terrorists from Zambia. They had planted landmines on farming roads, which had killed two European couples and their children and twenty-seven Africans on a bus heading into their tribal lands. In an ensuing contact with the security forces, several of the terrorists had been killed but most split up and fled in different directions.

Rex and I had just completed a mission against terrorist poachers in the difficult terrain of the Mupata Gorge and were on our way home for a rest, when we were diverted to intercept some of the fleeing remnants of this gang.

Concealing our Sabre Land Rovers beneath camouflage nets, we walked for two days to reach a waterhole on a dried-up river bed that was a well-known route to the Zambezi River, used before by terrorist groups to get in and out of Zambia.

The rains had been good and when we reached our destination the waterhole was, in fact, a small lake. There was a lot of game spoor around. It was obviously a popular spot for the animals – including elephants.

Our dilemma was where to site an ambush.

If we were too close and a herd of thirsty elephants arrived, they might not tolerate our presence. Not only would there be trouble but they would, in the process, compromise our position. I sent Rex and Pig Dog out to have a good look round and make their recommendations.

An hour later they returned and said they had found the perfect position. There was an anthill copse with shade overlooking the water. It was slightly elevated and had a great field of view.

Too good to be true. There had to be a catch?

'Well, yes,' said Rex with a twinkle in his eye. 'It's currently the home of a pride of lions, but we'll chase them off and move in.'

The big cats prowled around on the first night, vocally complaining, but thankfully they moved away and left us in peace.

Peace being a relative term, given there was a constant stream of thirsty animals through the day and night as we watched and waited for our prey to turn up.

We managed the ambush as we usually did, with Rex and Horse with his MAG in one group along with Fish and Mack. They would do six hours watching and waiting while Jonny, Nelson, Karate, Pig Dog and I rested behind them before our shift. With all the animal movement around us, it was an enjoyable time and staying alert and ready was easier than usual.

Across the lake directly in front of us, less than 100 metres away, was a low, rocky platform that descended gently to the water's edge. On one side of the sheet of rock, a tall dead tree was the favourite perching place of a beautiful, chestnut and white fish eagle.

It was my team on guard. I was enjoying watching the eagle through my binoculars when something startled it. It turned on its perch and looked at the lake in our direction.

'Be alert, guys,' I whispered. 'Something has spooked the fish eagle.'

A hammerhead stork we hadn't noticed in the reeds took flight and the frogs stopped croaking.

We moved the safety catches on our FN rifles. We were ready to open fire.

The fish eagle focused its attention on a small patch of reeds at the edge of the lake. We saw the movement in the reeds that had caught its attention. The eagle stretched out its neck and looked intently.

The plop in the water sounded like a tossed pebble but we could see nothing.

On the bank behind the reeds, a dozen mongoose suddenly appeared. They sat up on their hind legs like meerkats, eyes alternatively looking at the fish eagle and at the ripples in the water. Beyond the ripples, about three metres from the bank, the swirling shape of a large snake suddenly appeared.

'It's a big cobra,' gasped Pig Dog. 'It's trying to escape from the mongoose.'

As we watched, the fish eagle launched itself from its perch in the direction of the swimming snake. We could hear the *swish* of air through the huge

(*Above*) The Second Scramble for Africa as seen by the cartoonist.

(*Right*) Every afternoon a huge bull lumbered into our campground to feed on the nutrient-rich seed pods of the tamarind acacias. He would extend his trunk high into the air to reach the pods, and sometimes did a circus trick of standing up on his two hind legs to get even higher into the branches.

(*Above*) The Zambezi
River was compressed
between the hills of the
Mupata gorge, no more
than 150 metres wide
and very deep. The water
was crystal clear and we
could see shoals of *tilapia*
bream feeding below
while big, brown catfish
hovered just below the
surface.

(*Left*) We left Kanyemba
before dawn next
morning and found the
rough track the rangers
had told us about.
It wasn't much trouble
for the Sabres.

(*Above*) I'd just started my second spell as lead scout when a familiar, whirring bird call caught my attention. No more than 30 metres away, a dozen red-billed oxpeckers had spotted us and spiralled upwards sounding the alarm.

(*Right*) I could see at once the weeping holes of bullet wounds. We counted eleven of them. No more than 150 millimetres apart, they started in the big muscles of the rump and back leg and progressed in a line across the ribs and up as far as the shoulder. This elephant had been machine-gunned!

(*Above*) There were three desperately dangerous men ahead of us who knew we would be coming and one of them was armed with a deadly machine gun. They would be waiting for us and we'd need all our skills and guile to neutralise that advantage.

(*Below*) There were four fires with big logs that continued to smoulder and smoke. Above and around these were washing-line wires strung between trees and improvised posts that were festooned with long strips of meat. Elephant meat.

These smaller vultures were sitting in the mountain acacia tree, waiting for access to the carcass, and their attention on it was such that we managed to arrive beneath the tree without them taking flight in alarm.

Jonny noticed two grooves across the sand that were too straight to be crocodile markings. He followed them and hidden under low bushes found two kayaks. On the sand next to them lay four elephant tusks.

(*Above*) Author (right) cools down in the Rekometjie River with close friend Prof. John Hargrove.

(*Below*) John Hargrove's Tsetse Fly

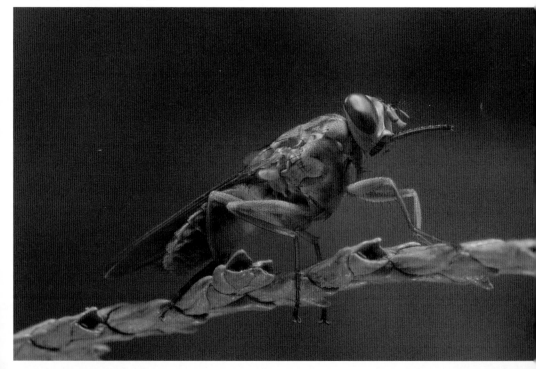

(*Above*) The French Alouette 3 helicopters flown by the Rhodesian Air Force about to take off at the start of Operation Dingo.

(*Below*) Six 'Paradaks' were used to drop the SAS and RLI Commandos who surrounded the southern side of the huge ZANU terrorist camp complex.

(*Above*) They came in low and fast, strafing the parade ground with their deadly 30mm front guns.

(*Below*) Because of the distance involved, command and control couldn't be from a helicopter so the air force organised two of their fixed wing 'Lynx' aircraft. The Lynx was in fact a Cessna 337 – an interesting aircraft with one engine 'pulling' in the usual nose cone position in the front while the other 'pushed' from behind and between twin tail booms.

(*Right*) Chinese trained ZANU terrorists pose with a bayonet. Picture recovered from the Chimoio attack.

(*Below*) On one side of the sheet of rock, a tall dead tree was the favourite perching place of the beautiful chestnut and white fish eagle.

'It's a big cobra,' gasped Pig Dog. 'It's trying to escape from the mongoose.'

ZAPU terrorists shot down two Air Rhodesia Viscount airliners used on the tourist route between Victoria Falls, Kariba and Salisbury. One hundred and ten tourists and air crew were killed in the two attacks. 'It was our boys,' said ZAPU leader Joshua Nkomo proudly to the world media.

The SAM-7 Strela ground to air missile system, supplied by the Russians to ZAPU and the South African ANC, whose plan was to shoot down an SAA 747 Jumbo. Thankfully that never happened.

Air Rhodesia
Viscount taking
on passengers
at Kariba. Both
aircraft were shot
down shortly after
take-off at Kariba
by the Soviet
missile system.

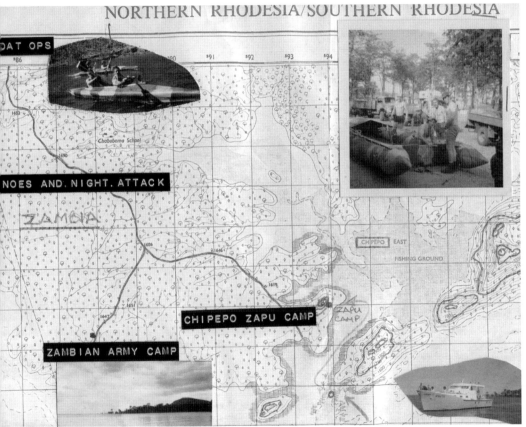

The author's map used on the Chipepo raid, with inserts of Armanel, the
Zodiacs and Klepper kayaks used in the attack.

Those parts of Mozambique so far unaffected by Frelimo were less than enthusiastic at the prospect of becoming part of Machel's anthill. What the country needed were Ant Bears – 'Sambani' – lots of them.

Afonso Dhlakama would eventually emerge as one of Renamo's leading political figures, but that was a long fourteen years away.

It didn't take rebel group Renamo long to design a flag.

(*Above*) The recruits started to arrive. By the end of their second week at the mountain, seventy-two new recruits had joined Rex.

(*Below*) As word spread, Fish was constantly at work. Health care was something new to this remote part of Africa. He treated all sorts of ailments and injuries, including removing a broken knife blade embedded in the neck of a middle-aged woman.

(*Above*) More and more women fighters joined Renamo as their influence spread north towards Malawi and south towards South Africa.

(*Below*) Afonso's group waiting in ambush on the road to Inhaminga. Two East Germans were amongst those killed in the ambush.

(*Above*) Entrance to the Frelimo Inhaminga base attacked by Comrade André and Pig Dog.

(*Below*) Pictures of Chicamba dam taken on an earlier SAS recce but later attacked by Renamo.

(*Above*) Chinese trained Frelimo pose with a
14.5 mm anti-aircraft gun and RPG bazookas.

(*Right*) Bob McKenzie, 101st Airborne and
C Squadron SAS.

wings as it power-dived towards the cobra. The mongoose fled, worried they might also be in the eagle's lunch plans.

Halfway across the lake, the eagle was at great speed; it was obvious this would not be the usual skimming attack with the talons deftly gripping a surface-feeding fish. This was a full-frontal, guns-blazing assault on what was a large and dangerous reptile.

Intent on escaping from the mongoose, the cobra didn't see the eagle coming and it struck the reptile with massive force. The snake ducked beneath the water, writhing and reeling at the force of the attack. The razor-sharp talons ripped into the snake as it dived. Spray and pounding wings shattered the calm surface of the water. The eagle took flight and climbed for a second strike.

It quickly gained height and circled. The snake resurfaced and swam rapidly, desperate to reach the cover of the reed beds, a bloody streamer trailing from behind its head.

The eagle threw back its head and uttered a long, shrill cry. A battle cry. A shiver ran down my spine.

The great bird turned into the second attack. Another power dive and a loud *crack* as it smashed into the reptile with massive energy and speed.

For a moment the bird disappeared, then suddenly, foam flying, it exploded into the air, gasping for breath. It struggled to get free of the water then flapped its heavy, wet wings and slowly, sluggishly lifted off the lake, dragging the cobra behind it.

The eagle circled, desperately flapping its wings struggling to keep airborne. Its talons were buried deep in the middle of the snake's back. The squirming cobra hung down and swung like a pendulum as the bird gained height. Looking stronger now, it turned and flew heavily towards the rocky platform next to its perch. It continued circling over the rocks and eventually, when it had reached thirty or forty feet above the ground, the eagle suddenly released the snake.

The cobra twisted silently through the air and thudded onto the rocks, bounced and lay still.

The eagle dived towards the snake, this time more slowly with wings raised, legs forward and powerful talons outstretched. The thump with which it again struck the cobra could be heard across the lake.

We watched as it straddled the dead snake, its usually pristine white breast sullied with streaks of blood. Its huge wings were spread in triumph. It was all over.

But, in the way of the wild, the victorious eagle didn't have it all its own way.

Two kilometres away, a tawny eagle saw the confrontation as it cruised the sky at just under a thousand feet. The big, brown eagle half closed its wings and flipped over into a low-angle dive. Four minutes later, it bounced on the ground a few yards away from the fish eagle that was by now consuming the mid-section of the snake.

A further two kilometres away, and at well over a thousand feet above the ground, a pair of white-backed vultures had seen the tawny eagle flip and dive. It was a signal they knew meant food and they too turned, compressed their wings and power-dived in the same direction.

As the eagle and vultures descended, they were seen by an ever-alert jackal that now trotted with some urgency towards the waterhole. Finally, in the water itself, a two-metre long monitor lizard had picked up the scent of blood and was already swimming towards the rock shelf where the fish eagle was feeding.

The tawny eagle was first to arrive; while threatened by the fish eagle it was not intimidated. Cleverly, it chose to avoid confrontation. It deftly gripped the tail of the snake and dragged it away from the posturing fish eagle that still gripped the middle. The separation was sufficient and both birds now fed on the snake.

The vultures, the jackal and the water monitor all arrived at much the same time and, being much bigger, simply ignored the two eagles and ran in to snatch and grab what they could in a frenzy of hissing, barking and snarling. Within a few minutes there was little left of the snake. The fish eagle took a strip of skin and flesh up to the dead tree perch, finished that off then went into the water for a bath.

Around midnight two nights later, Rex prodded Horse next to him as the frogs suddenly stopped croaking. Mack and Fish on either side of them silently pulled their rifles into the shoulder and peered over the sights.

An eerie silence enveloped the waterhole. There was a three-quarter moon and no wind.

Rex flicked the button to activate the light intensifier scope he'd mounted on his FN rifle. He heard the low, electronic whine as the device powered up and the green image flickered into focus.

'Terrorists,' he whispered to Horse. 'Two of them carrying AKs. Over there on the rocks where the eagle killed the snake.'

Horse peered across the water and saw two shadows moving where Rex had indicated.

'Got them,' he said.

'Mack? Fish?' queried Rex.

'Got them,' they replied.

'OK. I've got the one on the right in my scope. Fish, you aim there as well. Mack, you take the left. Horse, take your time and when you are ready open fire on the left target. We'll follow your burst.'

Horse shuffled a bit then, pulling the gun firmly into his shoulder, skilfully squeezed a double-tap at his target. Rex and the others fired as Horse then sprayed the area with a sustained burst of machine-gun fire nothing could escape from.

They stopped.

Rex held his rifle in the aim, scanning the ground with the light intensifier. Two bodies were slumped across the rocks. There was no movement.

Rex continued to hold the aim. 'I'm just going to make sure nothing more can happen,' he said, and with that he fired two well-aimed shots.

The rest of us joined Rex, and I had a look at the scene through the light intensifier.

We stayed alert for another half hour in case there were others behind with mortars, but nothing happened and the frogs began to sing again. I sent Rex and his crew back to sleep and my gang kept watch until first light.

We stayed in cover, watching the target, until the sun was well up and we could see the bodies clearly. There was some movement, but then I saw the tail of the big water monitor which again had been attracted by the blood and was feeding on something close to the bodies.

Rex took his team away from us then circled around behind the lake, looking to cut the tracks and establish just how many terrorists had come to that waterhole. Had we missed any?

He eventually called, saying he had found the tracks and there were just two and he was now going to inspect the bodies.

While Karate rigged up the HF G5RV antenna for my radio report, Pig Dog and I walked around the small lake to meet Rex. The water monitor watched us close to the safety of the lake, keen to get back to the feast of blood and brains before the voracious black ants overwhelmed everything.

We collected up the weapons and packs then dragged the bodies away from the water and close to an open patch where, an hour later, a helicopter landed to take everything away.

With the formalities completed, Rex asked what the next plan was. I knew instantly he had something in mind.

'This Nyakasanga River has a wide, fertile flood plain that extends a good five kilometres west of us,' he said. 'There are waterholes and many game paths. It is possible some of the other fleeing terrorists could have gone that way, so maybe we should go and have a look? We aren't short of rations; we could easily go for another three or four days across and down the flood plain before circling back.'

'And?' I asked, knowing full well there would be another reason.

Rex smiled slyly. 'Well, Mick,' he said. 'I've heard reports there is a herd of over a thousand buffalo down here. That really would be something to see. Bound to be good birdlife as well,' he added knowing I'd take the bait.

Pig Dog's eyes lit up. 'A thousand buffalo in a single herd? Wow!'

I laughed. 'That's a great suggestion, Rex. We've just had a successful ambush and there's no point staying here any longer. We were meant to be going home for R and R when they sent us here, so for the next four days we'll enjoy ourselves.'

I sent a signal back to base, letting them know of our plans and was applauded for our enthusiasm and proactive follow-up after the successful ambush. 'Yeah, right!' said Karate with his crooked-toothed grin as he wound up the radio aerial. 'SAS: Special Air Safaris. Game viewing and birdwatching at army expense our specialty.'

We had already been through many harrowing experiences together as a call sign. Many of them, like the recent poachers' operation, had been tough physically and dangerous to a point where at one stage I thought the unthinkable – that we had lost Rex. What we were doing now was an indulgence – although there was a legitimate chance we might find tracks of fleeing terrorists and the staff officers controlling the operation clearly agreed.

I'd been around long enough to know that anything could happen. I was looking forward to enjoying the next few days at a leisurely pace, but I quietly betted with myself that something would crop up before we had done our game-viewing and birdwatching circuit.

And I would have won the money.

We were on our third day, and hot on the trail of a massive buffalo herd that was heading down the flood plain towards the Zambezi River. We had stopped for a mid-morning brew and Karate routinely turned on the VHF radio. There was some general traffic between what was obviously an African Rifles' base station and its patrols. Reception was such that they could not have been too far from us; we guessed they were covering the Zambezi river line fifty kilometres away to our north.

The routine radio traffic was suddenly interrupted by an emergency call.

'Romeo Zero Alpha, this is Romeo Bravo Two. Urgent casevac request! Repeat, urgent casevac request! One of our call sign has been bitten by a cobra.'

The base station acknowledged.

I grabbed the microphone.

'Romeo Zero Alpha, this is Sierra One Seven, Sunray speaking. We have an experienced medic with us and we have cobra serum. We are currently located four kilometres west of the Nyakasanga River, in grid square Yankee Foxtrot Three Nine Seven Zero. It sounds as if we are close and if you want our help we are ready. Over.'

'Thank you, Sierra One Seven. Standby.'

Fish, who had been listening, came over and took the microphone.

'Romeo Bravo Two, this is Sierra One Seven, Starlight Medic speaking. Do you read me?'

An African voice replied and Fish acknowledged.

'To ensure this man's survival there are some instructions. You ready?'

'Go ahead, Starlight.'

'Roger. Firstly, do not cut the wound. Do not try to suck out the venom and do not apply a tourniquet. All I want you to do is fan the man's face, so he is still getting air and breathing. You copy?'

'Roger that, Starlight.'

'You have to convince him that help is on the way – that his injury is serious but not life-threatening. For him to survive it is critical he understands that and believes he will live. Tell him whatever you like but you must make him believe he will live.'

'Will do. Thank you, Starlight.'

As soon as Fish had stopped, the headquarters took over, advising they would take up our offer and a helicopter would be with us in about twenty minutes. They asked if there were any instructions.

I handed the microphone to Fish.

'We will need oxygen – you have probably already got that in the aircraft – other than that, speed. We have thirty to forty-five minutes maximum to play with before this man dies. Don't hang around.'

Fish dug into his pack and pulled out a green plastic box. He opened it to check the contents. There were three compartments. In one were two syringes in sterile packaging and in the other two were vials of serum: one for treating adder bites, the second for cobras.

He unfolded the accompanying information sheet describing the contents and treatment and read it out loud to us.

'"Cobras belong to a sub-group of snakes known as *elapids*. Their venom contains neurotoxins that spread rapidly in the bloodstream, causing respiratory failure and eventually death. It has been determined that even if only one-third of the receptor sites on the diaphragm muscle become blocked by the venom the victim will cease breathing. This process can take as little as thirty minutes. The only way to counteract the effects of cobra venom is to inject the appropriate antivenom shortly after the bite occurs. If antivenom is not available, life can still be maintained by an artificial respirator until the paralysis of the diaphragm wears off."

'It's going to be close,' he said, as we bundled his pack next to him on the back seat of the helicopter.

They landed in a swirl of dust next to where the injured soldier lay on the ground. The troops had lifted his head and rested it on his pack; two of his comrades fanned air over his face with their camouflage caps as instructed.

Fish didn't say anything. He had prepared the syringe in flight and on landing ran to inject the victim. He had asked the helicopter technician to follow him out with the oxygen cylinder and breathing mask; after the injection he pumped oxygen into the victim's lungs.

The technician ran back to the aircraft that was powered up ready to go and got a stretcher.

They put the African soldier on the stretcher and Fish and the platoon commander took an end each and carried the man to the Alouette.

They pushed him inside, and Fish jumped aboard next to him with the oxygen bottle he hoped would keep him breathing. A hand grasped his arm. It was the platoon commander.

'Thank you,' he said. 'Who are you?'

'A pleasure, Lieutenant. My name's Fish and Sierra One Seven is an SAS call sign.' And with that the helicopter whisked them away towards the hospital on the heights overlooking the great lake of Kariba.

Private Willy Mazunga lived on a tightrope between life and death for three days in the critical care ward of the small hospital. Within his body a great battle raged between the toxins of the snake and the antivenom serum, which itself was largely made up of toxins milked from snakes in captivity and modified to neutralize the original. When Fish injected the serum, it was almost like giving the man another snake bite and the impact on the human body was massive.

Fish knew that studies in India – where thousands were bitten every year by cobras – had revealed that one of the most important factors for survival was self-belief. They found that victims bitten by a cobra, who – for religious or fatalistic beliefs – thought they would die, did routinely succumb to the toxins. But those with a will to live frequently survived.

And so did Willy.

Fish was put up in the local army barracks while we finished our safari, but spent most of his time with Willy at the hospital as his internal battle raged. Sitting at the soldier's bedside, Fish explained what was going on inside him, likening it to some of the great military battles between the Zulu nation and the British more than a century earlier. Willy responded positively, and slowly but surely the tide turned and he began to regain strength.

The good news was forwarded to the platoon commander.

And after meeting up with the massive herd of buffalo, tailed by the pride of lions we had chased off our ambush site, we were duly reunited with Fish at Kariba.

A holiday town, it was a good place to meet. Expecting celebrations at the news of Willy's recovery, we were all surprised to find Fish more than somewhat subdued.

'What's the problem, Fish?' I asked. But he wouldn't own up to anything.

I left it at that, knowing Karate and Jonny would get the truth out of him eventually. Sure enough, we discovered he had fallen in love with one of the nurses at the hospital.

Nothing wrong with that, until Fish's regular girlfriend back in Salisbury found out about it.

Snakes sure can be troublesome creatures.

ZAPU's Secret Weapon

Isaac Ngonyama was the eldest son in a subsistence-farming family, living close to the Hope Fountain Mission about twenty kilometres south of Bulawayo. He did well at the mission school, but that only went as far as standard six and there were no further education options open to him.

During his schooldays, he had shown interest in things mechanical. Instead of playing football after class, he could be found at the mission workshops which housed two elderly Ferguson tractors, an even older three-ton Bedford truck and a variety of trailers and farming machinery used on the mission land. His interest was encouraged by the kindly staff and it was soon apparent he had the potential to become a good mechanic. On the completion of his schooling, one of the mission staff approached the owner of the local garage, Waterford Motors and asked if he would consider taking Isaac as an apprentice.

It didn't cost much to have a fifteen-year-old on the staff and there were several messy jobs his qualified mechanics regarded as beneath them. Isaac could do these and that would both please the mechanics and keep them productive, so the garage owner agreed to take him on.

Isaac and his family were overjoyed that he was working locally and training to be a mechanic. They lived near enough for him to cycle to work every day and he brought a small but welcome cash contribution back to the family on pay days.

The garage owner and staff were also happy with Isaac. They treated him well because he was polite, always keen to learn, and no job – no matter how messy – was a problem for him. As he became more competent, he was given more difficult jobs to deal with and his pay was increased. He enjoyed this and had no complaints about the pay and the bonus he received every Christmas.

However, as the years passed, he began to have doubts about his future at Waterford Motors. While he had clearly advanced to being on equal terms, technically, with the garage mechanics, there had been no indication as to when he too would be formally certified as a mechanic.

Whenever he raised the subject with the owner, there were apologies and excuses about how difficult it was to get an African, with his limited educational qualifications, a mechanic's certificate. Isaac knew his boss had tried, so there was no animosity against him or Waterford Motors and he continued to work as if nothing had happened. But deep inside there was a smouldering resentment against this discrimination.

He hid it well from both family and employer, but matters were to come to a head following a Saturday football match in Bulawayo between local team Kumalo Kings and the visiting Domboshawa Tigers from Salisbury. This was more than a league football match. This was tribal – Matabele, the royal house of Kumalo, against the inferior Mashona who had been subjugated by Chief Lobengula 100 or so years earlier. And the local team was determined to make sure that status remained on the sports field.

But it wasn't to be.

The Tigers had a better coach; they were fitter, faster and more skilful. They were up two-nil at half-time and went on to win the match by three goals to one.

The Matabele crowd, fuelled by gallons of the local millet beer, went berserk. They invaded the field while the referee and the Tigers team ran for cover in the changing rooms. Dozens of baton-wielding police descended on the scene and fighting on a grand scale broke out between the goalposts.

Isaac was sitting in the stand, watching in disbelief as the drama on the field developed, when two young African men, who had been sitting next to him, grabbed his arm and suggested they get out of there before they too were dragged into the conflict. Isaac followed them out of the stadium and into a beaten-up Datsun 120Y, which spluttered and stalled as it limped away from the action.

Along the way, Isaac pointed out the problems with the car and offered to fix them, explaining he was a mechanic working at Waterford Motors.

Being a Saturday night nobody was at the garage, so it was no problem for Isaac to change the oil and spark plugs, he put in a second-hand battery and found two suitably sized used tyres that fitted the small sedan. He left a note for his employer, saying he would pay for the materials himself the following week on pay day.

His companions were both grateful for what he had done and greatly impressed with his mechanical knowledge and skill. They suggested a drink at the local beer hall would be a good way to end the day.

Isaac agreed and over drinks he told them of his frustration with the obstacles he was facing in becoming a certified mechanic.

'We can fix that,' they replied. 'We can make you a super mechanic. You will no longer just fix old cars like ours. You will learn to fix all sorts of vehicles – huge trucks and heavy vehicles, perhaps even tanks. But to do that first you have to come with us to church.'

A smoother-running 120Y picked him up next morning and the three young men drove through Bulawayo and out to a township on the road to Victoria Falls.

'We are taking you to *Ibandla Zintandane* – also known as *The Church of Orphans*,' the younger of the two explained. 'It is a special church that organizes training for special people and we think you will be ideal. They will make you a mechanic and much more.'

At that stage, Isaac had no idea *The Church of Orphans* was a ZAPU cover organization, but he liked what he heard and what he was promised.

A month later, he was on a truck heading towards Kazungula, west of Victoria Falls, where the ferry would take him and a dozen other recruits across the Zambezi River into Zambia.

Initially, Isaac was based at the Joshua Nkomo training camp on a farm close to the Zambian capital, Lusaka. It was explained that he would at first undergo basic military training with the other recruits, but then he would be moved to a special detachment for advanced technical training. He would not just become a mechanic; he would also become a weapons' technician.

Isaac thrived in the environment. He wasn't just good at everything – he excelled – and he also demonstrated leadership qualities that impressed the ZAPU hierarchy. One afternoon they called him over and announced he was one of twelve cadres selected to go to Russia for specialist training.

Isaac, who previously had never been out of Bulawayo, found himself on a Russian Air Force Tupolev transport plane heading for Simferopol, on the Crimean Peninsula, north of Sevastopol.

There he spent the next six months with the Russians undergoing in-depth political and paramilitary training. Recognizing his mechanical skills, they extended his stay for a further six months, which were spent in one of the huge vehicle workshops, working alongside the Russian engineers servicing and repairing six-wheeled trucks, armoured personnel carriers, mobile artillery and tanks.

The day before his return to Zambia, he was called into the base commandant's office and congratulated on his work and progress through the training.

The commandant shook his hand and gave him a certificate with an ornate border and Russian writing he didn't understand but there in the middle, in bold font, was his name.

Isaac Ngonyama was now a mechanic.

And Isaac Ngonyama was now a highly trained and communist-indoctrinated ZAPU terrorist.

Back in Lusaka, ZAPU didn't waste time in sending Isaac off on the next phase of his development. He was to attend an advanced training course in Angola, run by two East German instructors. He was being sent there specifically to learn about, and take delivery of, a secret weapon that would change the course of the war with colonial Rhodesia.

Before leaving Lusaka, in the now familiar six-wheeled Russian truck, Isaac insisted on inspecting and test-driving the vehicle ahead of what would be a long journey over difficult roads. He learned the vehicle had never been serviced in the three years since its delivery from Russia.

It was not acceptable. He took his complaints to the hierarchy and demanded a service and maintenance regime be introduced immediately for all vehicles and equipment.

'Secret weapons and special missions are no use if our transport won't get us to the target area,' he said. 'On my return from Angola, I'll organize this routine servicing. It will be easy enough – the drivers can do it, but they will need training and if they are negligent they will be punished.'

Isaac had learned well from his Russian instructors and the ZAPU hierarchy liked what they were hearing.

The drab green truck initially headed north towards the Congo border, then veered west towards Mwinilunga, a small town on the border with Angola.

Once inside Angola the route kept them close to, and parallel with, the Congo border until eventually they reached the Benguela railway line in the province of Moxico. Here they again changed direction and followed the railway line west along a rough road that bordered the *Parque Nacional da Cameia* where the small settlement of Luso was located.

Luso was a siding on the railway the Portuguese had ambitiously built in an attempt to create a coast-to-coast rail link between Angola and Mozambique. They'd run out of steam not far into Zambia.

There was a school at Luso that had been taken over by the Russian-backed Angolan rebel group, MPLA, and made into a training base. It was a good location – miles away from the combat zones – too remote to be targeted.

Isaac greeted the gate guard and their ZAPU truck was admitted into the compound. He went forward to introduce himself to the training camp chiefs and get instructions. They were expected and an old, white-walled classroom had been reserved for them.

Facilities were basic, but Isaac was happy. It was a lot warmer than the Crimea.

The camp had around 150 personnel. Fifty were instructors, including two from the German Democratic Republic, their assistants and the camp service providers – drivers, cooks, cleaners and a small medical team. There were the twenty ZAPU men who had come with Isaac, another twelve ANC from South Africa, and the remaining sixty-eight were Angolan MPLA.

While most of the others were organized into groups for weapons training, Isaac, one of the ANC members and two MPLA were led to a small building away from the main complex by one of the East Germans.

An armed guard stood by the door. He came to attention and saluted the German, who returned the greeting, then unlocked the padlock securing the door.

The four trainees followed him inside the building then helped him open the steel-framed windows.

A long, wooden table with bench seating on either side was positioned in the middle of the room. On one wall was a schoolroom blackboard; the rest were bare, painted white a long time ago. A padlocked, heavy steel trunk was on the floor in one corner.

They were told to sit together on one side of the table.

The German, who was of medium build, clean-shaven with straw-coloured hair and dressed in dark green camouflage, stood in front of the blackboard and introduced himself.

'Good morning,' he said in heavily accented English. 'I am Captain Gerd Reinhold, from East Berlin in the German Democratic Republic. I am a weapons expert. I regard it as an honour to have been chosen to come here to pass on my knowledge and experience to those of you fighting for your freedom. For the next three weeks, I will be teaching you everything there is to know about a weapon that is greatly feared by Western forces around the world.'

He paused to look them over while they thought about this.

'Their fear is well founded,' he continued. 'The weapon is small enough to be carried and operated by a single man. That creates the opportunity to reach target areas where attacks would not normally be expected. Apart from the devastation of a successful strike, any surprise attack will also create panic amongst the security forces and that, in turn, usually presents additional good targets for the weapon.

'I use the term "good targets" deliberately, because you will not have many of these weapons, so selective targeting is critical. Every time you use the weapon you have to get maximum value. If there is any doubt then don't pull the trigger. Better to wait for another day and save the shot for something the enemy will remember for a long time.'

He left them wondering what on earth this weapon could be as he opened the steel trunk and laid a long, narrow, canvas zip-up bag on the table.

Gert Reinhold put his hands on the table next to the bag and leaned towards the recruits.

'You are all fighting forces with well-developed intelligence agencies. Your early success with this weapon depends very much on you keeping it secret until you are ready to strike. Keep the weapon in this bag at all times so it cannot be seen. Tell nobody about it.'

On the night of 2 September 1978, Isaac and eight trusted ZAPU comrades crossed the fifty-kilometre widest stretch of Lake Kariba in the Zambian Army's black-hulled, high-speed launch, *The Black Bitch*, negotiating flooded forests before landing on the Charara shoreline, no more than ten kilometres from the airport at Kariba.

Having dropped them off, the launch returned to Zambia. It would come back the following night to extract them after the mission.

Isaac led the group towards the Kariba airport. They initially hid in cover, but later in the day moved in closer to the airport.

They waited in the thick, thorn scrub until Air Rhodesia flight 825 from Victoria Falls flew over them.

It landed at Kariba to pick up tourists, who had spent the day marvelling at the engineering wonder of the hydroelectric project and the wildlife associated with the biggest man-made lake on the planet.

The final leg to Salisbury would take just over an hour.

The passengers were flying on a Vickers Viscount, a four-engine, turbo-prop aircraft that was quick, comfortable and had an impeccable safety record.

But none of that would count when Isaac fired his secret weapon as the Viscount took off over them on the homeward leg.

Holding the Strela SA-7 Grail over his shoulder, he first activated the power supply of the launcher. A moment later, the gyros had stabilized and that put the sights on target. He pulled the launcher trigger for the first time, and that activated the seeker electronics. If the target was producing a strong enough signal, and if the angular tracking rate was within the acceptable launch parameters, the missile would then lock onto the target. A light in the sight mechanism would illuminate and a buzzer would sound. Isaac would then have less than a second to again press the trigger.

He remained calm; and launched the missile while the aircraft was still in the climb phase of its flight.

When it was only five and a half metres away from Isaac, the rocket sustainer motor activated and accelerated the missile to a speed of 450 metres per second. Once it reached peak speed, the final safety mechanism deactivated and the missile was fully armed.

The missile's infrared seeker head kept it on target with a spinning reticle that measured the amount of incoming infrared energy and worked out where the centre of the energy was coming from.

The Vickers Viscount had no chance.

The missile hit the inner starboard engine and exploded.

With the fuel and hydraulic lines ruptured, a fire started that could not be put out. The second starboard engine failed almost immediately and, heaving wildly, the aircraft began a rapid descent.

With only two engines, the pilots attempted a desperate crash-landing in a cultivated field. The landing was initially hopeful but then the skidding airliner hit a ditch and cartwheeled.

Of the fifty-six people on board, eighteen somehow managed to survive. Five were strong enough to leave the wreckage and go in search of help.

Isaac and his ZAPU terrorists reached the wreckage.

The thirteen survivors lay next to the downed aircraft.

The AK-47s opened fire.

Isaac and his gang were picked up later that night by *The Black Bitch* and returned to the safety of their base at Chipepo, hidden away amongst the islands and inlets on the Zambian side of the great lake.

From ZAPU's point of view, Isaac's first strike with the secret weapon could not have been better. Leader Joshua Nkomo wasted no time in letting the world's media know it was 'his boys' who brought down the airliner. He cleverly sidestepped the issue of killing the survivors.

Initially, the Rhodesians were in shock and denial. Nothing like this could happen.

But in the days that followed, the disbelief was replaced with fury and hate.

They would get even, no matter what.

At the time our SAS team was in Mozambique, in action against Frelimo terrorists on the border with Malawi. Others followed the ZAPU tracks to the lake and it was clear they had escaped back to Zambia, but nobody knew exactly where they had gone or what to do next.

Air Rhodesia put on a brave face. It took precautions such as flying out across the open water of the lake after take-off at Kariba, but normal service resumed and soon tourists were again winging their way between Kariba and Victoria Falls.

Meanwhile, Isaac and his terrorist group had, as a precaution, moved back to the training farm outside Lusaka.

He had one missile left.

He would wait until the situation settled down before striking again. The longer he left it, the greater the impact would be on the enemy.

Five months later, Isaac and his ZAPU terrorist group returned to the Chipepo base. The Zambian Army platoon that operated *The Black Bitch* was pleased to see them back and excited at the prospect of more action.

On the night of 11 February 1979, Isaac and his group again crossed the lake and were dropped off in the same location they had used on the first attack.

Isaac led the team through the night towards Kariba airport. After the first attack, he'd realized he didn't need to get as close as he had been, so this time he selected a spot nearly a kilometre further away. There would be less chance of detection as they sat in the deep shade of an African sausage tree and waited for the aircraft to arrive.

At around 1600 hours, they watched as the aircraft from Victoria Falls came in to land and collect passengers before the final leg to the Rhodesian capital, Salisbury.

Just over an hour later – a bit behind schedule – the white and blue Viscount was climbing over Isaac's position. He held the aim; the infrared guidance system locked on and within point eight of a second the missile was launched.

The aircraft went down and all fifty-nine passengers and crew lost their lives.

Isaac Ngonyama would have suspected he was now the most wanted man in Africa.

What he wouldn't have known was that he'd also just run out of luck.

Retired Royal Navy Lieutenant Commander Bob Ellis was the Kariba harbour master. On 12 February 1979 he had been in the Charara basin, laying marker buoys on the edge of a flooded forest close to the route taken by the ferry that operated between Kariba and Binga, 200 kilometres up the lake. He'd not finished the tricky job that day so had anchored *Armanel* – his twenty-metre work boat – in shallower water for the night.

He had heard the explosion of the plane crash and listened to the dreadful news over his radio.

He was still up at midnight, sitting on the deck with a final brandy, when he heard the sound of boat engines. Picking up his big, naval binoculars, Bob saw a fast dark-hulled launch heading towards the shore about 400 metres away from him. He didn't recognise the boat – he'd never seen it at Kariba.

He could make out the shape of two or three crew in the front.

'What was a boat like this doing in these waters at this time of night?' he wondered.

It returned within twenty minutes, heading back towards the Zambian shore at high speed. Bob watched with interest and noticed it now had several people in the back.

It was a pick-up. Then, suddenly, realizing what was going on, he went below deck and switched on his radar.

Armanel was equipped with the latest Furuno marine radar to chart and monitor thousands of acres of flooded forest, shallow reefs and a constantly changing water level, so Bob had no trouble tracking the launch across the lake, but lost contact as it approached the Zambian shoreline. Looking at his charts, he could see it was an area of many islands and several inlets, some of which tracked well inland, and at the end of one such inlet the name 'Chipepo' was marked on the map.

Bob lost no time in getting on the RT, and instructed the duty operator at Kariba to inform the police immediately.

Just before 1000 hours the following morning, a Rhodesian Air Force Canberra took high-altitude photographs of the area around Chipepo.

At 1500 hours the brigadier ordered an urgent meeting in the SAS operations room.

The ten of us who made up his special task force, Sierra One Seven, sat in front of the map display his team had rigged up that showed us the detail of the lake and ground around Chipepo.

The brigadier welcomed us and came straight to the point.

'Gentlemen, this is about getting even with the ZAPU gang that shot down the Viscounts,' he said.

'After both attacks they seemingly just disappeared,' he continued. 'They don't have helicopters so extraction by boat was always the most likely explanation, and now we know that is the case and we know exactly where they came from.'

He told us about the black boat being radar-tracked towards Chipepo. He pushed a button and the white projector screen rolled down out of its housing.

'This morning the Canberras flew a photo-recce mission over the area and have come up trumps.'

He pushed another button and a black and white picture appeared on the screen. It showed the islands screening the long, narrow entrance into Chipepo. And there – at a mooring a few metres from shore – was a black boat.

He pushed another button and a magnified picture of Chipepo came on screen.

Close to the boat mooring was a building that looked like a single schoolroom, about fifteen metres in length with steps at each end, suggesting there would be doors and the way in and out of the building. Parked outside was the unmistakeable six-wheeled Russian truck that we already knew well from previous operations.

'This is clearly the ZAPU base,' said the brigadier. 'And over here,' he pointed to two similar looking buildings, 'is where their Zambian Army accomplices are located.

'I have deliberately used the word "accomplices" because that's what they are. The boat belongs to the Zambian Army. In using it to transport the ZAPU gangs across the lake, to shoot down the airliners, they are equally responsible for the atrocities.

'Usually we have avoided contact with the Zambian security forces, but there is no political expediency in this case. You have clearance to take them out at the same time as the ZAPU terrorist gang.'

We all enjoyed the sound of that.

We sent Karate away with the team to get started on drawing the stores while Mack, Rex and I worked out with the brigadier what we were going to do.

Time was of the essence. We didn't know how long the ZAPU group would stay at the Chipepo base, and the country was clamouring for action.

The brigadier didn't give us time to think about it. 'You're going in tomorrow night,' he said.

We would fly into Kariba with our boats in the morning. A Rhodesian Army national service company was based at Kariba with one of our SAS majors, Harry Harvey, in command. We had absolute trust in Harry's discretion and knew he would be keen to give us a hand. We needed transport to get from the airport to where we would launch. A three-tonne truck and a Land Rover would do. The brigadier made the call and that was organized.

We would use our Zodiac inflatables to get us within striking range then transfer to the Klepper kayaks for the silent approach to the base. Mack suggested we assemble the kayaks before leaving and carry them ready-to-go on an additional Zodiac.

We would need five kayaks, because with two targets all ten of our team would be involved.

'I need some extra men, Sir,' I said. 'With carrying the kayaks we'll need three Zodiacs and, once we have done the business, I want them to come in to pick us up. The sooner we are out of the area the better, because it's a long way back and I don't want to be caught out on the open water in broad daylight. So I'd like six more men to come with us to operate the Zodiacs.'

'Sounds good. Who do you want? We have B Troop available.'

I'd commanded B Troop myself some years before, so gave him the names of six men I knew would be good to have with us.

We discussed the attack plans.

In the early hours of the morning Rex, Karate, Simmo and Jonny would give the Zambian Army platoon something to think about while the remaining six of us would eliminate the ZAPU gang. We'd blow up their black boat on our way out.

'Mick, there is one thing that worries me about this operation,' said the brigadier once we had the general idea worked out, 'and that is navigation. Specifically, you finding the target.

'I well remember what you reported when paddling on Lake Cahora-Bassa at night. How the lake surface merged with the sky so there was no horizon. Here, there are countless islands and inlets and you have at least fifty kilometres of lake to cross. The Zodiacs have no navigational equipment and, in the dark, I'd say there is a good chance of you getting lost.'

'Yes, Sir,' I replied. 'I can't argue with that and it's been worrying me all afternoon, but I have an idea that might help. You know Commander Bob Ellis, don't you?' I asked.

'We are related,' he laughed. 'Bob married one of my sisters.'

'Even better,' I said. 'In your briefing, you told us how Bob tracked the Zambian launch using the radar on his boat. How about coming up to Kariba with us and you and Bob go out on the lake in his boat? Bob can use the radar to track us, and you can guide us in to our kayak launch point with VHF comms. Once we are in that close there's no way we will get lost.'

'Your staff college training's coming through, Mick,' he beamed. 'I'll enjoy that.' He got up to make the telephone call.

In spite of the mad rush, the start worked out to perfection. I had a good feeling about the operation.

Harry and I had been on a number of covert operations together. I enjoyed his company and had a lot of time for the man, so it was good to see him on the runway as the DC3 taxied towards the small airbase located a discreet distance away from the main civil aviation terminal at Kariba.

He'd organized a covered RM Bedford to meet us and had brought his own Land Rover. With him was Bob Ellis.

'Mick,' said Harry once we were on the ground. 'Get Rex to organize all the gear onto the truck, while we take you and the brigadier down to the harbour to show you what we have arranged. The truck driver has been briefed so he knows where to go.'

I jumped in the front with Harry while the brigadier chatted away to Bob in the back. The road twisted around the lake's edge past the resort hotels and we headed towards the hydro dam wall. About a kilometre short of the wall was a deep-water, rectangular inlet which was Bob's harbour. Three or four boats, including *Armanel*, were moored on the water. There was a wide, concrete boat ramp with rails leading into a large, grey, corrugated iron shed that was both a storeroom and a boat service and repair area. Some white-painted, portacom-style office buildings were off to one side – straggly bougainvillea vines adding a bit of welcome colour.

Harry and Bob got out of the Land Rover and together pushed open the sliding door of the shed. A large trolley sat at the top of the boat ramp rails with a wire cable attached to a big mechanical winch. They would be used to haul boats out of the water for servicing.

'As you can see,' said Harry, 'there is plenty of room here to assemble the Zodiacs and prepare for the operation away from prying eyes, and Bob is happy for you to use the winch to launch the boats – saving time and effort.'

The brigadier and I nodded in appreciation. It wasn't often we let others in on the organization of an SAS operation, but this was looking good.

Bob Ellis asked for our attention. He explained how he had used the radar on *Armanel* to track the Zambian launch, but how he lost the signal as it closed in on the Zambian shoreline.

'I've been looking at the charts. I can see how some of the islands close to the Zambian shore would have screened the radar,' he said. 'What I suggest is that the brigadier and I leave well ahead of you, so I can position *Armanel* where we will be in line of sight behind the islands. That will be much better for us guiding you in close to your target.

'*Armanel* does ten knots at full speed and your Zodiacs do more than twice that, so we'll have to get underway early if we are to reach a position where we can be most effective. Brigadier, we need to leave in about two hours, which gives us just enough time for you to say a quick hello to your sister.'

I shook my head and couldn't help laughing. The start of our operation had been well and truly hijacked, but the good feeling I'd had earlier just kept on growing.

We left the harbour just after 1900 hours.

The lake was mirror smooth. With the Zodiacs at their full speed of between twenty and twenty-five knots, I estimated we would reach the island we had selected as the kayak launch point in a bit less than three hours.

From the island, it would take another one and a half to two hours paddling to reach Chipepo.

Attack time would, therefore, be between midnight and 0100 hours. I was happy with that. It was a good time to attack and left us with just enough time to get back to Kariba before dawn.

As we skimmed across the lake, the brigadier made contact advising they had us on radar and instructing us to make a slight alteration to our course: 'Go left about twenty degrees, Mick,' he ordered. The other boats were listening and followed the adjustment as we altered course with our compass.

There was no moon but the sky was illuminated by millions of stars. As we approached the Zambian shoreline, we could make out the shape of islands directly in front of us.

'Maintain your course for another ten minutes, there's no need to slow down just yet. Bob advises you are still in deep water,' said the brigadier, easing the nervous thoughts I was having about running a rubber boat into a flooded forest at twenty-five knots.

'Ease up now, Mick,' ordered the brigadier. 'We want you to make a ninety-degree left turn in the next five minutes.'

We turned and found ourselves in a wide channel with islands on both sides.

'Two kilometres straight ahead to touchdown. There is a sandy beach on the open-water side of the island you are heading for with deep water all the way in. We will be listening out. Good luck!'

We were now on our own.

We reached the beach. It could not have been better for us. Soft sand and calm water as we unstrapped the Kleppers and started on the final leg into the target.

Before leaving, I spoke to B Troop commander Phil Hammond, who was leading the Zodiac team.

Phil was another Kiwi SAS man like Pig Dog. He was a great officer and a stickler for detail so there were no stuff-ups with B Troop. He'd cleaned up our mess after a big ambush on the Chewore River a couple of years previously and I felt I owed him one. It was great to return the favour and have him and a few of his boys along with us on this operation.

'Phil, as soon as you hear the explosions, get the Zodiacs on the water and come in to join us. We don't want to hang around, so our first priority is to get out of there as quickly as we can. But, as you well know, things can happen, and if any of our team hit trouble we'll be asking you to come in and give us a hand.

'I see you have an RPG bazooka on every boat. Brilliant. If the shit hits the fan that's exactly what we might need to get us out of it.'

'Good as gold, Mick,' he replied, using a Kiwi expression I really enjoyed.

We paddled in to Chipepo. It was easy going and we made good time.

As we approached the *The Black Bitch's* mooring, we stopped and used both infrared and our passive light intensifiers to see if there was any likely opposition. Nothing was seen so we went straight in and left our kayaks on a beach, amongst wooden dugouts and small fibre-glass fishing boats.

Rex and his team moved off towards the Zambian Army barracks while my group closed in on the ZAPU target.

It would take Rex about half an hour to reach the barracks. Meanwhile, my team would move in close to the ZAPU camp and wait for Rex to start the action.

Our plan was simple.

Rex and his team would silently lay three bunker bombs against the outside walls of the two Zambian Army barracks.

The bunker bombs were a home-made improvisation Karate and I made together.

We had a double-skinned kettle back at base we used to melt the high explosive known as Pentolite. It liquefied at exactly 100 degrees – boiling point. Once we had it in liquid form, we would pour it into a family-sized

Coke bottle with a knotted Cordtex tail inserted before the explosive cooled. We ended up with a four-kilogram high-explosive device that could be used individually or linked together to get a simultaneous detonation of any number of the bombs.

It was simple but lethal. We'd brought six of them along.

After they had buried their dead the Zambian Army might not, in future, be so keen to get involved with shooting down civilian airliners!

Rex stopped as they reached the two barrack rooms and scanned the area using his light intensifier. There was no activity. It looked like they were all sleeping.

Karate and Simmo crept around the back of one of the buildings and laid three bunker bombs against the block wall. They linked the three explosive devices together with a Cordtex line then attached the detonator with a short length of safety fuse.

'Ready to go when you are, Rex,' said Karate into the whisper mike.

'OK here as well,' said Rex who had done the same to the other barracks.

'Initiate the charges,' he ordered.

Three minutes later the two buildings exploded. The walls blew in over the sleeping soldiers and the roofs collapsed.

As the dust settled, Rex and his team approached. Without mercy, they sprayed the two ruined barracks with sustained gunfire.

Next they turned their attention to the three Land Rovers parked outside.

On the back of each vehicle was a metal frame with a webbing strap that housed a five-gallon petrol jerrycan. They emptied the fuel from these containers over the Land Rovers then stood well clear as Rex lobbed a white phosphorous grenade into the middle of them.

The Zambian Army part of the mission was complete.

We, meanwhile, had silently moved to within twenty metres of the ZAPU base and were waiting for Rex to start the show.

I'd put Fish along with Horse and Mack on one end of the building where we could see a door above two or three steps – that was their target. With Pig Dog and Nelson, I'd gone to the opposite end to cover the doorway there. As soon as we heard Rex's explosions, Fish and Pig Dog would put bazooka rockets through the two doors.

With Mack on one side and me on the other, we would then run up to the shattered doors and each lob a phosphorous and a fragmentation grenade into the building. We'd then duck out of the way as fast as we could because Horse would fire through the doorway with his MAG machine gun while Nelson, who was carrying an RPD, would do the same at the opposite end.

The ZAPU terrorists would have a choice: they could stay inside with the grenades or they could run through the doors and into the machine-gun fire.

For good measure, Fish and Pig Dog each had another two bazooka rockets.

We were crouched down and waiting when suddenly we saw a figure approaching us.

Nelson signalled *stay* to me, stood up and walked towards the man.

'*Sabona*, Comrade. You are out late tonight,' he said in impeccable Ndebele.

Startled, the figure started to say something but before any words came out, Nelson struck as fast as a biting viper. The butt of his RPD flashed upwards and connected with the point of the man's jaw. Without a sound he crumpled and fell to the ground.

We pulled him over to where we were crouched and tied and gagged him. He lay still next to us while we waited.

The thunderous crash of high explosives shattered the silence of the night as Rex's bunker bombs exploded.

Whoosh! Pig Dog and Fish let fly with the rockets.

Mack and I sprinted the twenty metres to the edge of the building and threw our grenades through the shattered doorways.

The machine guns opened fire then there was another *whoosh* as the bazookas fired for the second time.

After the final rocket attack we stopped firing. I ordered Fish's group, on the opposite end of the building, to stay where they were and cover their door while the three of us moved in to clear the inside.

A figure suddenly bolted out of the far door, only to be bowled over as he ran into fire from Fish's group.

Everything became quiet.

We moved cautiously into the barrack room; amongst the wreckage and smouldering bedding we found seven bodies.

In a corner that would have been sheltered to some degree from our fire was a bed that was still intact and hadn't been slept in. On top of it was a pack and a long, narrow, zip-up canvas bag. Pig Dog picked it up and undid the zipper.

'Oh my God!' he said, as we immediately recognized what it was.

We'd never seen one before but we all knew it was the Strela.

What we didn't know was that it belonged to the man lying tied and gagged on the ground outside the shattered ZAPU camp.

Phil roared in with the Zodiacs, and we lost no time in loading the kayaks and our prisoner, while two of his team attached limpets to *The Black Bitch*. Her days were over as well.

We stopped at our staging island, to properly secure the kayaks before the long ride back across the lake, and I checked in with the brigadier who was anxiously waiting for my report.

'Sunray mobile, this is Sierra One Seven. You read me?'

'Fives, Mick,' replied the brigadier immediately. 'Hope all's well?'

'Affirmative. No problems. It all went like clockwork, thank you. Hundred per cent result and we also scored two bonus points for you. First, I have aboard a live member of the ZAPU gang and request you organize Special Branch police to meet us at the harbour. He will require some medical attention – we broke his jaw. Fish has given him a morphine shot but he's not comfortable. Roger so far?'

'You broke his jaw?' the brigadier responded incredulously.

'Yes, Sir. Long story, will tell you later. Secondly, we have recovered the weapon used to bring down the airliners. I'm not sure what to do with it. Do I hand that over to Special Branch as well?'

There was a stunned silence for a moment.

'You've had a big night out, Mick,' he finally replied. 'Yes, hand it over to Special Branch then best we keep our usual low profile. Once you have handed everything over, pack up immediately and I'll get Harry to take you straight down to the airbase. You'll be home and well out of the way before lunchtime.'

We closed down the radio and powered up the twin forty-horse Evinrudes.

Return to Angola

For three days and nights, Special Branch police interrogated the captured ZAPU terrorist we had brought back from Chipepo.

Their interrogation techniques were not cruel and brutal, but they would wear down and demoralize a prisoner until he reached the stage of exhaustion and despair. The prisoner's jaw had been broken by the butt of Nelson's RPD, so he was physically uncomfortable from the start. On the third night, he asked to be allowed to sleep and promised he would tell all next morning.

And he did.

His name was Isaac Ngonyama, he told Special Branch. Then he proceeded to give an account of his journey that had started at *The Church of Orphans* in Bulawayo; his time in Lusaka; of being sent to the Ukraine and then to Luso in Angola for training on a secret weapon.

The interrogation team stopped him at that point and produced the zip-up canvas bag we had brought back.

'Is this the weapon?' they asked, handing him the bag.

Isaac undid the zip and removed the Strela.

'Yes,' he said, caressing the launcher.

'Show us how it works,' they ordered and Isaac obliged, demonstrating and explaining the missile launch sequence.

His interrogators were pleased. 'Would you like a coke, Isaac?' they asked.

He was given one and was also offered a cigarette. Isaac relaxed. But now it was crunch time.

'Was it you who used this weapon to bring down the airliners?' demanded one of the officers.

Isaac admitted it at once, and went on to describe how he had been presented to ZAPU leader Joshua Nkomo after the first strike.

'So was it Nkomo and the ZAPU hierarchy that planned the airliner attacks?' they asked.

'No,' replied Isaac. 'The German at Luso told us to be very specific with our targeting, but at that stage we had no firm plans and were mainly thinking about shooting at Rhodesian Air Force planes and helicopters. I got the idea of bringing down the airliners from the ANC man, who said they were going to use theirs to shoot down one of the new South African Airways Boeing 747 jumbo jets in Johannesburg.'

There was a stunned silence as the interrogators realized the significance of what Isaac had just told them.

'The ANC were at Luso?' they asked incredulously.

'Yes,' said Isaac. 'There were twelve of them, but only one was trained to use the Strela like me.'

On night five, Isaac Ngonyama was sedated with a tranquilizing injection. Handcuffed and in a semi-conscious state, he was put on a boat and taken ten kilometres offshore from Kariba.

With no comprehension of what was happening, Isaac was dropped into the deep, dark waters of the lake.

With the capture of the ZAPU gang member and the recovery of the Strela, the brigadier decided to stay on in Kariba with Bob Ellis and his sister to monitor events as they unfolded. He knew they would get good intelligence from the capture, but never in his wildest dreams could he have imagined the news from Special Branch when they met on the fourth day.

An air force plane took him back to Salisbury later that morning. On arrival he went straight into an urgent, top priority meeting with the Rhodesian ComOps general and the air force air marshal.

The ComOps leaders were told about Luso, the presence of the ANC, and a plan to down an SAA jumbo with a Strela from somewhere in Kempton Park, a well-populated industrial area in line with the Jan Smuts runways.

'We can't hang around with this,' the brigadier said. 'I have pre-empted your authority and booked two seats on the SAA flight to Johannesburg, leaving at 1700 this afternoon.'

Turning to the air marshal, he explained: 'The second seat is for you or one of your officers because, with the ANC connection, I'm certain the SADF will want involvement in anything we do. I'm thinking Mick should again direct a night attack with the Canberras, like we did on the Malawi border, but this time with a combination of our own Canberras as well as some South African aircraft. Together we'll wipe Luso and the East Germans off the face of this earth.

'I'm also keen to get the South Africans involved because I'm going to need their help to get Mick and his team back home.'

'I'll see you at the airport this afternoon at 1600 hours,' said the air marshal.

As the SAA Boeing 737 finally stopped outside the international terminal at Jan Smuts, an unmarked black Mercedes drove alongside and parked next to where the front boarding staircase was being positioned. The brigadier and the air marshal left the aircraft and were ushered into the vehicle, which took them across the airport complex to a hangar with C130s lined up outside. The Mercedes headed towards a Super Frelon helicopter that was warming up off to one side of the giant freighter planes.

They landed outside the SADF headquarters in Pretoria twenty minutes later and were escorted into the building by armed guards.

The brigadier had requested a meeting in an Ops room with detailed map coverage of Namibia, Angola, Zambia and Rhodesia, because the operation he was proposing would cover all four countries and he needed to show them why.

After the official greetings, the brigadier opened proceedings by giving the assembled South African Defence Force hierarchy the background to the Chipepo attack, and a detailed description of our SAS raid that had eliminated the terrorist gang and resulted in the capture of a ZAPU member along with the weapon which brought down the airliners.

There was a gasp from the audience as he opened a zip-up canvas bag and laid the Strela SAM-7 on a table in front of them all.

He already had their undivided attention, but you could have heard a pin drop as he went on to describe the camp at Luso where Isaac and an ANC terrorist had been trained to use the weapon by an East German named Gerd Reinhold.

And then the climax of the presentation!

'ZAPU had no premeditated plan to shoot down an Air Rhodesia Viscount,' he said.

'Isaac Ngonyama got the idea from the ANC man who was being trained with him. His stated intention was to position himself somewhere in Kempton Park where he would shoot down an SAA 747 jumbo as it took off from Jan Smuts.'

The brigadier paused and watched as jaws dropped in shock and disbelief.

'Yes,' he said, acknowledging the reaction. 'Up in Rhodesia, we too couldn't believe anything like this could happen. But it has – twice!'

He paused again to let that critical point sink in with the South Africans.

'I'm now going to take you back a few years and describe an operation involving one of our SAS teams in northern Mozambique.' The brigadier related how, in the dead of night, we had used distress flares to indicate the location of a Frelimo training base with 300 terrorists for the Canberra bombers. The bombing had been done with pinpoint accuracy and there were no survivors.

'My proposal is to use the same team and proven technique to destroy the Luso training camp in Angola. With the ANC involved and what is at stake, we thought a combined operation would be appropriate. In general terms, the air marshal has suggested Squadron Leader Bernie Vaughan leads the attacking party as he has the experience of working with the SAS. We will commit three Rhodesian Canberras to the operation and were thinking that perhaps the SAAF might like to participate with another four Canberras on the raid?'

'Absolutely!' exclaimed the South African Chief of Defence Forces without any hesitation.

'Is there anything else we can do to assist in this operation?' he asked.

'Thank you, General. Your support is greatly appreciated and yes, there is one more thing you could help us with,' replied the brigadier.

He outlined the operation he had planned and there were nods of approval as it all unfolded.

'Where I need your help is with the extraction of my SAS team. They will be too far away for helicopter recovery, but as there will only be four of them this is what I have in mind.' He went on to explain his plan.

The South African faces lit up with a combination of amusement and admiration.

'No problem, Brigadier,' smiled the general. 'We will get your boys back in one piece.'

Next morning while the air marshal was busy with the South African Air Force, the brigadier was given a car and driver to take him to the CSIR – the Council for Scientific and Industrial Research – which was also located in Pretoria. He had arranged to meet his old friend the professor, who had given the SAS a special super glue that had helped secure the explosives in another operation, which had brought down Zambian bridges and halted the influx of Russian armour.

The professor greeted his old friend warmly on arrival.

'Great to see you, Peter,' he said smiling and shaking his hand.

'Thank you for sending me that most interesting account of how your SAS team marked a terrorist target at night for the Canberra bombers. I struggle to express my admiration of your innovation and the courage of the men who made it all happen.

'Your request this time was much easier than the bridges' problem. The solution is both readily available and ideal for what you want to achieve,' he said.

'ICAO – the International Civil Aviation Organization – makes the rules about aircraft used by all international and local carriers. One of those rules is that in addition to the usual navigation lights, the aircraft must also have warning strobe lights. It's a safety feature and the requirement is that the strobe lights should, in clear skies, be visible from at least twelve miles away – that's eighteen kilometres in our language.

'What better solution is there for Mick and his team marking the target at night?' he continued. They can illuminate the target markers well in advance of the attack and, unlike the flares you used in Mozambique, they won't burn out. It means there is much more time for the bombers to get themselves lined up with the target and, perhaps more importantly, more time for Mick and the boys to get well away from the danger zone.

'Not that that seemed to worry them too much in Mozambique, but better all the same,' he added.

He put four translucent, polycarbonate cases on a table in front of the brigadier, each housing a strobe light complete with a mounting that had a sharp steel fork that could be driven into the ground to provide a stable platform.

'I know you only wanted three,' he said, 'but I've put four together for you in case one is damaged if you are doing a parachute entry.'

The brigadier was effusive with thanks and as the professor fired up one of the units to demonstrate its capability, he was even more appreciative.

Mick and his team would be much safer with this gear and the night bomber pilots would be ecstatic.

The following morning, we were given word the brigadier wanted to see Rex and me with Fish and Karate asap in the SAS operations room.

We saluted on arrival.

'Morning Gentlemen,' he said. 'Before you sit down, is my memory correct in remembering you four were the ones with the flares that night on the Malawi border?'

'Your memory is good, Sir,' I replied.

'Excellent. Take a seat. I have another operation for you in which a terrorist camp will again be attacked at night by the Canberras, but this time we have made things considerably safer for you on the ground. And perhaps that is just as well, because in addition to your friend Bernie Vaughan with three Rhodesian aircraft leading the attack, there will be another four South African Canberras with them.

'This has all come about as a result of information obtained from the ZAPU man you captured at Chipepo.' The brigadier proceeded to tell us about Luso, the ANC presence, and the plan to shoot down an SAA 747 in Johannesburg.

We listened as spellbound as the SADF chiefs had been the day before.

'The night bombing concept you came up with has massive appeal. The enemy are asleep and concentrated in the camp area. They don't expect to be attacked at night – in fact, at Luso they spoke of the base being well out of reach. They can't see or hear the attack coming, and because it all happens so quickly there is no time for them to make use of any anti-aircraft defence systems they may have.

'But, for the concept to work, the target has to be well marked. There were limitations with what we had available in Mozambique and, because of that, you ended up way too close – well inside the danger zone, in fact. We got away with it but I don't want to take that risk again, and we don't have to.

'Come round the table and have a look at these,' he said, opening the taped-up cardboard box the professor had supplied with the strobe lights and his improvised mountings.

'They are powered by a nine-volt battery that will keep them going continuously for about an hour, I am told.' He switched on one of the strobes. A dazzling, electric blue light flashed in our faces, so bright we turned our eyes away.

'Brilliant,' I said. Immediately realizing that not only would it be good for us, but Bernie and the other pilots would be able to see the lights from a long way out. There would be so much more time for everyone, and the bomb aimers would have the target markers all the way in to the release.

I picked one up. 'Fantastic. Not too heavy,' I said.

'Yes,' said the brigadier. 'I thought you would approve. CSIR are indeed good friends of ours. Now please take your seats and we'll have a look at the maps and your mission in detail.

'We'll start with the target detail,' he said dropping down the projector screen. 'For once, this is probably the simplest part of the operation.

'A Canberra did a photo-recce run over the area early yesterday morning. We have found what matches the training camp description given to us by the ZAPU man from Chipepo. We can't see it on these monochrome pictures, but he told us the roofs of all the school buildings taken over by the MPLA are painted red; given the training camp is also right alongside the railway line, you shouldn't have any difficulty finding and identifying the target.

'Don't be concerned about this settlement,' he said, pointing to twenty or so mud huts pictured on the western side of the school buildings. 'This is all terrorist accommodation. The nearest civilians are at least forty kilometres away.

'The air force plan is to fly up towards the settlement of Luena, about 100 kilometres west of you, then change course north-east and follow the railway line in to the target. They may not be able to see it in the dark, but that won't matter as the South African aircraft have Doppler systems that can use your radio transmissions to guide them in towards you until they visually locate the strobe lights.

'So, that being the case, make your inverted "V" marker, with the strobes at a point of your choosing, on the west side of the camp complex.'

'Sounds good, Sir,' I said. 'You say there are no locals within forty or so kilometres of the camp? That far away and in MPLA country the last thing we want is to be compromised.'

'Mick, we can never completely rule out the possibility of locals being around, but all indications are that you shouldn't be disturbed around the camp. You may get mortared or fired at by rockets and anti-aircraft guns, but compromise by locals is highly unlikely,' he said, trying to keep a straight face.

'Mortared and shelled? Am I missing something here?' I asked nervously.
The brigadier turned to the map coverage of the area.

'The training camp is located on the north-western edge of the *Parque Nacional da Cameia*. The park is a granite shield with low woodland and open tussock plains in the north, while the south is mainly swamp and reed beds associated with the upper reaches of the Zambezi River. It's over 1,400 square kilometres of deserted national park. The game has long gone and the ground is unsuitable for farming, so there are no people.

'And that,' he said with a triumphant glint in his eyes, 'makes it perfect for a field firing range.

'The ZAPU man described how they could fire the 82-millimetre mortars, 122-millimetre rockets and 14.5-millimetre KPVs into the hills from within the training camp.

'Clever set-up. And we are going to drop you right in the middle of it. For us it's the perfect drop zone.

'Mick, you had no problem dodging the mortars, rockets and 14.5 fire during the camp raid on Cahora-Bassa,' he said with a smile. 'I'm sure you can do it again in Angola.'

Well, we'd just bloody well have to.

'OK, Sir, so you drop us into the field firing range, we dodge all the artillery, then we put out the markers and the Canberras destroy the camp. What then?' I asked. 'We will be hundreds of kilometres inside Angola. That's a hell of a walk back through Indian country.'

'Twelve hundred kilometres, in fact,' he said. 'But don't worry, you won't be walking out.' The brigadier told us what he had arranged with the South Africans and why only four of us would be doing the job.

For the remainder of that day, we put together everything we'd need for what they had called Operation Vanity.

'Guys, I have to tell you there is one thing that worries me about this operation,' I said later as we sat together in the stores. 'It's not MPLA, fear of compromise or the bombing that worries me. It's the weather.

'For a start the weather could screw up the bombing mission. If it's hosing down, they will put it off until they have a clear night. Same applies to the brigadier's plan for getting us out.

'What is supposed to be a four or five-day mission could easily turn into twice that or longer. We will be in a high rainfall area so water won't be a problem, but to me that national park sounds a bit like the eastern highlands here in Rhodesia. It's high so there's a good chance we will be wet and cold.

'For a start I reckon we should all take a blanket as well as our nylon sleeping bags. If we are warm, we'll sleep well and if we sleep well, we'll work well.

'We should all take extra brew kit to last at least ten days. Rex, I'll get some cash from payroll while you get a Sabre to go down to your butcher mate in Greendale. We want twenty packets of shaved biltong and chopped dried boerewors mixed together – each packet enough for a day. That's five packets each and they must be sealed in plastic bags so the meat stays dry.

'With brew kit and protein we'll have the ability to stay out there for as long as it takes.

'What we have to come to terms with is the fact we will be 1,200 kilometres from the nearest friendly border. If things go wrong with the plans to pull us out, then this could turn into a long and tricky escape and evasion exercise. And, as you well know, escape and evasion exercises are all about survival.'

Late afternoon, the brigadier called for a meeting and we again met in the operations room.

'Some good news for you,' he said. 'The South Africans have offered to drop you in from one of their C130s. They fly much faster than the DC3 Dakotas and their more sophisticated navigational equipment means they can locate the drop zone with absolute certainty.

'Moreover, you can exit from the back ramp that will be lowered on reaching the drop zone. It means you won't have to sit for five hours in the freezing conditions of an aircraft without a door.'

'That's great news, Sir, thank you,' I replied. 'We are all set to go, but we spent some time this afternoon looking at what we will do if we can't get out as planned because of bad weather. If it's OK with you, we would like to show you on the map coverage what we have in mind?'

We had selected two alternative pickup locations, each progressively further away from the planned pickup point. If those couldn't work then basically our plan was to start walking due south towards the border with Namibia.

At the start we would be in an unpopulated national park; then sparsely populated tribal lands before again reaching national parks that extended all the way to the safety of the border. Along the way, we could implement the extraction plan if the weather and the ground presented that opportunity. But if push came to shove we would walk all the way back.

'Good work, Gentlemen,' said the brigadier. 'I sincerely hope it doesn't come to that but, whatever happens, I will be monitoring your progress. At worst we'll get you out once you are in range of helicopters.'

Next day we boarded a Rhodesian Air Force DC3, at the civilised time of nine in the morning, and took off on the start of our Angolan adventure.

The Dakota initially flew south-west out of Salisbury towards Victoria Falls. From the falls, the aircraft took a more westerly bearing that followed the course of the Chobe River on the northern border of Botswana, where there was the greatest concentration of elephants on earth.

The lush floodplains of the Chobe were eventually replaced by dry *mopane* woodland as we continued west and into Namibia and the Caprivi Strip. It got drier and drier as we finally reached the dusty mining town of Rundu, on the southern border of Angola, where the South Africans had army and airbases.

We had several hours to kill before boarding the C130, so I took out my binoculars and went birdwatching. In these remote, arid areas there were larks and other bird species that weren't found elsewhere in Africa; an airbase was the perfect environment for a number of them.

I asked our hosts to let base security know they had a birdwatcher on site before wandering off across the low, yellow grass surrounding the airstrip.

Rundu was a good place to start the operation because, as we had noticed in our contingency planning for a long walk back, the first 300 kilometres to the north were unoccupied national park.

The C130 took off in the dark at 2000 hours and initially headed west before circling round and climbing back over Rundu and the Okavango River.

The climb continued over the empty national park areas just north of the border, until the aircraft eventually levelled out at 12,500 feet and settled on a course of nine degrees – just east of north. The *Parque Nacional da Cameia* was some 1,200 kilometres away. Cruising at a speed of 540 kilometres an hour, we would get there in about two and a quarter hours.

The four of us sat together at the front of the cargo bay with two South African parachute dispatchers. At our flying altitude, the temperature inside the unpressurised aircraft would get down to about minus eight degrees, so we were grateful for the blankets they had given us before take-off. We put them over our heads and wrapped them tightly around us as we sat in the uncomfortable, saggy canvas seating.

Anyone who has ever flown in the back of a C130 will know that sleep is impossible! The engines were noisy and immediately above where we sat were the two hydraulic systems that operated the wing stabilizers. There was no escape from their incessant wheezing and hissing. We tried ear plugs but to little avail.

We sat and shivered, trying to doze through the flight until thirty minutes out when the dispatchers stood up and called for action.

We complied with relief.

On another operation, the C130 flight engineer had told me that if they made things too comfortable, we paratroopers wouldn't want to jump out. No risk of that. We couldn't get out quick enough.

With the dispatchers assisting, we strapped on our main canopies and reserve parachutes. They did a double-check ensuring all was OK, then we synchronized our altimeters.

Once happy with the parachutes, we then strapped our packs to the steel D-rings on the webbing beneath the reserve chute. Finally we secured the quick-release device that would free the packs from our bodies once we had deployed the parachutes; they would then dangle safely below us on a three-metre nylon rope.

At last, tightening the helmet strap and minor adjustment of our goggles, we were ready to go.

A red light came on at the back of the aircraft and the rear loading ramp began to open.

The two dispatchers led us towards the gaping hole at the back of the plane, and held us where the ramp was hinged with the fuselage. The wind swirled, the aircraft rocked and rolled and the noise was deafening.

We stood waiting anxiously as the pilots closed in on the drop zone.

The red light changed to green.

'Go! Go! Go!' yelled the dispatchers.

With our heavy loads we staggered down the ramp until the turbulence blew us off. We fell tumbling away from the aircraft and out into the dark space above Angola.

First priority was to get stable. I got into position and soon had control. Second priority was to look around and find the boys. They too had stabilized and were close. All good.

We stayed close together as we hurtled towards the ground at terminal velocity – around 200 kilometres an hour.

The plan for the C130 was to dispatch us over the northern quadrant of the *Parque Nacional da Cameia*, between fifty and thirty kilometres south of the target area. To help with our orientation we had decided to deploy the chutes early – we'd pull at 6,000 feet. That would give us time to look at the ground and make a call on where we would land. With the forward drive of the Para-Commander free-fall parachute, we could fly a considerable distance from 5,000 feet above the ground, and we hoped to take full advantage of that.

But first we had to concentrate on the drop.

At our descent speed, it would take just thirty seconds to reach 6,000 feet, so I kept my eye on the altimeter on my left wrist and focused on staying good and stable.

As 7,000 feet flashed past, I signalled to the others. We turned and separated to give ourselves plenty of airspace as the parachutes deployed.

I reached across to my left shoulder and pulled the ripcord. The pilot chute sprang out, dragging the main canopy behind it. There was a low rumbling as the Para-Commander opened, I felt the tug on my shoulders and my feet swung up to waist level as in the space of 200 feet I was slowed down to the gentle descent rate of the parachute.

I had a quick look round to make sure we were still well separated while I dropped my pack. I operated the quick-release device. The pack dropped and oscillated gently three metres beneath me.

Time now to get my bearings.

The night was clear with a waning quarter-moon setting in the west. I pulled on my right toggle to turn the parachute until I was in line with the front stars of the 'Plough' – we would fly due north and see what happened.

I glanced round to see the others following me and closing in.

Looking ahead for the first time, there were open grassy areas with patches of low trees stretching into the distance for as far as I could see. It was looking good and we'd fly as far across this country as we could while slowly descending.

There was no wind to speak of but, as I approached my chosen landing place, I turned the Para-Commander 180 degrees to slow the forward momentum we had developed in the descent. The parachute stalled as my feet touched the ground. Stand-up landing! Nice.

The others landed safely within twenty or thirty metres of me.

I got out of the parachute webbing harness, opened my pack and took out the Russian-made AKM we had decided to carry. I put on a magazine and loaded.

The others followed suit then we turned our attention to bundling up the parachutes, which we stuffed into black plastic rubbish bags. We added our helmets, goggles and the pack harness with the quick-release device, and then put the four bags out of sight under some low bushes.

We presumed we were in the *Parque Nacional da Cameia* but had no idea exactly where. We'd walk for a couple of hours to clear the drop zone then bed down. Maybe tomorrow we would be able to work out exactly where we were.

The going was easy, across low grassland with occasional patches of stunted woodland and small streams. Around 0100 I called a halt and we crawled under the canopy of the stunted, windswept trees, where we spent a comfortable night. We were all glad we had brought a blanket.

After a welcome brew next morning, Karate rigged up the HF radio antenna and tapped out a Morse message to the brigadier, letting him know we were OK but yet to establish our exact location.

Rex and Fish meanwhile wandered off on a circular patrol of our campsite to see if there were any signs of life and anything we should be worried about.

They returned, reporting a network of narrow tracks through the grass and burrows that would have been made by springhares – so named because that member of the rabbit family had extended back legs that propelled it along like a kangaroo. They were also tasty and would be a good food option for us if we started to get short of rations.

Rex reported that, as far as he could see, the ground was flat. There were no visible features that might help us work out our location. In a way that was useful. We knew there were hills immediately north of our target and if we were close we'd see them. It meant we were still well south of our objective.

We started to walk.

At first we were cautious, checking the ground ahead with binoculars, but by mid-morning it was patently obvious there was no regular human traffic through that area, so we relaxed and pushed on. The going was good and by the time we stopped for an extended break, some five hours later, I was confident we had covered at least fifteen kilometres – probably more.

'We'll keep going until it gets dark,' I said. 'Even if they dropped us fifty kilometres out we should start seeing some landmarks by the end of the day.

'We really can't go wrong,' I added. 'If we keep heading north, we will eventually run into the railway line – it's just a matter of time.'

We continued through the afternoon in perfect weather – blue, cloudless skies and cool air. There were a few birds but no sign of game animals and, happily, no human presence.

Just after 1600 hours, we dropped down into a stream crossing then climbed up a rocky incline that was steeper than anything we had previously encountered. It still wasn't much of a climb, but it was just enough extra elevation for us to see the low outline of hills on the horizon.

We pulled out the maps and looked through binoculars. Lining the map up with the compass, we tried to match what we could see with the drawn features on the map. We were still more hopeful than certain of where we were, but we now had a reasonable idea and that boosted morale. There were still twenty to thirty kilometres to walk but we were closing in on the target area.

The night was clear with a million stars lighting up the sky, but the temperature dropped into single digits. We found another low, wooded copse and curled up underneath in our blankets, luckily avoiding most of the heavy dew that soaked the grass that night.

We made an early start and Rex pushed the pace. Our packs were heavy and, in spite of the good going underfoot, it was hard work, but the air was cool and there was plenty of water along the way. We made good progress.

By late morning, the range of hills was noticeably closer and then just before 1600 hours we heard explosions. It was mortar fire. I took a compass bearing – 335 degrees north-west and about ten kilometres away.

We pushed on with renewed energy. We were nearing the edge of the great plateau that broke up into pointed hills and dropped steeply into the deep valley where the railway line and our terrorist camp were located.

That afternoon as we edged steadily forward, the hills to our right suddenly erupted as mortar bombs fired from the camp exploded on the unmarked targets of their field firing range.

We stopped to watch the show and make our approach plans.

We needed to be far enough away to avoid detection during the daylight hours before the bombing, but close enough to observe the camp and proceedings without getting mortared or shot at with rockets.

We needed to work out exactly where we would place the markers and how best to get there after dark. Finally, we had to plan our escape route once we had activated the strobe lights for the bombers.

We looked at the options with binoculars.

Rex handed the glasses back to me. 'Mick, take a look at that feature,' he said, pointing to a rounded hill some 400 metres away in the direction of the mortar fire.

'On the south side you can see it drops into a wooded saddle, not far below the summit. And from the saddle there is a small stream that runs around the side of the feature and down into the valley. We can base up in the saddle where there is cover, and we can use the stream to guide us down to the railway line.'

It was a great option.

'Perfect,' I said. 'And with any luck we won't get mortared.'

We moved into position.

Below us and off to the right, we recognized the red roofing of the camp and the adjacent mud huts the brigadier had pointed out on the air photographs. The railway line and a road passed next to the camp. We could see plenty of human activity and Fish tried a head count with the binoculars. His estimate was 150 to 200 terrorists.

'Mick,' he said after giving us the numbers. 'I've been thinking about the strobe lights. I don't know what your plans are but I don't think we should leave them behind. After the bombing we should go back and collect them. If we do that there will be no indication of our involvement. The MPLA will just think of it as an air attack. If we leave the strobes behind and they find them, they will realize a ground force was also involved and that could start a manhunt we don't want to be part of this far from home.'

Fish had once said that what he liked about the SAS was that we were soldiers who used our brains, and he'd just proved that.

'Great logic, Fish. Thank you,' I replied immediately.

'I was also thinking of collecting the strobes after the attack, but your reasoning is way better than mine. I wanted the strobes back to help us get out of this place afterwards.'

'Well, that's two bloody good reasons,' interjected Rex. 'And, while we are on the subject, I too was having some thoughts about them. We should pace out the distance from the edge of the camp to where we plan on putting the front light. Then we should pace out exactly the same distance to where we will position the back strobes. The bomb aimers will then have an illuminated indication of how far in front of the lights the target starts.'

'And it will be even better for them if we use our fourth strobe at the back and in a straight line with the front marker,' added Karate.

With a team like that how could we fail?

That night we rigged up a big antenna and tapped out a coded sitrep to the brigadier. We let him know we were in position and ready for the attack anytime from the following night. To give us time to collect the strobes and get well away from the area before daylight, I requested an attack time of around midnight. We were told to keep listening as he would have an answer for us within an hour.

We got the reply.

At midnight the following night, the Luso training camp would be obliterated.

The following day was spent watching the target, working out how best to make our approach and where we could position the strobe lights. We also got some rest because we had a big night ahead of us.

There was one other thing we learned and it came as no great surprise. It soon became obvious that our first extraction option was a non-starter.

The brigadier had asked the South Africans if we could be extracted from the operational area using one of their Beechcraft aircraft, usually reserved for VIP flights around South Africa. He'd done his homework: with a range of around 2,500 kilometres and a 45-minute reserve flying time, it could do the round trip between Rundu and *Parque Nacional da Cameia*. His plan was for us to find a road it could land on, and the first and obvious suggestion was that we try the road alongside the railway line.

From the outset I thought it was too close to the target. After the bombing, there was bound to be some reaction from the MPLA, who had a large base at Luena, about 100 kilometres away to the west and on that same road. However, it was a suggestion worthy of consideration.

But during the day, as we watched the occasional truck and a few buses laboriously negotiating the ruts and potholes, it became clear the road had had no maintenance in many years. And that being the case, there was no way an aircraft could use it as a landing strip.

It confirmed what we already expected – we'd have to do a lot of walking to find a suitable place where the plane could land.

What worried us more was that during the day the wind had changed. The gentle easterly we'd enjoyed during the drop had been replaced with a fresher breeze from the west and in the distance we could see clouds building. They were still a long way off but were definitely heading our way. There was no way of telling how fast they were moving. We would just have to cross our fingers and hope they stayed clear until after the bombing.

Once it got dark, we packed up and moved carefully down the hill, following the line of the stream that headed towards the railway line where it flowed under a low bridge. We would leave our packs under the bridge while we closed in on the target to position the strobe lights.

The bridge was about 400 metres away from the camp; far enough, we decided, to be safe from the bombing and we could take cover under the concrete bridge piers. It was a good place for us.

On our side of the terrorist camp there was a narrow belt of woodland and then a cultivated field that extended almost all the way back to our bridge. It couldn't have been better for positioning the strobes.

We moved cautiously over the cultivated land towards the trees next to the camp. Once in the cover of the trees, we stopped while Rex took a night scope and silently moved towards the edge of the camp. He reached the edge of the treeline. In front of him and no more than twenty metres away were the mud huts.

A dog barked – the last thing he needed. Through the night scope he watched the dog sniffing the air and looking in his direction. It was time to move out, he thought and backed off.

Rex started pacing back towards us.

He had counted out ninety paces by the time he reached us. That converted to eighty metres. He then added the extra twenty metres to the huts and then a second twenty metres as we moved away from the trees into the open field where we would place the front strobe.

Finally, he took a compass bearing. One hundred and twenty metres on a bearing of fifty-two degrees to the target.

Karate put his strobe onto the mounting and pushed the steel stake into the ground.

Meanwhile, Rex again followed his compass and paced out what we reckoned would be 120 metres back from the front light.

He made a mark and I put my strobe into the ground.

I stood up, facing the target, and spread out my arms to line up the back markers of our inverted 'V'. Rex and Fish moved thirty metres away on either side of me and fixed their strobes.

We were all set to go. All we had to do now was wait for the aircraft then switch on the lights.

It looked like the weather was going to play ball. We could see the odd lightning flash and heard the distant rumble of thunder to the west, but it was a long way from us. There was a clear night sky above us and we were warmer than we had been up on the plateau.

At 2325 hours the VHF radio crackled into life.

'Sierra One Seven, this is Cyclone Five Green Leader. Do you read me? Over.'

'Strength five, Bernie,' I replied. 'Good to hear your voice again. We are all set here and waiting for your instructions.'

'Roger, Mick. Thank you. What's the weather like in your location?' he asked.

'Clear skies and a light wind, maybe five knots from the west. Some big weather to the west of us but it's a long way off – so it's all good here.'

'That's good news, because we are in heavy cloud and probably heading into that big weather you described. I'm going to change course to get into your clear skies. Stand by. I'll be asking you to help in about thirty seconds.'

We waited, wondering how we could help Canberra bombers flying somewhere in the night sky at 400 miles an hour.

Bernie's voice came over the air.

'Mick, how many radios do you have?'

'Two VHF and one HF,' I replied.

'Great. Now put your second VHF set onto channel ten. Tell me when you are ready.'

Karate turned the switch to channel ten and nodded.

'All set, Bernie.'

'Excellent. Now press and hold the transmit button on the microphone for thirty seconds. Release it for ten seconds then repeat for a further thirty seconds. Reckon you can do that OK?' he asked with a chuckle in his voice.

'Dunno,' I said as Karate held down the transmit button. 'Bloody difficult for us counting to thirty.'

We followed instructions and as the second thirty seconds was counted, I called 'Transmission ends. That OK, Bernie?'

'Wait one. Yes, good. But we'd like you to do it one more time to confirm our fix on your position.'

We repeated the procedure.

The South African Canberras would have used their navigational technology to turn the flight in the direction of our signal. They would now be heading directly towards us. It was time to get moving.

Karate took the second radio and jogged off towards the top flare.

Rex and Fish moved into position next to their strobes.

'Sierra One Seven. Green Leader. We are all set now. What have you got for us, Mick?' he asked.

'We have four lights for you, Green Leader, in the same inverted "V" we used last time, except there will be three lights at the back. The single front light is 120 metres from the start of your target, on a bearing of fifty-two degrees. Roger so far?' I asked.

Bernie acknowledged.

'One hundred and twenty metres in a straight line back from the front light is the centre rear light. That line is also fifty-two degrees. Thirty metres on either side of the centre rear light are the side markers. The distance between the two centre flares is exactly the distance to the edge of the camp. You with me, Bernie?' I asked. 'We thought that distance indicator would help you.'

'Couldn't be better. Brilliant,' he replied. 'We are about twenty minutes out. Time to light up and get out of there.'

We turned on the strobe lights and waited for Karate. He joined us a minute or so later and together we hurried towards our railway bridge.

Bernie adjusted the direction of his formation to fifty-two degrees and they dropped down to three thousand feet above the ground. The bomb doors opened as the flashing strobe lights guided them in towards their target.

Bernie was in the centre of the 'V' formation, leading the three Rhodesian Canberras. He was carrying eight 250-kilogram high-explosive bombs while the aircraft on either side of him each carried three hundred Alpha bombs. The four following South African Canberras, flying five hundred feet higher and fifteen seconds behind the Rhodesians, collectively carried sixteen 250-kilogram bombs and six hundred Alpha bombs.

Each Alpha bomb weighed just seven kilograms, but the outer case was packed with hard rubber balls, so when it hit the ground they bounced the bomb forward for up to twenty metres before exploding between three and four metres above the ground.

It was a deadly weapon. And 1,200 of them would rain down moments after the six tonnes of high explosive hit the mud huts and the old school buildings that made up the Luso terrorist training camp.

There would be no survivors.

As the Canberras roared over our railway bridge, I had the fleeting thought that the Luso camp occupants would hear the jet engine noise and wonder what was happening. But the bombs would already be on their way down as they had such thoughts; it would be too late to do anything.

Too late for even a second thought.

I felt no sympathy.

It would be easy for them in comparison to the terror the passengers on the stricken airliners would have experienced in the final moments of their lives.

Later I asked the team what had been going through their minds at the time of the attack.

They too had been thinking about the Viscounts.

As the last thunderous explosions died over the Luso training camp, we scrambled up the bank from under the bridge and jogged across the field to recover the strobe lights.

We could still hear the familiar soft whistle of the Avon jets as the Canberras disappeared into the distance when Bernie checked in to see if we were OK. Not for the first time, I told him that I was glad they were on our side, as I pulled my back centre strobe out of the ground.

'Those lights were fantastic, Mick,' he said before leaving us.

The brigadier would be pleased to hear that but my thoughts now were how they could do the job again for us.

We had to get out of this place.

Karate returned, carrying a smashed strobe light. Polycarbonate was tough stuff but it was no match for the Alpha bombs. We threw the broken light into the stream under the bridge. We'd be long gone if it was somehow found later.

We followed our stream back into the hills, climbing back up to the flat plateau of the *Parque Nacional da Cameia*. We cleared the broken hills just as the first light of a new day arrived. It was hard work and we had been out all night. We ducked into the first copse of low woodland and pulled out our sleeping bags.

We set off again around midday, following a compass bearing of 190 degrees. After 100 kilometres we would meet the headwaters of the Luena River, another forty kilometres further on we would reach a major road close to the small settlement of Lucusse.

Our hope was the road would be good enough for the Beechcraft to land on. If that wasn't to be, there was an airstrip at Lucusse and we'd sneak in and use that while nobody was looking.

These were our only sensible options. There was another main road to the east of us, and we knew the Portuguese had built an airstrip at a settlement known as Cazombo, but that was over 220 kilometres away and to get there, we would have to cross the upper reaches of the Zambezi River and negotiate acres of swampland and reed beds around it.

So we headed south across the open tussock and scattered low woodland of the great plateau. Knowing exactly where we had started meant that reading the map wasn't difficult. The going underfoot was easy and the ground was gently undulating. We made good progress.

We stopped not long after dark to make some dinner and report back to the brigadier. We'd covered about twenty kilometres that afternoon. If we could average thirty kilometres a day, it would take us another four days to reach the road. If the ground conditions remained reasonably favourable we could achieve that easily.

The following day was the same easy-going country and we again made good time, but on the third day our optimistic time and distance estimates went out the window.

As we approached the Luena River basin the flat plateau became broken hill country. We picked our way down off the granite and found ourselves in a maze of eroded gullies running between sheer pinnacles of soft sandstone.

Looking at the map and the many dry oxbow lakes, this was obviously an ancient course of the river. Earth movements, flooding, or both, had redirected the Luena River that now was fifteen to twenty kilometres away.

We made our way laboriously through the labyrinth that seemed quite endless and, with constant twists and turns around the pinnacles, it was easy to lose one's sense of direction.

We got through it all just before last light and made camp. We hadn't got as far as we would have liked, but on the credit side we weren't under pressure and there was plenty of water around.

We let the brigadier know where we were.

Halfway to where we hoped we could be picked up. Another seventy kilometres to go.

On the fourth day, we ran into yet another belt of eroded gullies and pinnacles and again progress was slow. We had used most of our army rations by then and that night we opened the first packet of biltong and dried boerewors sausage.

The nights were cold but we made hot tea and we had our blankets.

On day five, we eventually cleared the broken country and made camp in green woodland close to the Luena River. The next forty kilometres to the road would be easier, but as we got closer the chance of us bumping into locals increased significantly. They would be no physical threat to us, but we did not want to be seen and we especially did not want our presence reported.

We needed to stay invisible.

How often was that the case with the SAS? I mused to myself.

The Luena River consisted of shallow, stony stretches that ran into deep pools on bends in the river. It was easy enough to cross and we pushed on at a good pace. There were a few small animals and birds around but still no sign of human activity.

I called a halt at midday.

'We'll have something to eat and get some rest here until last light,' I said. 'We are closing in on the road and, to avoid compromise, we'll now move at night. The going looks OK so we should still make good progress.'

There were nods of agreement, as we each opened our third packet of biltong and dried sausage.

We walked all night on soft, sandy soil through open, scattered woodland. By keeping to our south-south-west bearing, our course would hopefully bring us to the road at least twenty kilometres west of the settlement at Lucusse. We knew that area was not heavily populated and figured it was far enough away to be safe from compromise.

At night in the featureless terrain precise map-reading was impossible. It didn't really matter because we knew we would eventually hit the road, but it still came as a big surprise when, shortly before dawn, the trees suddenly stopped and we walked out onto it.

Joy of joys, it was a two-lane, tarmac road with evenly spaced white-painted lines as centre markings. Even better, we were on a long straight. The road disappeared into the distance on either side of us. It looked as though we had a couple of kilometres of runway for our Beechcraft.

Perfect!

We backed off into cover, out of sight from the road but close enough for us to hear and observe human or vehicle traffic. We took it in turns to keep watch while the others slept and made a note of whatever traffic came by.

There was nothing until the first bus came past at 0910 hours and thereafter there was the odd truck, a few cars, a couple more buses and a tractor towing a trailer. It was not a busy road.

Later in the day, Karate rigged up the antenna and tapped out a Morse message giving our location, details of the road and requesting a pickup time of 1900 hours the following evening. It would be dark by then but we would use the strobes to guide the aircraft down onto the road, and the pilots would have daylight to assist with navigation for most of the three-and-a-half-hour flight to reach us. On the return leg there would be no issue finding Rundu and landing at the airbase in the dark.

The brigadier acknowledged our request and told us to listen out for the aircraft on our usual ground-to-air VHF channel three.

A truck came past at 1730 hours and that was the last traffic of the day.

We tucked into our second-last bag of biltong then, as it got dark, we ventured back out onto the road.

Standing on the white centre line, I tried to imagine the aircraft coming in to land.

'There isn't much wind,' I said to the team, 'but it's from the west so first we must get the plane to approach from the east.

'I was thinking we should use my strobe to mark the centre line of the road. I'll just sit it on the ground on one of these white lines. We'll then position the other two strobes opposite each other on either side of the road to indicate the width of the landing strip. With these indicators the pilots can line up the plane with the road.

'What I'm not sure of is how far the side markers should be from the centre light.'

'Not too close,' Fish offered. 'I don't know what their landing speed is but those twin-engine aircraft come in pretty quick.'

'One hundred metres?' I asked.

'We'll ask them,' said Rex. 'But 100 metres sounds about right.'

We walked down the road for fifteen minutes checking the surface, making sure there were no potholes or other obstacles that could get in the way of our extraction plan.

The road was good.

All we had to do now was wait.

On the last day, we made do with a brew and bits and pieces we had left in the way of rations. We had one protein bag left. If something delayed the pickup plans we'd make that last a couple more days, and then we'd have to start hunting lizards.

By 1800 hours we were packed up and waiting for it to get dark when the VHF set came to life.

'Sierra One Seven, this is Lima Echo Three. Do you read me? Over.'

'Reading you fives, Lima Echo Three. Good to hear you. It's been a long walk,' I replied.

'*Ag* man, that's what you okes do!' the pilot replied and we could hear him laughing.

Karate mimicked his heavy Afrikaans accent and we too had something to laugh about.

'Lima Echo Three, we have a few things planned for you but would appreciate your advice,' I said. And went on to describe how we were going to mark the road with the strobes and asked him how far apart they would like them to be.

'One hundred and fifty metres would be good,' came the reply. 'We will come in low over your back light and try to touch down between the two forward markers. The road centre line should stand out well in the landing lights. We are looking forward to this. We've never landed on a road before.'

We could sense their enthusiasm. They were clearly getting a buzz out of doing this recovery.

'Lima Echo Three, we will wait for you on the left side of the road between 500 and 600 metres past the front lights. We have small torches and will still be on air. Once we are on board, you have about two kilometres of straight road for take-off.

'Sorry, one last thing. We will make our weapons safe at the last minute – just before getting on the aircraft.'

'Good thinking, Sierra One Seven. The last thing I want is to be shot up the arse while driving you home.' We could hear him laughing again.

We moved out onto the road and positioned the strobes. We got them going as we heard the aircraft in the distance and headed down the road to our pickup point.

'Got you visual, Sierra One Seven. Man, those lights are good.'

'Roger that, Lima Echo Three. We are in position and all's good down here,' I replied.

The aircraft roared over us then circled round to line up with the strobe lights. The wheels came down and the landing lights came on. We watched nervously as it got closer and closer.

The Beechcraft touched down a few metres short of our side lights. There was a low bounce, the nose wheel came down and they were on the road. We heard the engine pitch change as they slowed down, but they were still going at a good rate as they headed towards us.

'Welcome to Angola, Lima Echo Three. Good to have you here,' I said.

'Thank you, Sierra One Seven. Keep well clear until I have stopped the aircraft. The first officer will open the passenger door and the baggage hold then signal for you to come forward. Approach the aircraft from the rear. Just dump your gear in the hold then get on board. We won't be hanging round.'

As the aircraft got closer we signalled with our torches and the pilot acknowledged. I turned off the radio and we all unloaded our AKs, slotting the breach round back into the top of the magazine.

The door behind the wing opened and some short stairs popped out. The first officer got out of the aircraft and opened a hatch behind the door. We crouched down on the side of the road waiting for his signal.

'Come on, guys,' he shouted. 'Let's go!'

We doubled forward, shoved our packs, webbing and rifles into the hatch then climbed in the back of the plane.

I was last to board with Karate in front of me.

Karate suddenly stopped at the foot of the stairs and looked up at the first officer.

'Sorry, Sir,' he said. 'I've lost my boarding pass.'

There was a moment of bewildered silence before I pushed him forward.

'Get on the plane, you bloody idiot!' I cried as howls of laughter came from inside the aircraft.

We heard the baggage hatch slam shut then the first officer hauled in the steps and closed the door firmly. He checked we were strapped in as he made his way to the cockpit, where the skipper had already started the plane rolling.

The engine noise increased and there was an exhilarating surge as the aircraft leapt forward on the road, rapidly gaining speed.

The two supercharged Lycoming engines powered us up into the night sky.

Pseudo Gangs

I t's probably fair to say that at some time in our lives we all have been involved with things which, with hindsight, we should have steered well clear of. For me, one of these was involvement in the setting up of pseudo gangs in the Rhodesian war.

What we started grew into a highly successful anti-terrorist unit called the Selous Scouts, but regardless of that I wish I'd had nothing to do with it.

The reason was that in the early pseudo gang operations we lost three really good men. Men I'd recommended; men we were unlikely to have lost if they'd stuck with the SAS.

Although the concept of using 'turned terrorists' to seek out and destroy their own kind had been used much earlier in the Philippines, the term 'pseudo gangs' came out of the Mau Mau uprising that started in Kenya in 1952.

The Kenyan Police Special Branch organized captured and converted Mau Mau into gangs with Kikuyu-speaking African troops. These gangs were effective in infiltrating the Mau Mau organization and in orchestrating their ultimate defeat.

Some of the Rhodesian police and military had been involved in the Kenya Emergency and knew about pseudo gangs. It was inevitable they would try to do the same.

The first experiment was in 1966 with a Special Branch-led exercise involving the SAS. It didn't meet with universal approval or much enthusiasm, but Special Branch persisted and as the security situation in the country deteriorated the concept was resurrected.

It was logical Special Branch would turn to the SAS for support, given we had a history of working with them on operations and they knew we could be relied on to keep our mouths shut.

And in that respect they liked the fact that we didn't report to the Rhodesian Army.

ComOps managed all Special Forces and their operations so we reported directly to the general – chief of ComOps, whose team included an air marshal and director of the CIO – Central Intelligence Organization.

It was no great surprise then to be called into the brigadier's office and to find Special Branch officer Vic Opperman talking about pseudo gangs.

Vic had been running a small team consisting of three turned terrorists and three African police constables. They had worked out some good operational techniques and Vic was now keen to give them a try in the operational area, but he had a couple of important issues.

The main one was he didn't know how much the turned terrorists could be trusted.

The pseudo gangs operating against communist guerrillas in the Philippines and Malaysia, and those against the Mau Mau in Kenya, had not had a single defection in all three campaigns.

It was a remarkable statistic, even more so because there was never any reluctance to turn on their previous comrades. Just the opposite, in fact.

We knew that, but at the time of our meeting we didn't know if they would apply to our country, our people and the war we were involved in.

So Vic was looking for an insurance policy.

He wanted a couple of SAS men to join his gang, to ensure there would be no double-dealing by the turned terrorists that could lead to the compromise and destruction of the group.

In addition, he pointed out that members of a pseudo gang would require some basic military tactical skills for survival – if nothing else – and this too could be provided by the SAS.

And SAS involvement would solve the issue about the timely dispatch of accurate intelligence.

What Vic was asking made sense, as did the formation and deployment of these gangs, for the all-important reason that within Rhodesia itself intelligence had virtually dried up.

The terrorist groups had infiltrated the tribal lands of the country and lost no time in subverting the local community. Dissent was immediately and ruthlessly put down.

Word soon spread of the brutal beating and killing of so-called 'traitors'. With it being obvious that police and security forces could not adequately protect them, the local population had no choice but to assist the terrorists and keep quiet.

Such violent subjugation of a local population was almost impossible to oppose by security forces. As Vic said ruefully, 'If the terrorists break an arm, what do we do? Break two arms?

'The only way to break the stranglehold,' he explained, 'is to use pseudo gangs to confuse the local population and destabilize the real terrorists. It is disheartening to learn that erstwhile comrades have changed sides. It creates distrust and uncertainty amongst them and, as pseudo operations gather momentum, many will start thinking that maybe they are on the wrong side.'

In Kenya it was concluded that pseudo gangs accounted for more Mau Mau than any of the large military operations.

Rhodesia desperately needed similar success.

'Mick, I'm not prepared to let Nelson go,' said the brigadier. 'He's much too valuable to us. Who else have we got who's fluent with the African languages? And can we spare them?'

'Two immediately come to mind,' I replied. 'Andre Rabie is so fluent if you closed your eyes you'd swear an African was speaking. His buddy Alan Franklin isn't as good but he'll understand everything being said.

'They are an ideal choice, really. Both are exceptionally good bushmen and both are currently with the Tracker Training Wing up at Kariba, so a secondment won't affect our own operations in any way.'

'Good,' said the brigadier. 'But it won't be a secondment. If they want to be part of Vic's operation they can volunteer for it. Pseudo operations aren't everyone's cup of tea.'

The brigadier and Vic travelled to Kariba, where both Andre and Alan had no hesitation in volunteering to lead Vic's gang.

I was given the job of looking after them all; making sure they had everything they needed, doing the army liaison and getting them secretly and safely in and out of their chosen operational areas.

Vic called the shots in terms of operational deployment, and he based that on the latest field intelligence gathered from colleagues or from sources he ran himself.

The Centenary farming area in the north-east of the country was chosen for the first operations. Terrorists were operating there and had done damage. We hoped to track them down.

Before the deployment, we housed the gang in a secluded barn on the property of a friendly farmer and police reservist. We dressed them in rough clothes but gave them good Chinese webbing, AKs and an RPD machine gun. Andre and Alan also carried a selection of grenades.

Hidden deep inside his pack, Andre carried a VHF radio with spare batteries and the code sheets. We gave him the call sign 'Golf One'.

Two days earlier, I had been to the local joint operational headquarters where we briefed the police and army commanders, and with them established a 'frozen area' where the gang could operate without fear of running into our own forces.

After dark on the first night, I drove a Land Rover with a covered back canopy out to the barn. Andre and Alan had both grown beards to hide their features and were blackened up. The gang looked frighteningly authentic and clearly excited about the operation.

I'd shown Andre the start point on the map, and got him to sit next to me in the front of the Land Rover so he could map-read from the outset. We both needed to be absolutely sure we knew exactly where we were when we dropped off the gang.

The dirt road we were following was crossed by power pylons adjacent to our frozen area. It was easy to find and we were both happy we were in the right place as I bade them farewell and good luck.

Unless Andre wanted something different, we would meet there again in six nights' time. I'd take them back to the barn for a rest, clean-up and a decent feed. Vic would do the debriefing before we headed into the second round, two or three days later.

I have to say the pickups were a bit unnerving. Sitting on my own in the Land Rover, in the dark, and then suddenly to have six armed terrorists walk up to the vehicle. My mother once told me I was too trusting. It wasn't something I wanted to remember on those nights.

At the end of the fourth week, we were all sitting together enjoying a beer at the barn. The gang had been well received wherever they went, including in the labour-force villages of some big farms where farmer and worker relations were reported to be good. Remarkably, not a single report had come in from police sources about their presence in the area.

Golf One had also established that a real terrorist gang had been in the area a month previously but had returned to Musengezi, a river system to the north that ultimately led to the Zambezi.

The gang were getting useful information and had already gelled into a good team. They all seemed to get on with each other and Andre was clearly revered as a leader. That didn't surprise me. He was like that in any company.

Next day, Vic turned up with another four turned terrorists.

It was fascinating to witness the mixture of astonishment and relief when two of them recognized one of the Golf One team. They had all trained together in Mozambique. The four newcomers immediately became more relaxed with the realization they were not the only ones to have changed sides.

With the extra manpower, Vic now wanted the gang split into two teams of six led by Andre and Alan. He had two compelling imperatives.

Further north and east in the area of Mt Darwin, the body of an elderly and well-known prospector, Len Koenig, had been found riddled with bullets at an old mine site.

Len had been in his eighties and his retirement days had been spent reworking the mine tailings, trying to extract gold unrecovered by the old extraction techniques. He was brutally killed by a terrorist gang leader armed with an RPD machine gun.

Forensic tests on the cartridge cases left behind linked the weapon to the murders of a number of African businessmen and local leaders, including two schoolteachers.

Alan was to become 'Golf Two' and take his team into the Mt Darwin area to try and locate the gang responsible.

Andre meanwhile would move a little further north where a TMH46 landmine, planted by a new terrorist group, had just killed a farmer and his wife.

I went to the local joint operations' centres and again tied up the critical frozen areas for the two groups. But I left with nagging doubts about these operations.

The chiefs at the two centres I visited were clearly expecting our gangs to locate and destroy the terrorists involved in these latest incidents. The 'we want kills' cry was also coming from higher echelons, and increasing in volume as time passed without the fledgling gangs making a strike.

'But is that what we really wanted?' I wondered.

As soon as our gang opened fire they would be compromised. We might get the odd terrorist, but thereafter there would be no more local intelligence. Our cover would be blown. Our efforts would be at an end in that area.

Far better, surely, for the gangs to get the information about the terrorist groups then pass it on to the Fireforce reaction troops to deal with?

Our gangs would have to lie low or hightail it out of the area during the action, but we wouldn't be compromised.

'Phew! That was a close call!' we could say to the locals afterwards then continue to milk the intelligence.

We had talked about this, and while we didn't disagree on the merits of passing on the intelligence, the pressure was on to get kills, and I could see Andre and Alan were intent on delivering that.

Looking back, it was probably the right call at the time.

Vic took Alan away to the more distant location while I dropped off Andre and his 'Golf One' team.

Alan's Golf Two team started at a subsistence farming village, not far from the mine site where the murder of Len Koenig had taken place. There were only women there on the first night. They told them they wanted food and would be returning the following night to collect it.

On their return they were met enthusiastically by an elder male. They ate the prepared food with him and listened intently as he described how there was another group of comrades in the area. The tribesman said he was sure they would be pleased to learn of their arrival and suggested he organize a supply of the local millet-fermented beer they could all enjoy together.

The die was cast. They would meet again at the village in three nights' time.

Alan reported back, and we all waited anxiously as the night of the arranged meeting finally arrived.

ZANU leader Kennedy Zwamutsana and his gang approached the rendezvous confidently and without caution. Nobody knew of the pseudo gangs at that time.

Kennedy saw the Golf Two group huddled together, and stepped forward as one of the group detached himself and walked towards him.

'Comrade!' he cried in delight, recognizing a man he had been with at the ZANU Lithuli Camp near Lusaka.

He took his hands away from the RPD machine gun slung across his chest and stepped forward to embrace his friend, and at that moment Alan opened fire.

The other members of Golf Two followed suit and lobbed grenades at the bewildered ZANU gang members as they tried to flee.

Kennedy and two others died and a fourth was captured the following morning by security forces.

Len Koenig's murder and the killing of the others had been avenged. The first pseudo gang had struck in fine style. The military hierarchy were ecstatic. They'd got their kills.

After the action, Alan sent one of the comrades across to the local headman who had watched in horror and disbelief.

'This Kennedy was a traitor,' he said. 'We were sent here to kill him.'

It was a good try at maintaining credibility but it couldn't last long. ZANU would eventually realize the truth and they would be fearful.

The time of the pseudo gangs had arrived.

Andre, meanwhile, was making little progress, and the news of Alan's success simply added to his frustration and determination. Alan had proved the pseudo concept worked and now it was his turn. The Golf One gang had to make a kill.

Andre persisted and the information looked more promising. Eventually, he was shown a small arms cache by locals who had been helping the ZANU gang in the area. He took the stick grenades and boxes of AK ammunition.

That was a success story in itself, but it wasn't enough for Andre, who kept probing away, determined to catch up and eliminate a terrorist gang.

Out of the blue, Vic Opperman received a report of a gang of terrorists operating in an area close to Andre's location. But was it a real gang or had somebody seen and reported Golf One?

The first priority was to contact Andre, both to warn him and to make doubly sure the report wasn't about them. Andre was contacted and gave them his location. It was well over ten kilometres away from the reported sighting.

The army went into action and a commando team was dropped into the area to hunt down the terrorists.

They were following a stream when ahead of them they heard voices. Advancing stealthily forward, they saw the unmistakeable shape of an RPD machine gun that had been placed on a rock next to the stream. A terrorist then stood up.

The lead scout aimed carefully and pulled the trigger. The terrorist figure dropped as the commandos swarmed forward looking for more kills.

'Oh my God!' cried the lead scout as he reached the fallen terrorist.

It was Andre. The instructor who only recently had trained him in the art of tracking.

As the news reached me, I got our SAS doctor, Richard King, to join me on the helicopter sent to recover the body and the rest of the gang who, miraculously, had managed to escape the action without further injury or loss of life.

Richard was from Wellington in New Zealand. He had studied medicine at Edinburgh University, adding additional spice to his life by joining the SAS D Squadron that was located there. On completion of his internship he applied for a transfer to C Squadron, and for a number of years we were blessed with a fine doctor.

Richard and I laid Andre's body on a table in the police station at Mt Darwin. He had been hit in the temple with the heavy, high velocity round of an FN rifle.

'Mick, even if this happened in an operating theatre with the best surgeons in the world ready and waiting, there would have been nothing they could have done for him,' Richard said soberly, as I looked aghast at Andre's body.

What a waste!

How could something like this have happened?

In the event there were two reasons for Andre's death.

Sadly, both were a result of his own mistakes.

Firstly, he had misread the map.

He had reported his position as being close to a farm dam. But what he didn't know, what none of us knew, was that a second dam had been recently built in the same general area and it wasn't yet marked on the topo maps.

Andre had got the wrong dam, but what really created the confusion was he had used the wrong code in reporting his position.

We used a simple 'Shackle code' that changed every day, and Andre had used the wrong day's code. The error was such that it put him much further away and seemingly safe from the follow-up, and so the commandos proceeded with their fatal action.

The Golf One group were inconsolable but, remarkably, one of the turned terrorists told Vic they had to go back. They had to compensate for the killing of Andre by making contact with and killing terrorists. And four nights later that's exactly what they did, with one terrorist killed in the action.

Events were now moving swiftly to create a new unit comprising these pseudo gangs, and the general at ComOps had somehow convinced his old friend, Ron Reid-Daly, to come out of retirement and run the unit. Ron and the general had served together with the SAS in Malaya and shared many successes in the Rhodesian Army thereafter.

Ron was the ideal choice. He had the intellect and wit, his service record was impeccable and he was the master at man management.

While Ron's appointment was being ratified, the pseudo gang activity continued.

Robin Hughes replaced Andre with Golf One and they were soon back in action.

Robin was a part-timer with us. He was a parks and wildlife ranger stationed in remote game reserves and was an outstanding bushman and tracker. We had seconded him to the Tracker Training Wing, where he ran the bush survival and tracking courses with Andre and Alan. He was fluent in the local African language and was a logical replacement. On top of that he was keen to avenge Andre's death.

Robin and his group had been working an area, and were hot on the trail of a gang of six ZANU terrorists who had murdered several locals in the area; one of their landmines had also killed two policemen in a Land Rover.

I had pulled them out for a resupply and rest and sat in on the debriefing with Vic. They had learned the local population were beginning to use the terrorist groups to settle old scores. They told us how a man, whose wife had been molested by one of the neighbouring villagers, let the ZANU gang know the offender was in fact a police informer.

They found his mutilated body a couple of days later floating in the local cattle dip.

The following day Vic came in with urgent news.

We had to deploy the gang again that night. He had an impeccable source that had told him the ZANU gang were meeting at a beer drink.

They had been told there was another gang operating in the area and they were keen to meet.

As you can imagine, so were we.

I knew the area where the meeting would take place quite well, so decided to guide Golf One to the isolated village myself. It was the only involvement I ever had with the groups in the field.

We left in the covered Land Rover just on last light. The team was full of nervous anticipation and Robin was fizzing at the prospect of a contact.

We reached the drop–off point and I moved the Land Rover off the road.

I led them on paths I knew would take us to the village and once we had the thatched structures in sight, I left them to it.

'Good luck,' were my last words to Robin. I would never see him alive again.

I made my way back to the Land Rover and returned to base.

Robin's gang reached the village and was warmly welcomed. They sat down with their backs against some large rocks and were given beer. Robin, realizing he would not pass close scrutiny, hid himself next to the wooden poles of a cattle enclosure about ten metres away from the group where he could see and hear everything.

The beer flowed and discussions continued, when the real gang walked in on the scene.

But as the six terrorists came face-to-face with Robin's group, something must have perturbed them. Perhaps they recognized one of the group? Whatever it was they were clearly alarmed and started to raise their weapons.

Golf One opened fire.

A brief exchange of fire followed. Two terrorists were killed and a third was wounded and captured by local security forces the following day.

When it was over, Robin was found sprawled on the ground next to the cattle enclosure railings he had used for cover.

I again recovered the body.

We concluded he'd been hit by a stray bullet. The terrorists would not have seen him.

It was a fluke. Incredibly bad luck.

Golf One was well and truly compromised.

It was time for a rethink about the way pseudo gangs operated. When Ron Reid-Daly came in to take over, I let him know I thought intelligence gathering should be the focus with others doing the killing; that while the gangs might occasionally be forced into using arms themselves, it should be the exception and not the rule.

Ron didn't disagree. And the pseudo gangs were ultimately highly successful in setting the scene for successful contacts by the Fireforce groups stationed in each operational area.

A month or two later, Alan Franklin was killed when he crashed his motor cycle. It wasn't an operational fatality but – like Robin – he was dead all the same.

I was glad to move on.

I was looking forward to getting back into more conventional SAS bush warfare operations, but it was a vain hope.

The pseudo gangs paled into insignificance in comparison to what the brigadier had lined up for us next.

We were going into Mozambique and we were going to start a civil war.

The Antbears

Frelimo leader Samora Machel was an avowed Marxist-Leninist, and his aim was to run Mozambique strictly along those lines. In practical terms that meant he would try to turn the country into a huge anthill.

Ants form highly organized colonies that may occupy large territories and consist of millions of individuals.

These larger colonies consist mostly of sterile, wingless ants forming castes of 'workers', 'soldiers', or other specialized groups. The colonies are described as 'superorganisms' because the ants appear to operate as a unified entity, collectively working together to support the colony.

There is no dissent in an anthill. The life of an ant is strictly controlled and instinctive and they don't know anything else.

But humans do, and that's where Machel's obsessive doctrine was always bound to fail.

The Portuguese exploited the country and the cheap labour, but they didn't interfere much with the basic social structure of the African tribes living in Mozambique. Families lived in villages where they grew crops, had livestock and sought food from hunting and fishing in common tribal lands. As with most indigenous people around the world, their land was sacred. Nobody physically owned it but they all belonged to it.

When Frelimo came along all that changed.

Villagers were rounded up and forced to live in camps next to the terrorists. They were a protective shield; they provided food for the terrorists; they were the unpaid porters of arms and equipment.

No facilities were provided for these populations. They made their own flimsy A-frame shelters from cut branches and thatch. There were no schools, no doctors or hospitals, and there was no freedom. They were slaves.

Anyone showing dissent would be brutally beaten and often shot. Women were molested at will. Any unwillingness on their part would be regarded as dissent and they would be dealt with in the same way.

So against this background it was hardly surprising that pockets of resistance to Frelimo started to emerge amongst the local population.

At the time of the Portuguese exodus from Mozambique, Frelimo influence was widespread but scattered and mainly in the northern half of the country. Those parts of Mozambique thus far unaffected by Frelimo were less than enthusiastic at the prospect of becoming part of Machel's anthill.

What the country needed was antbears.

The antbear or aardvark is a pig-like creature with a long snout that can sniff out ant and termite colonies. With their powerful claws, they dig into the colonies and consume as many as 50,000 ants in a night.

We were about to mobilize them.

I saluted and walked into the brigadier's office. 'Morning, Sir,' I said, and then repeated the greeting to the visitor sitting opposite him in one of the armchairs arranged around a coffee table.

Ken Flower was head of the CIO – the Rhodesian Central Intelligence Organization. With a neatly trimmed, thin moustache and ruddy cheeks, he had old-school policeman written all over him; he'd done well and had been running the CIO for over twenty years.

He stood up and shook my hand. 'Good morning, Mick. Good to see you again.

'The last time would have been at least three years ago, at the Bindura joint operations centre,' he continued. 'I recall you describing what you called your "Stepping Stones" theory, where the terrorist groups use one tribal land after another as stepping stones to progressively advance their presence into the country. It was very well researched and one of the best presentations I've ever heard from military intelligence.'

'Thank you, Sir,' I replied. 'And I remember you commenting that it was a pity the operational commanders found it so hard to counter this obvious terrorist strategy. As true as it was the general wasn't at all happy about that remark. I remember his face going as red as his hatband and collar dogs.'

Ken laughed and turned to the brigadier. 'Mick's right. El Supremo was pretty pissed off with me for saying that.'

I took a seat with them and the brigadier started proceedings.

'Mick, your recent involvement with pseudo gangs will be good background to what we have in mind for your next operational commitment. The start date is two weeks today, but there is no end date.'

He paused as I raised my eyebrows.

'Ken and I have agreed there is nobody better than your Sierra One Seven team to help start a civil war. I'll let Ken explain.'

'Mick, when you were on operations in Mozambique or Angola, did you ever meet or hear of the Flechas?' Ken asked.

'No, Sir,' I replied. 'I've never met them, but Colonel Costa da Silva mentioned them in passing when we met him at Nampula before our Furuncungo operation some years ago. He didn't say much about them, but it sounded as if they were pseudo gangs or vigilante groups, maybe both – I don't know any more than that.'

'Pseudo gangs and vigilante groups are a good description. The Flechas were set up by the DGS – the Portuguese Secret Police – to conduct special military operations and to gather intelligence in both Angola and Mozambique. They consisted of small units, mainly African bushmen but with Portuguese officers. In Mozambique they were led by Álvaro Cardoso and had some success against Frelimo.

'When the Portuguese pulled out of Africa, the Flechas were left high and dry like everyone else in Mozambique, and not surprisingly turned to us for help. They wanted us to support their ongoing efforts to destabilize Frelimo.

'I liked the idea,' he continued, 'mainly because I believed they would, in the process, bring us valuable intelligence about ZANU operating in Mozambique. So we went along with it, but unfortunately it was a disaster. There were too many white Portuguese involved and in no time they were reported by the locals to Frelimo and several of them were captured. The remainder fled, and most eventually made their way to Angola to join a CIA-supported resistance movement.

'On the positive side, however, this experience did get us thinking. If we could get a resistance movement going in Mozambique, it could potentially pressure Frelimo into abandoning their support for ZANU. If that happened, ZANU would have to turn to Zambia for assistance, and without 800 kilometres of Mozambique border to worry about the Rhodesian security forces could easily contain them there.

'With the ZANU military threat largely neutralized, the country could then get on with finding a political solution to these conflicts.

'Mick, you would agree this is a cause worth committing to?' he asked.

'The logic is good, Sir, especially since we also know that a big proportion of the local population want nothing to do with Frelimo. But I wouldn't have a clue as to how we get all this going.'

'Don't worry about that, Mick,' he replied. 'We've already done it for you.

'What really got things moving was the arrival here of Orlando Cristina. He's a colourful character, you'd enjoy him. He was born in Portugal but lived most of his life in Mozambique. He and his father were professional big game hunters and ran a successful safari business in the north-west corner of the country, close to the Malawi border.

'Orlando married an African woman from the local Niassa tribe and immersed himself in their culture. He was introduced to Frelimo and spent some time with them before the Portuguese found out and put him in jail.

'A friend of his father, a wealthy businessman from Beira, got him out of jail and persuaded him to help with anti-Frelimo propaganda and the setting up of a Mozambique army to oppose them. They got it started but it didn't come to much, and when the Portuguese abandoned Mozambique, Orlando came here.

'He talked us into starting anti-Frelimo propaganda broadcasts and we set up a radio station in Gwelo, known as *Voz da África Livre*. Broadcasting in both local languages and Portuguese, Orlando set about promoting the *Resistência Nacional Moçambicana* as a liberation movement against Frelimo. "Renamo", as he abbreviated it, had an immediate impact. Frelimo hit back, branding it *The Voice of the Hyena*. We had reports of individuals deserting Frelimo to go looking for Renamo, and people all over Mozambique looking for this mystery organization. It was remarkable.

'The problem was that it didn't exist. We knew we were onto something special, but we had no idea at that stage what we could physically do about it. But then we got lucky. Our broadcasts reached the ears of one Andre Matsangaissa and he came here looking for the source.

'Matsangaissa is a 26-year-old former Frelimo platoon commander. He has endless enthusiasm and energy and hates Frelimo with a passion. They put him in jail because of his vociferous opposition to their policies, in particular the confiscation of his family's property. He managed to escape and with another two ex-Frelimo soldiers mounted a raid on the jail. A number of the guards were killed and the survivors fled. He then released all the prisoners – over fifty of them – and gave them a choice: they could either go their own way or join him in the struggle against Frelimo.

'Over a week later, and after occasional skirmishes with Frelimo patrols along the way, the three of them and twenty-eight new recruits reached the Rhodesian border and told us they were here "to start the second war of liberation" in Mozambique. It was a remarkable turn of events.'

Ken Flower paused and poured himself a glass of water from the jug on the table.

'All that happened just over three months ago. As you can imagine, we were excited about it because suddenly we had a charismatic leader together with thirty men, all with a grudge against Frelimo and all of them keen to start a war. But first we had to work out what we were going to do, and while that was going on we had to put these men somewhere out of the way, and get them better organized and prepared for their future role.

'I put Dudley and Danny – your two ex-SAS men – in charge and they took them to an unoccupied farm north of Umtali belonging to Danny's family who leased the land out for grazing.

'We got the group cleaned up and into some old police uniforms, then I got a local doctor to check them all. A few were carrying injuries from prison, but nothing too serious, and all have since been declared fully fit.

'Danny built a firing range and lost no time starting their weapons' training. We gave them AK-47s and plenty of ammunition and he reports they are already greatly improved. Andre Matsangaissa joins in everything and spurs them all along. They now call him "Commander Andre" and he's itching to get back into action in Mozambique.'

'And that's where you come into the picture,' said the brigadier.

'When Ken initially briefed me on this, I immediately thought of what our colleagues in 22 SAS are currently engaged in with the Sultan of Oman's forces. They have a squadron working full-time with the Omani troops – most of them are Baluchi from Pakistan. It's a two-pronged campaign: they fight the communist Adoo from the Yemen, but put as much if not more effort into winning the hearts and minds of the local population, who struggle to scratch out a living in the desert conditions. With the locals on side, the Adoo have no chance.

'Mick, we want your team to do much the same with Renamo in Mozambique. But with more emphasis on training and organizing them as a terrorist group against Frelimo,' the brigadier continued. 'A big part of that will be to ensure they get the local population on their side and actively helping them, including with recruitment.'

I listened, my mind spinning. This would be completely different to anything we had ever done before and I was excited about it. We knew the bush; we knew the strengths and weaknesses of the terrorist groups better than anyone. We were invisible and we could strike anywhere.

My biggest fear was we might be dragged down by this ragtag and bobtail bunch we were meant to work with. They had to buy into what we would be doing for them and who gave the orders. If they didn't, then I'd have no hesitation in walking away from it all. Ken and his CIO bunch could go jump.

I was going to make sure the brigadier and Ken Flower knew my feelings on that score from the start. Respectfully, of course.

Ken picked up the story.

'Mick,' he said. 'We want you to work in two separate groups. Andre Matsangaissa wants to operate in the Gorongoza district, to the north of Chimoio. It's where he is from; he knows his way around and assures us he will be well supported by the local population. His deputy, Orlando Macomo, and several of the others come from the Sitatonga area, which is about 200 kilometres further south, and that is where they want to go.'

'Sitatonga,' I said. 'I have been there.'

They both looked at me in astonishment.

'Actually I have been there twice. It's the southern extremity of the Chimanimani Mountains. About ten years ago I went there with a scientific expedition to record the birdlife. The border with Mozambique runs through the middle of the mountain chain. We based up on the Haroni River that flows through the jungle covering the lower slopes and I walked to Sitatonga Mountain from there. It's a massive rainforest, trees forty or fifty metres high. You could hide an army in there.'

'So it looks like Rex will be going north with Andre,' smiled the brigadier.

'And he'll be pleased about that because he knows the Gorongoza game reserve,' I replied.

The following morning, we drove up to the farm near Umtali in the Sabres, smartly kitted out with our sand-coloured berets, badges of rank, medal ribbons and our SAS wings. I wanted to make an immediate impression on these men. I wanted them to see they would now be working with the professionals. Working with the big boys. To emphasize that point I put Rex, Horse, Jonny and Nelson in front as we were taken to meet the Mozambicans, who'd been assembled outside the tobacco barn where they were billeted.

It was clear from the outset that Danny already had a good rapport with the group, and he'd done a great job priming them for us. He had told them about our exploits against Frelimo, ZANU and ZAPU. They were in awe of what we had done and excited at the prospect of meeting us.

One of the taller men, with high cheekbones and a thick, black beard, stepped forward and saluted.

'I am Andre Matsangaissa, Renamo commander,' he said. 'We have been told much about you and are very much looking forward to having you with us.'

I returned the salute and went forward to shake his hand.

'Good to meet you, Andre,' I replied. 'We too have heard a lot about you. Together we will make Renamo a force that will be greatly feared by Frelimo.

'Who is your deputy?' I asked.

A shorter, stocky man stepped forward and saluted. 'Orlando Macomo,' he said.

I shook his hand as well, and then proceeded to introduce our team. When I got to Nelson he spoke to Andre in the local language. Andre replied and they both laughed.

'He is another Manyika,' said Nelson. 'We will have no trouble communicating.'

'Andre,' I said. 'There is a lot we want to talk to you all about but, before we start, I have a request. We have been told you will be operating in the Gorongoza area, while Orlando will be further south around Sitatonga. Rex knows Gorongoza so his team will be with you. I have twice been to Sitatonga so it makes sense for me to go with Orlando.'

Everyone sat down in the shade of a big jacaranda tree, with Andre and his men grouped around Rex and his team on one side and Orlando and his men on the other with my team. With Rex I'd put Horse, Simmo, Mack and Pig Dog. Fish, Jonny, Nelson and Karate would come with me.

Nelson and I stood up in front of the two groups. Andre had a few more men than Orlando but the balance was OK.

I started by telling them what they already knew about Frelimo gathering together people and making them slaves, but they had never heard this likened to the making of an anthill. I could see their amusement and comprehension as Nelson explained it in their language. It prompted some animated chatter amongst them.

'What the country needs – what you will become – is antbears!' I exclaimed. 'Antbears, that with their claws will rip open the Frelimo organization and tear it apart.'

'*Sambani*!' shouted Nelson using the local name for an antbear.

'You will be the *sambani* of Mozambique!' he cried, stepping forward and challenging them.

'*Sambani*!' they shouted in unison. '*Sambani! Sambani!*'

Nelson had heard my communist ant theory before and had told me that throughout Africa the antbear was a revered animal, greatly admired for its bravery in the face of biting soldier ants and in some societies regarded as having mystical powers.

I hoped Andre Matsangaissa and his gang could relate to this. It would be a unifying identity; one they badly needed to help with the all-important recruiting.

So far so good.

'Commander Andre,' I said. 'I know you want to start the action against Frelimo immediately, but I am asking you to be patient. Before we start shooting Frelimo, we need to be ready and we need more people – more *Sambani*.'

'Building up our support without alerting Frelimo is critical to our success,' I added, 'and we have learned from ZANU exactly how we can achieve that.'

With Nelson interpreting, I went on to describe my 'Stepping Stones' theory to them. We would do the same around Gorongoza and Sitatonga. Frelimo would be unaware that forces against them were building, until we decided the time was right to strike.

I then told them about Chimoio and that it had been destroyed because ZANU forgot the basic principles of guerrilla warfare: *Better to keep moving. Better to stay in small groups and disperse far and wide. Stretch the resources of the enemy to breaking point.*

And how ZAPU had miscalculated, in turning to heavy Soviet weaponry and a more conventional approach to warfare. That we had destroyed them because they couldn't stop us blowing up the bridges and roads, laying mines and ambushing their convoys. It would be the same with Frelimo in Mozambique, I told them.

It was lunchtime. I'd given them a lot to think about so I called a break.

Two hours later, Danny led us all down a narrow farm track until we came to some trees flanking a field of low grass, where I asked everyone again to sit in their two groups.

'In our fight against Frelimo, it is vital that we look after the local population. We need their help as recruits, we need them to be our spies, and we will need to get food and water from them. We must encourage them to help us.

'I have ordered a number of battery-powered radios, because we want them to listen to our radio station – the Voice of free Africa. We will give a radio to every village that agrees to help us.'

I took a small transistor radio from the pack I was carrying and tuned it to the Gwelo radio station. Orlando Cristina was in fine voice. I had no idea what he was saying, but Andre's group did and there were shouts and cheers as they listened.

'We will also give every village seeds and fertilizer and help them make gardens. We will get them to grow our food. We will get them to plant maize, tomatoes, pumpkins and beans in summer, and in winter kale and spinach. They can use these vegetables, but there must always be some for us.'

Andre said something to the men, in his local language, and there were nods and replies of obvious agreement. I looked questioningly at Nelson.

'He says this is the way we will win, and it is clear that they all agree with him.'

'Good,' I said. 'Tell them the major is happy they understand the importance of this.' Nelson reiterated everything in their language just to drive the point home.

'What I'm going to show you now will give you a big advantage over Frelimo.'

I dug into my pack and pulled out a VHF radio.

'First, you will have communications. You will be given radios, so that when Andre sends out patrols he can give each one a radio so they can report back to him. They can tell him where they are. They can pass on intelligence about Frelimo. They can request help or supplies.

'Even better, these radios can talk to aircraft.'

I'd heard the unmistakeable sound of a DC3 Dakota in the distance. I switched to the usual air-to-ground channel three, turned up the volume so they could all hear what was being said and picked up the mike.

'Cyclone Three, this is Sierra One Seven. Do you read me? Over.'

'Sierra One Seven, this is Charlie Three, reading you strength five. We are about ten minutes out. What have you got for us, Mick?'

'Thank you, Charlie Three. We have a large DZ for you that I'll mark with orange smoke. Light breeze from the east around five knots.'

'Roger that. Give us the smoke.'

I nodded to Pig Dog, who lobbed a smoke grenade out onto the grass. A bright orange cloud erupted and started to drift down the field with the following wind.

I turned to Andre and his men and explained.

'Where we are going, it is too far to carry in all the supplies and equipment we will need. Instead, they will be dropped to us by these aircraft. We use the smoke so they know where we want our supplies dropped, also so they can see how much wind there is because that will push the parachute.'

I got them all to stand alongside me, so they could watch the show as the Dakota turned and lined up with our drop zone. As it closed in, we could see activity at the open door and then out dropped a wooden pallet with black cargo netting. A white parachute opened as it fell away from the aircraft. The pallet oscillated gently beneath the parachute canopy that drifted past us and landed in the grass about eighty metres away.

I thanked the air force while the others ran excitedly towards the pallet.

Rex, Pig Dog and Nelson got them organized on the grass around the pallet, and showed them how to collapse the parachute canopy so the pallets would not get dragged and damaged if there were strong wind conditions.

'This time we can give the parachute back to the air force so it can be used again,' said Rex. 'But that will not be possible when we are operating with you, so then we will keep everything. Everything will be useful to us.'

He let them feel the canopy nylon and the cord. There was a lot of material in a parachute that, together with the wooden pallet, could be used for many things, he told them.

Inside the cargo netting we had another surprise for them. I had asked our quartermaster to get me thirty-one old, infantry backpacks, one for each of these Renamo soldiers. As Rex and Pig Dog unloaded them from the pallet, they were lobbed across to the men who grabbed them eagerly.

There were cries of surprise and delight when they opened the packs and found they each contained a parachute-nylon sleeping bag; a green, lightweight nylon shelter; a plastic poncho; a web belt with two pouches and two water bottles. There was an aluminium mess tin with a knife, fork and spoon set and a rifle-cleaning kit.

Andre stepped forward and stood next to me. He ordered the men to put on the backpacks and then he addressed them.

I had no idea what he said, but it was delivered with a passion and an authority that cut through the air and demanded attention. I looked and listened in admiration. Andre was a natural.

At the end the men, as one, lifted their AKs above their heads and shouted, '*Sambani! Sambani! Sambani!*'

The antbears had a leader. A leader with strength and charisma.

I suddenly felt good about all this.

Two other events of note happened that afternoon.

After Andre's address, I noticed a short, solid-looking young man wearing thick-rimmed, black spectacles playing with the radio I had left on the ground under the trees. He was twiddling the knobs and talking into the mike, copying what I'd said.

'Who is that, Andre?' I asked, pointing to the man with my radio.

Andre laughed with enjoyment when he saw what was happening.

'That is Afonso Dhlakama. He was a Frelimo platoon commander like me. He was with me when we took the prison and will be my deputy in Gorongoza. Afonso is quiet but he is clever. He is very different to me but he too is a leader.'

Andre was not just a natural leader; he was also a good judge of character.

Afonso Dhlakama would eventually emerge as one of Renamo's leading political figures. But that was a long fourteen years away.

'Who will be Orlando's deputy?' I asked.

'Phillip,' he said, and pointed to a slim, clean-shaven man standing next to Orlando. He too had high cheekbones, like Andre. I'd always thought that to be a characteristic of the tribes from Ethiopia and Somalia. Their blood must have somehow reached Mozambique.

I asked Andre to get everybody together again as we had one last surprise for them.

'Tomorrow we want to see how you can shoot, and then we will start making the plans for our operations: where we will start and what we will do when we get there. Today we have one last thing for you. I will let Nelson and Dudley explain.'

I stepped to one side. It would be interesting to see the reaction to what we were about to do.

Nelson and Dudley stood together, Dudley holding a worn, leather briefcase.

'Frelimo treat everyone as slaves,' Nelson began in their dialect. 'Their leaders, like Samora Machel, have all the wealth. They ask their soldiers to fight and die for them, but the soldiers are not paid. Machel keeps all the money.

'Renamo will not be like Frelimo. If you are a soldier with Renamo you will be paid.

'Who will the locals in Mozambique want to join?' he demanded. 'Will they want to join Frelimo and be treated as a slave? Or will they join Renamo who will treat them well and give them pay?

'They will want to join the *Sambani!*' he shouted.

'*Sambani! Sambani! Sambani!*' they all shouted in response.

Nelson let them settle down, then he called Andre forward.

'Commander Andre, you are the leader and you have the responsibility. You will be paid $75 a month from today.'

Andre's jaw dropped; then while the others all looked on in silent amazement, Dudley stepped forward, dipped into his briefcase and gave Andre the money.

'Orlando, Phillip and Afonso you are deputies. Deputies will be paid $40 a month.'

They stepped forward and took their first-ever pay packet.

'The Renamo soldiers will each be paid $20 a month,' said Nelson, as Dudley walked over and started handing out $20 notes to the disbelieving Mozambicans.

Ken Flower had had no hesitation in agreeing to the suggestion to pay these rebels. It was a master stroke.

Thirty-one paid rebels and ten SAS men were ready to start a civil war in Mozambique.

More Game for Gorongoza

Our second day at the farm with Renamo was spent on the shooting range, where we introduced them to white phosphorous grenades and the RPG7 bazooka, which they all wanted to carry. Bazookas were cool with guerrilla groups everywhere.

We also showed them how to lay the TMH46 anti-tank mines we intended using to give Frelimo a taste of the medicine they had dished out to the Portuguese on so many roads in Mozambique.

We did some tactical training with them on the third day, teaching them about ambushes and camp attacks.

The Renamo bunch were, without exception, great students. They were full of enthusiasm and energy, spurred on by their talented leaders and deputies.

On the fourth day we discussed how we would reach our operational areas, where we would initially base, and what we would do in the first six weeks.

We also had to do some planning ourselves.

For both groups it would be a long walk in and we didn't want to be too heavy. We would need an air-supply drop soon after reaching our first base locations, and that needed to be organized in advance along with procurement of the items we wanted.

We needed to have some plans in place in case any of our SAS men were killed or injured.

Finally, we had to work out what we were going to do for R and R.

While we were happy to be helping, this wasn't our war or our country. We had our own lives to live, somehow, through all of this. The 'no end date' to the operation, imposed by the brigadier, was a tall order by any standards and it needed to be tempered with regular breaks when we could briefly return to a life of some normality.

We decided that, after every six-week period, three SAS men from each group would be choppered out for ten days leave and the remaining members would fly out on their return. We could also use these helicopter trips to bring in any additional equipment we might need in between airdrops from the Dakotas.

For the deployment of the troops, Rex organized a covered, five-tonne Mercedes truck with a driver and escort. His team drove up to the farm to collect Commander Andre and the eighteen men who would be the Gorongoza arm of Renamo.

Not too far north of the farm, the road wound down a steep escarpment into the Honde Valley and the catchment of the Pungwe River. Fed by perennial high country streams, the Pungwe flowed clear and fast through the terraced Rhodesian tea estates, continuing south-east into Mozambique. After 120 kilometres it reached the western boundary of the Gorongoza National Park, then turned due south, eventually reaching the coast at the port of Beira.

West of the national park area there was the small settlement of Gorongoza. Further east, a larger town called Inhaminga was located on the road and rail links from the coast to the northern Mozambique provinces and Malawi.

It had been agreed that Rex and Andre would operate between Gorongoza and Inhaminga, with the road and rail link between Beira and Umtali their southern boundary.

Rex and Andre had discussed the best route in and opted to initially follow the Pungwe River, retracing the route Andre and his merry men had used to reach Rhodesia after the prison escape.

'Rex, around here there is a ZANU base camp.' Andre pointed to the map they were studying and circled a river junction some sixty kilometres inside Mozambique.

Rex's eyes lit up with interest.

'It was well concealed and took us by surprise, but we were not afraid because we knew it could not be Frelimo, who live in garrisons these days. We entered the camp and were greeted by six ZANU comrades. They all carried AKs but were friendly and welcoming.

'They told us they looked after the Pungwe Camp that was used by groups from Chimoio on their way into Rhodesia, and sometimes by groups already operating in the country that came back for ammunition and food supplies.

'We told them we were Mozambique freedom fighters. They gave us food and warned us about Rhodesian Army patrols on the border.'

'Andre, you understand these ZANU terrorists are our enemy?' asked Rex.

'Yes, I understand that,' he replied. 'And, if they are your enemies, they are now ours as well.'

'That's good, Andre,' Rex replied. 'Because, on our way in, we are going to destroy this camp and anyone we find there. It will be a good way of testing what you have learned from our training.'

Andre smiled and looked Rex in the eyes. 'At last some real action,' he said.

What we were doing wasn't exactly pseudo gang business; nevertheless, our deployment was made that much safer by keeping police and army out of the Honde Valley on the day of Rex's departure.

They were dropped off where the road was closest to the border with Mozambique and headed due east towards the Pungwe River, some twenty kilometres away, where they spent the first night.

The following day they stayed on the north bank of the river. After thirty kilometres walking they would reach a road. The river junction where the ZANU camp was located was another thirty kilometres further east from that. It would take four days to get there.

Along the way Rex continued their training.

He put Andre and one of his men up front with Pig Dog to learn how to move through the African bush. Learning how to be invisible. Learning to look for signs.

Andre rotated his men so all got to experience working with Pig Dog.

On the second day, Rex did several mock-attack drills where he and Horse, who carried an RPD, moved forward to join the scouts while Mack and Simmo led the others in a wide flanking movement.

On the fourth day, Rex stopped the party in the early afternoon. In the distance loomed a sheer granite mass that the map showed as being close to where Andre believed the ZANU camp was located.

Renamo would now get the next phase in their SAS training.

They would lie in cover for the remainder of the day then move through the night to the granite feature, which Rex believed would give them both good cover and a great view of the surrounding area. From there they would look for the camp. If they located it, they would move in after dark to surround it and launch an attack at first light the following morning.

Rex gathered them all together just before dark and pointed out their destination.

'Andre, I want you and Afonso to lead us there,' he said, and went on to show them how to use the recta compasses we had given them.

'At night, it is important for those of you in front to remember there are more than twenty men behind you. You must keep everyone together and that means going slow. Even when it is flat country and easy going you must still go slow in front. The men at the back will have to go faster than you to keep up. That's the nature of travelling at night.

'We will keep it slow,' said Andre, appreciating the wisdom and experience of this big SAS man.

They reached their destination around midnight. The hill was in fact a series of gigantic outcrops interspersed with deep cracks and gullies filled with thick vegetation. They immersed themselves deep in the cover and bedded down for what remained of the night.

At first light, Rex took Andre and Pig Dog on a clearance patrol of the area, to get the lay of the land and to assess the risk of discovery in their current location. They climbed a steep slope covered in dense woodland that thinned out as they approached the bare sheet rock of one of the granite domes. Crouching in cover, they had a perfect view of the surrounding area.

A smaller river, flowing in from the north, joined the Pungwe about 400 metres away. Andre pointed to a thicket close to the junction. They could see wisps of smoke drifting above the canopy.

'That is the camp,' he said.

'We will be safe here,' said Rex. 'We'll go back and make a brew and some breakfast then we'll come back to watch and work out how we will attack the camp.'

Once back with the group, Rex got Andre to organize the men into four-man teams and then he spread them out tactically in the cover of the gully. Rex explained that while they were not expecting trouble they should always be prepared for it, and be prepared to defend themselves. A guard roster through the day was organized.

Rex and Andre were sharing a brew when Rex suddenly lifted his head – sniffing the air. Smoke! Standing up, he saw a thin, blue-grey plume wafting through the branches behind him. He grabbed a water bottle and, with Andre following, ran towards the smoke.

One of the Renamo teams sat around a small fire heating a mess tin. Rex leaned forward and snatched it out. He poured water over the flames and kicked the hissing sticks apart with his boot.

Rex gave the mess tin back to one of the men. 'We have to stay invisible,' he told them quietly. 'Stay here. I will be back in a moment.'

He returned a minute or two later with his small gas cooker. He lit it and put the mess tin on top.

'We have to stay invisible,' he said again to the Renamo men who were watching – silent and apprehensive.

Andre was furious, but Rex took his arm.

'Relax, Andre. I don't think any harm has been done. And this is our fault, not theirs. We didn't think to get them gas cookers like ours. I'll get our boys to share their cookers today. Meanwhile, talk to your men and make sure they understand: You won't survive unless you all learn to be invisible.'

Andre nodded and went off to spread the word while Rex wondered what the next tactical blunder might be.

Arrogance and ineptitude could be the biggest problems with this deployment. Rex and I had discussed the issue. If it came to a point where it jeopardized our own safety, the only sensible option would be to bid farewell and leave them to it. None of us wanted to do that and it was a call we hoped we wouldn't have to make.

While the Renamo men made breakfast and a brew, Rex took Mack, Pig Dog, Andre and Afonso back to the observation point they'd used earlier. He pointed out the camp location where smoke still seeped through the woodland canopy.

'You see the smoke, Afonso?' he asked pointedly. He was happy to see Andre smarting at the question.

For the next hour they watched the camp and made plans for the attack.

The two rivers met at an acute angle, creating a south-pointing V-shaped wedge of ground between them. The camp was located in the centre of this 'V'.

Rex decided he would put two four-man stop groups on the Pungwe River on one side of the 'V' and another two on the opposite side stream. Each stop group would be led by one of the SAS men.

Rex, Andre and the remaining five men would initiate the attack in a sweep line from the north, forcing any fleeing terrorists towards the river lines and the waiting stop groups.

Through the day, the SAS men took their teams up to the observation post to show them the camp and to explain where they would be going and their role in the attack. Everyone seemed to understand, and the nature of the ground would make it pretty simple.

A half-moon came up at 2230 hours as the Gorongoza antbears moved silently towards the camp and their positions.

Pig Dog branched off with the stop groups.

He positioned the groups with Mack and Horse on the side stream, on the western side of the camp. He then picked his way carefully along the edge of the Pungwe River to position Simmo and his own group on the opposite side of the camp.

Pig Dog used the whisper mike on the VHF set to let Rex know they were all in place.

Rex acknowledged. He kept his group together in a bunch, hidden in cover some 150 metres from the camp. As first light approached, they'd spread out and move in on the camp.

All they had to do now was wait.

As the sky began to lighten, Rex led them forward to the very edge of the camp. The Renamo men spread out on either side of him.

Rex would start the action by firing into the nearest thatched bivvy, and they would do the same while slowly advancing through the camp.

Rex's attention was on the three men off to his right, when Andre and the two Renamo left of him suddenly opened fire. Swivelling round in alarm, he saw a ZANU terrorist drop in the hail of fire. Rex darted forward and fired into the bivvy in front of him.

'Move!' he shouted, waving them forward on both sides. He dashed forward a few metres. A figure stood up and sprayed the area around them with automatic AK fire. Rex dropped to a knee and dispatched him with a rapid double-tap. He looked up and saw other terrorists running away from them. They all fired at the fleeing terrorists and another one dropped.

They continued their advance, firing into each bivvy as they made their way through the camp. There was good control and Rex was satisfied with the way the Renamo team handled the situation.

However, in the stop group on the Pungwe side of the camp, Pig Dog was far from happy.

When the shooting began, two of the Renamo men stood up and joined in, firing blindly. Worse, they then left their position and began to advance towards the camp. Pig Dog ran forward, grabbed the men and led them back.

'Stay and watch,' he commanded as they again crouched down in cover.

Pig Dog heard shots from the direction of the stops on the side stream, followed by a burst of sustained fire that would be Horse with his RPD.

The firing stopped.

Rex kept everybody down in cover and on high alert. They watched for half an hour then radioed Pig Dog to close in on the camp, while Horse and Mack held their positions.

'And Pig Dog, tell me when you reach the edge of the camp. I'll let Andre and his men know so there are no accidents.'

Pig Dog and Simmo arrived and settled in behind Rex, who then ordered Horse and Mack to close in on the camp. A minute later there was a burst of fire in their direction. Horse came on the radio, letting Rex know they'd found a wounded survivor who foolishly tried to be a hero by firing at them.

With everyone assembled, Rex organized them into two groups. Pig Dog and Afonso led one on a wide sweep around the camp while he and the others did a detailed search of the bivvies.

'Keep anything useful you find,' said Rex. 'Take their clothes. If there is blood it can be washed out. It will all be valuable to you later. Bring what you find back here so we know what we have got and can share the load of carrying it.'

An hour later, Pig Dog returned with three boxes of AK ammunition, a TMH46 mine and a quantity of tinned food. He'd spotted a track leading to a rocky outcrop and found the small cache in a dry hollow under a large boulder.

Additionally he and the group reported finding four dead ZANU. They took their weapons and the dark overalls they had been were wearing, along with two pairs of boots and two pairs of sandals made from car tyres.

They were added to the pile of weapons and equipment Rex had collected in the camp itself, where they had found a fourth body in a bivvy to add to the total of three ZANU killed during the assault. In all, eight ZANU terrorists had been killed.

Rex believed they had accounted for about half the number occupying the camp at the time and he wasn't unhappy with that. For a first attempt it was a good result and, apart from the stop-group incident, Renamo had done well.

They loaded up the captured material then burned the camp.

There was another sixty kilometres to go, but spirits were high and they started to sing.

While the rhythms and harmonies changed, there was a constant underlying beat and they marched to that. Now and then the beat would be emphasized by a hard stamping of the feet before reverting back to a quieter tempo. Rex later described it as 'hypnotic' – like walking in a trance. It enveloped the SAS men who, though they didn't sing, found themselves completely in step with their Renamo comrades.

The kilometres disappeared beneath them.

Gorongoza Mountain was a 200 square kilometre ancient volcano complex that rose to more than 1,500 metres above the surrounding plains of the game reserve. Over time streams had eroded the softer sediment, leaving a maze of sharp crater rims and deep gullies that didn't see the sun. The rich volcanic soil and high rainfall supported a thick woodland cover with palms and tangled vines. Where there were natural clearings, grass grew above one's head.

South of the mountain was the vast national park; on either side and to the north were scattered local settlements, including the one where Commander Andre's family lived.

Rex and Andre agreed that somewhere close to his family would be the best place to get themselves established.

Through the mountain ran a network of tracks used by local hunters stalking the abundant monkeys and rock hyrax. Andre knew these tracks and led them deep into the mountain maze. Rex could see this would be an ideal location. Guards could be placed in elevated positions and would have a wide field of view over the surrounding country. They would get advanced warning of approaching trouble and would have the choice of manning a deadly ambush or disappearing deeper into the mountain.

The Gorongoza antbears made camp in a clearing surrounded by broken bare rocks and waited for their first supply drop. They had already made contact with the locals. Many of them knew Andre and his family and were immediately supportive.

Andre had asked for their help carrying the supplies and equipment back to the camp, because the drop zone would be some distance away on flatter, open ground. He had told them they would be rewarded and over fifty locals had joined the Renamo team as they waited for the aircraft.

Seven white parachutes with pallets covered in black cargo netting drifted down as the locals watched excitedly. They had never seen anything like this before. Andre addressed them then they all ran off towards the pallets.

Rex and the SAS men undid the parachute harnesses and netting, and the locals hefted the boxes and sacks and took them to Andre who was supervising the collection.

With everything unloaded, Rex examined the contents.

'How many individual families are here?' he asked Andre.

'Six,' answered Andre after some questioning.

With the boys helping, Rex made six separate piles each consisting of one large brown sack and two large cardboard boxes. He then asked Andre to call for everyone's attention.

Rex started by saying there was one pile for each of the families helping them. He asked Andre to translate and get the families to stand next to a pile that would be theirs.

Rex opened one of the sacks. Inside were six *badzas* – the African hoe – and a medium-sized watering can. There were cries of surprise from the locals.

He then opened one of the boxes and showed them the contents.

There were two bags of fertilizer, two balls of twine and several packets of seeds. He pulled out a small, red transistor radio from its protective wrapping, took two of the supply of batteries and put them in the radio and switched it on. He twiddled the knobs to get the frequency of the Voice of Free Africa and turned up the volume. He gave the radio to the village headman.

'It is for you,' said Andre. 'Listen to the messages and tell everyone.' There was laughter and excitement amongst the locals. For them this was Christmas.

Rex finally opened the third box – a standard army issue ten-day ration pack.

Andre took over, explaining they would need their help to overthrow Frelimo, but that they were determined not to be a burden to those who supported them.

He explained that in the next few days they would help them make gardens where they would grow their food. He said they could feed from the gardens but there must always be some for the Renamo fighters. The gardens would take some time to grow; meanwhile, they had the army ration packs.

There were smiles and nods of understanding. We had started well in the battle to win the hearts and minds of these people.

Over the next few days Rex and Simmo, with help from some of the men, built the base camp.

They had large canvas tarpaulins dropped in and used them to create shelters where, together with pallets and netting, they could keep their supplies dry and safe from vermin.

Horse was put in charge of the gardens.

At each of the six villages they dug the beds, applied fertilizer and sowed the seeds. Using branches, twigs and the twine they had been given, Horse then got them to make low shelters with a light covering of long grass for each bed. This would protect the seedlings from the sun and heavy rain and help retain moisture in the soil.

Andre and Afonso meanwhile started moving around the district, letting the locals know Renamo were in the area and looking for support and recruits. They were well received and learned there was no Frelimo presence nearby; the nearest garrisons were well over a hundred kilometres away at Chimoio and Inhaminga.

The recruits started to arrive. By the end of their second week in the area, seventy-two new recruits had joined them. Rex ordered another airdrop to arm and equip them. Amongst the mail and personal items for the SAS team that was included, he was surprised to find a large envelope addressed to him. He opened it and found a hundred small envelopes, each holding a twenty dollar note. Renamo wages!

As the word spread, recruits would arrive in droves.

The training of these new men was progressing well, and Rex was pleased to see some of the Renamo contingent emerging as leaders beneath Andre and Afonso. He called for a meeting with the two of them.

'Things are going well here,' he said. 'But we Europeans have a saying: "all our eggs are in one basket". It means that everything we have is in one place and if something bad happens at that place we will have lost everything.

'To avoid that we must move into new places. We have spoken to you about this before and I think the time is right to start our expansion. Would you agree with that?' he asked.

The two Renamo men nodded in agreement.

'Andre, I want you to take forty men and head east towards Inhaminga, a hundred kilometres away. I want you to set up a camp like this in good cover somewhere between fifty and sixty kilometres from here. Far enough away so the airdrops to you will not be noticed by Frelimo at Inhaminga.'

Rex showed him on the map where he thought it would be best to make the camp.

'Start recruiting like we have done here. Also, I want you to take a small team to make a reconnaissance of Inhaminga. There is a garrison there as well as a political prison. My thinking is we should commence our offensive with a mortar and bazooka attack on the garrison. While that is happening, you attack the prison and bring the prisoners back with you as recruits, same as you and Afonso did at the start of all this.

'Pig Dog and Horse will go with you, and I want Pig Dog to accompany you on the reconnaissance of Inhaminga. You already know how good he is. He can also lead the attack on the garrison.

'One more thing, Andre,' continued Rex. 'While you are attacking Inhaminga, I want Horse with three of your men to follow the main road and railway line south of Inhaminga for around six kilometres. There the map shows the railway line crossing the road. I want Horse and his group to lay a TMH46 mine under each track of the railway line. The first train that comes along will be blown off the lines and badly damaged and, in the process, it will completely block the road. No traffic will be able to use the road until they clear the mess on the railway line.'

'Three attacks at the same time. Frelimo will not know what to do,' Andre replied, his eyes dancing with excitement.

'It will be more than three, Andre. While you are busy at Inhaminga, Afonso will be in action somewhere else and I will be leading another team to a third location.

'Two hundred kilometres south of here, the major will be doing the same with Orlando and his team. These multiple attacks, widely spread across the country, will stun Frelimo. They will wonder what is going on and what they can do about it.

'After the attacks, we will just disappear. Next time, we will attack in different places far away from these initial strikes.'

Rex looked at them both. 'Do you both see and understand what we are doing here?' he asked. 'Remember what we told you about this sort of warfare?

Keep moving. Stay in small groups and spread far and wide. Stretch the resources of the enemy to breaking point.'

They nodded in understanding.

'You are helping us greatly,' said Afonso quietly.

'Thank you, Afonso. You are also to take forty men and move to the south side of the mountain, about thirty kilometres away. Set up a base and start recruitment from the settlements of Vinduzi and Gorongoza. Mack and Simmo will join you.

'When the time comes to attack, you will have two objectives. The first will be to destroy the road bridge across the Pungwe River. That is about eighty kilometres south of Vinduzi. Simmo will show you what to do with the explosives.'

Rex showed him the location on the map.

'At the same time, I want Mack with twenty of your men to set up an ambush on the main road about halfway between Dondo and Inhaminga. To get there you will have to walk through the centre of the national park. It will be a long walk – about eighty kilometres – but there is plenty of water in the park.

'After the attack at Inhaminga, Frelimo are bound to send reinforcements. You will attack and destroy that force in your ambush. Mack will show the men how best to do this with explosives and bazookas.'

Afonso smiled. 'That will be more exciting than blowing up a bridge,' he said. 'I will lead the ambush party.'

'Yes,' said Rex. 'But blowing up the bridges is important. While you both are busy, I will be taking a team to blow up a bridge near Tica. It is about eighty kilometres away to the north-west. With these two bridges down and the road and rail blockage at Inhaminga, Frelimo cannot reach us by vehicle in this area. If they find out we are at Gorongoza Mountain, as I am sure they will eventually, they will have to walk to reach us. If that happens we will be watching and waiting for them.'

Afonso looked at Andre. 'He thinks of everything.'

The Sitatonga Sanctuary

I used four covered Land Rovers, two with trailers for all our gear, to take Orlando Macomo and his Sitatonga antbears to their new hunting ground. There were eighteen of us, plus the drivers and their escorts.

We headed south out of Umtali and eventually turned off the main road towards the small settlement of Melsetter, the centre of the vast forestry enterprise that dominated this area. There was a police station, a hotel, a small school and a general store with fuel pumps. It was a neat and tidy place with tall eucalypts providing shade in summer and wood for the fires in winter.

I stopped the convoy in the main street in front of the general store. We'd been driving for nearly four hours. It was time for a break and to stretch our legs. It was also our last chance to take advantage of civilization before the journey to Sitatonga.

Nelson got everyone together, and I asked him to explain they could buy whatever they wanted from the store, but there must be no tobacco and no alcohol. He told them none of us smoked because the smell was too strong in the bush. We could smell Frelimo when they smoked but they couldn't smell us.

There were nods of understanding as they filed into the store to spend some of their first pay packets.

Nelson and I sipped our cold Cokes and stood with the store owner as the antbears went shopping. The store owner was an affable Greek character and I'd told him these were new recruits. He was happy to have their business and help with questions – mainly about price – that came from the men via Nelson.

Every one of them bought an Okapi pocketknife. The blade folded into a groove cut in the resin-coated, brown wooden handle. It was made from good quality German steel and held a good edge. They were popular; millions would have been sold throughout Africa.

In addition to the knives they bought boxes of matches, bars of soap, candles and tubes of XXX mints. Three of them brought out machetes, and another two had small axes. I'd not thought about bringing these, but they would be useful. I told them to put them back as I would get some dropped in with our air supply. They exchanged them for cheap, Chinese-made sunglasses, not nearly as practical but they looked very cool.

We headed towards the wall of bald rock that was the Chimanimani Mountains, then turned south and drove on parallel with the range until it dipped down at the southern end. I managed to find the rough track the scientific expedition I'd been part of had used some ten years earlier.

We bedded down for the night in a field of wild lasiandra, the purple of the blooms matched by the glowing beauty of the mountain range as the sun dipped below the horizon.

'It's good you know where you are going, Mick,' said Nelson, as we had a breather about halfway down the steep track that would take us to the Haroni River, hidden somewhere in the misty rainforest below us.

'You see where the bare rock of the Chimanimani Mountains tumbles down and meets the rainforest?' I asked, pointing at the hills several kilometres in front of us. 'Beyond that there is a granite mound. That mound is Sitatonga Mountain. That's where we will be based. This track takes us down to the Haroni River. There is another track that follows the river through the forest to Sitatonga. Once we are off this steep slope the going will be quite easy and cool because we will be in deep shade.

'You're right about it being good to know these tracks. I'd hate to try and bash my way through this country. And there is another problem it brings. The trees are too high for an airdrop. We will have to find somewhere more open.'

Nelson called Orlando over to join the discussion.

Orlando told us the country opened up on the opposite side of the mountain and that there were settlements, including his own family village. He said there would be no difficulty doing an airdrop there and he would organize the villagers to help us carry everything to our camp.

With that worry over, I settled down to enjoy the walk through a primeval forest of gigantic trees, where black and white samango monkeys looked down on us and big hornbills with huge, yellow beaks flew away braying like donkeys.

It took two and a half days to reach the mountain.

One of the big advantages we had when operating in Mozambique was that neither Frelimo nor ZANU had aircraft. If they'd had helicopters they could have made life fairly difficult for us, but they didn't and as a result they had to move by road and, to a lesser extent, by rail. That made them vulnerable and we'd amply demonstrate that to them in the months ahead.

For the moment, it meant I could safely locate our base camp out in open country, away from the rainforest, where it was drier, lighter and where there were fewer mosquitoes. We were in a malaria zone and every morning Fish dosed us up on prophylactics and made sure we applied plenty of repellent.

Orlando and Phillip lost no time in making contact with the local population living in scattered villages on the eastern side of Sitatonga. They reported the locals were happy to see them and were willing to help as best as they could.

On the third day, I asked them to bring in as many locals as possible because I'd organized an airdrop for that afternoon.

We got a good response and between thirty and forty local men and women with several children sat in the shade, waiting expectantly. It would be a new experience for all of them. The children especially were excited and kept running off to look for the plane they had been told was coming.

'Sierra One Seven, this is Charlie Three. Do you read me? Over.'

I turned up the volume of the VHF set so everybody could hear.

'Greetings, Charlie Three, reading you strength five,' I replied. 'We'll mark the drop zone with orange smoke. There is no wind to speak of and, if possible, a south to north run would suit us. We are all well clear of the DZ on the western side.'

The pilot acknowledged and we soon heard the characteristic rumble of the big rotary engines as the aircraft closed in on us.

There were shouts of delight from the locals and the Renamo men as the white parachutes opened and four pallets loaded with supplies floated gently down towards us.

In return for their help in carrying everything to our campsite, we gave the locals some gardening tools, a small, red transistor radio that we tuned to the Voice of Free Africa, and some army rations. Orlando explained how we were going to make communal gardens, which we expected them to look after while we were away fighting Frelimo. It was plain to see they were happy with this arrangement.

I put Nelson in charge of making the gardens with the locals. Jonny and a couple of Orlando's men helped me build our camp and the training areas.

I sent Fish with Orlando to scout as far as the settlement of Dombe, about thirty kilometres away to the east where Orlando's family lived. Karate and Phillip would go south to recce the sparsely populated area along the Buzi River.

In the weeks that followed the recruits began to flow in, aided in no small way by Fish and his medical bag.

As Orlando's group moved towards Dombe and his tribal home, they stopped at the villages of the local headmen, telling them of their mission to oust Frelimo. They would give them one of the little red radios, tuned, of course, to the Voice of Free Africa. And Fish would be introduced as a doctor: if any of the local community were sick or injured they were told Fish could fix them.

As word spread, Fish was constantly at work. Health care was something new to this remote part of Africa. He treated all sorts of ailments and injuries, including removing a broken knife blade embedded in the neck of a middle-aged woman.

There were many cases where he could not diagnose the problem, but he had a good supply of aspirin; remarkably, a tablet and a pat on the head usually did the trick.

I hadn't realized how effective this medical service would be in winning the hearts and minds of the locals. I asked for the news to be passed on to Rex, and ordered a good supply of the items Fish had listed for our next resupply airdrop.

Meanwhile, south towards the Buzi River, Karate and Phillip had news that really got me buzzing.

They too had been welcomed by the locals. They had established a base camp on the Buzi River and already had several volunteers as new recruits. I'd told them about Fish's success with his medical bag and Karate did his best to copy that. He would never be as good a medic as Fish, but his efforts were equally well received.

Using the local knowledge of the new recruits, they patrolled south-east from the Buzi and eventually reached national grid power lines. The trees had been cleared for twenty metres on either side and a vehicle track ran beneath the pylons. It would be used for inspections and maintenance by the power company engineers.

'Mick, I couldn't believe our luck,' said Karate when discussing it later. 'There were no recent vehicle tracks, but the locals told us it was used occasionally. They said the power lines crossed the road to Espungabera, well south of us, and the vehicles came up the track from the road and went as far as the Buzi River.

'Then, just as they were telling us this, we suddenly heard the sound of a vehicle approaching. There wasn't any cover to speak of, but we were concealed in a dip where a dry stream bed crossed the power lines. I had a quick look and could see a white 4 x 4. It obviously wasn't Frelimo so Phillip and I stood in the middle of the track with the others alongside. I told them not to shoot unless I did.

'The vehicle was going slowly, but they braked hard when they came over the rise and saw the AKs pointing at them.

'Phillip shouted at them, telling them to stop or they would be killed, and they did. There were three of them wearing blue overalls and white hard hats. They got out of the vehicle with their hands in the air.

'They were all scared stiff, but one of them shouted something. Phillip responded by opening fire. The others followed suit.

'After the shooting, Phillip ordered the men to drag the bodies away, well off the track. They returned with their boots, overalls and three white hard hats.

'He told me the man had said they worked for the power company, and that Frelimo were their friends. It was a bad mistake and the poor bastards ended up dead. I asked Phillip if he had thought about taking them as recruits. He shook his head and said they would have betrayed us to Frelimo.

'And then, Mick, I suddenly realized we had wheels!'

The vehicle could not have been better for us. It was a white Toyota Trooper; a tough 4 x 4 with a powerful diesel engine and low-ratio gearing. It could go just about anywhere. It had two spare wheels, the second secured to a sturdy roof rack alongside an aluminium ladder.

Karate drove it back to their camp on the Buzi then was guided along footpaths that eventually led him to our camp at Sitatonga Mountain.

I added two forty-four gallon drums of diesel and a handpump to my next airdrop request.

The Toyota solved a problem that had been worrying me increasingly since our occupation of the Sitatonga Mountain area. We were getting excellent support from the locals, but it soon became apparent that any meaningful Frelimo targets were a long way from where we were.

In a way that was good for us, but to go on the offensive meant we would have to travel long distances on foot and that would take a lot of time and create logistical problems. Added to that, the closer we moved towards the coast the more settled and open the country became. We would be exposed.

But with wheels, we could drive to within striking range of our targets then escape quickly back into the vastness of Africa. If I was careful with my target selection, there would be nothing to suggest we were operating from the Sitatonga area.

These were the advantages I needed to really kick-start this revolution against Frelimo.

I spread the maps out on top of a table made from one of the airdrop pallets.

The first thing that caught my eye was a road that ran through Dombo, where I'd sent Orlando and Fish. It went all the way up to Chimoio on the main Umtali to Beira road, about 140 kilometres away. But about halfway there was a branch road that initially tracked west towards the Rhodesian border before swinging due north towards the Chicamba Hydro Dam.

Perfect!

A couple of years earlier, I had done a recce of this dam. We knew it provided power to the regional towns of the Manica province as well as the port of Beira. As such, it was strategically important to Frelimo and thus an obvious SAS target. But it was well defended by a Frelimo battalion with Russian tanks, and for some reason there were political sensitivities, so we were never given the go-ahead to make mischief.

But things were different now. This would be a Renamo initiative. They didn't care about political sensitivities. Doing serious damage to the facility would be regarded by them as a great start to their campaign, especially since they'd also get a fair crack at Frelimo in the process.

My attention turned again to the road between Dombo and Chimoio, and this time I looked at side roads that ran east towards the coast. One, I noticed, crossed the Buzi River then continued north-east where it met the main Umtali to Beira highway at a bridge that crossed the Pungwe.

We knew a thing or two about destroying bridges, and if we dropped the Pungwe River Bridge, it would cut communication to and from the coast. I was unsure about doing the same to the bridge over the Buzi because that could attract attention to our base location. I knew that sooner or later

Frelimo would find out where we were, but the longer I could delay that the better it would be for the Renamo recruitment campaign.

I called over Nelson and Orlando.

As Nelson explained things, Orlando shook his head.

'There is no bridge across the Buzi River,' he said. 'People and vehicles cross on a ferry boat.'

'A ferry? What is this boat like, Orlando?' I asked. He described a typical car ferry with ramps at each end and a high, narrow bridge for the skipper on one side of the vessel.

A light bulb in my brain flashed on.

We had wheels and we could also have a boat. We could control the Buzi River crossing without having to destroy anything or attract attention to ourselves, and dropping the Pungwe River Bridge had just got a whole lot easier.

We'd take a team in the Toyota across on the ferry and drive up to within striking distance of the bridge. We'd use timing devices to initiate the explosives; we would be well clear of the area when the charges blew.

There was another flash of the light bulb.

Once the Toyota was safely back on the south side of the Buzi River, we'd use the ferry to take us downstream.

The Buzi and Pungwe rivers met and flowed into the sea opposite the Port of Beira. Separating the two rivers where they met was a mangrove island.

Hidden behind the mangroves, we could fire our 81-millimetre mortars from the deck of the ferry and give the port and the Frelimo garrison there a fair old pounding. We would do this at night and, while they were licking their wounds and wondering what was happening, we would quietly sail back up the Buzi to the ferry crossing.

Night one, we'd cut power from Chicamba.

Night two, we'd drop the Pungwe Bridge.

Night four, we'd launch the mortar attack on Beira.

With Rex up to similar mischief to the north of us, Frelimo would be bewildered and dazed.

I'd get the CIO to up the propaganda broadcasts after the raids. *The Voice of the Hyena* would be heard across Mozambique.

Renamo was alive and in action.

Frelimo beware!

The Antbears Strike

Midway through our seventh week out in Mozambique, I sent a signal to the brigadier requesting we be taken out for some R and R, and a debriefing ahead of the offensive action. We were picked up by helicopter two days later, leaving Renamo to get on with recruitment and training during the ten days we were to be away.

The request was prompted by me wanting to make some changes to the teams, and to assemble the explosives and accessories we would use to down the bridges. I also realized that the brigadier and Ken Flower would be itching to get first-hand detailed reports of how it was all going.

'Rex, I'm sorry,' I said, 'but I'm going to take Mack away from you. I've got a Land Cruiser and a ferry boat with diesel engines, and I need Mack to keep them going for us. In exchange I have asked for Andy Johnson to join you. He's a class act, as you know, and on a par with Fish as a medic. Fish's medical expertise with the local population has been a huge advantage to us, and Andy will do the same for you around Gorongoza. Not only that, but we are about to go into action and there will be casualties. You need a medic.'

'No problem, Mick,' said Rex, and laughing added, 'the only thing that pisses me off is that you've got a Land Cruiser and I haven't.'

'But you'll be working on that, no doubt?'

'You bet,' he said.

Through the next two days, Rex and I went over progress with the brigadier and Ken Flower. At the start there were just thirty-one Renamo. We now had well over two hundred and the recruits kept coming in. We were well received by the locals, and a combination of our activity and the Voice of Free Africa meant we were winning the hearts-and-minds battle.

The rest of the boys, meanwhile, were busy preparing weapons and equipment for our return journey. Karate picked out a Russian 82-millimetre recoilless rifle. It was heavy, but we had the Toyota. Both teams took two 81-millimetre mortar tubes. We put them aside with the shells, bombs and explosives that would be airdropped in to us on our return.

On day three, we left the SAS for seven days of living in jeans and tee shirts and without rifles.

As good as it was to have R and R, by the end of the break we were all excited at the prospect of getting back and starting the action. We had, inevitably, grown close to the Renamo teams we were with. The teacher-classroom relationship was still there, but the class was getting better and more confident all the time.

On our return, Rex and I called a meeting with everyone in our respective groups. We explained that we had reported on the progress of Renamo. We told them the CIO was happy with what had been achieved, but that we had to keep up the recruiting and spread our influence in Mozambique. If Renamo could do that the weapons and supplies would keep coming.

We also explained that we had arranged for some new weapons to help us with the first attacks against Frelimo, and explosives to blow up the bridges.

The weapons and supplies arrived the following day, and the next three days were spent on mortar training. Karate took over the recoilless rifle. He'd use it against Frelimo at Chicamba. We needed his skill to ensure we hit the target with the first one or two rounds before the heavily armed battalion guarding the power station could retaliate.

Karate had picked three Renamo to work with him. After this opening attack, they would take over the weapon for use on future operations.

On day four, Rex's teams began their long marches to the south and east but, as was often the case in the military, things didn't go exactly to plan.

Afonso's Renamo group with Andy Johnson made their way into the Gorongoza game reserve. It wasn't long before they bumped into four national parks' staff, working on a windmill water pump. Afonso explained who they were and what they were doing, and couldn't believe his luck when the game rangers offered to drive them across the park in their three-tonne truck.

The game rangers dropped them off next to a river bed and told them to follow it upstream. So instead of walking for four days, they reached the road where they were to ambush Frelimo early on day two of the operation.

The location could not have been better.

There was no shortage of water, granite outcrops with thick tree cover right up to the edge of the gravel road. A lookout on top of one of the granite outcrops would be able to see the road for some distance on either side of the ambush party. They could give early warning of a likely target coming from either direction.

Afonso and Andy climbed the outcrop to survey the general area, then dropped down onto the road itself. The two of them came up with an innovative ambush plan that would be easy for the men and covered both possible approaches.

They chose a sharp corner in the road as it twisted between the granite outcrops as the place where they would initiate the ambush. Andy concealed two ten-kilogram slabs of plastic explosive against the side of a granite boulder, no more than five metres from the road edge. He attached a length of Cordtex detonating cord to each slab and ran the line behind the boulder where he taped on an electrical detonator. He connected the detonator leads to two thin, black wires on a reel then ran out the cable to their position in cover just over 100 metres away.

On top of the outcrop, two men would keep constant watch and would have a radio to speak to Afonso if something was seen. Close to them would be four men, two armed with RPG bazookas and two carrying RPD machine guns. The rest of the men would be with Andy and Afonso in their shaded cover next to the road.

The idea was that if a target came along, Andy would initiate the ambush by blowing the plastic explosive as the vehicle reached the corner. The bazookas and machine guns would fire down onto the target from above. The men led by Afonso would engage the target at close range from the edge of the road.

Everything was set up and all they had to do then was to wait. Andy had stretched out and was starting to nod off when the radio came to life.

'Frelimo!' Afonso shouted. 'A truck and a van coming from the south!'

Everybody buckled up their web belts, grabbed their weapons then hurried into position. They were well hidden in the cover of the boulders and grass as the two vehicles approached.

Andy risked a look. The lead vehicle was a green, three-tonne truck with about twenty armed Frelimo troops on the back. The second vehicle he recognised as a VW Combi – dark blue with a white roof. Was the truck an escort for VIPs in the Combi, he wondered?

The truck slowed right down to negotiate the sharp bend. He touched the battery terminal with the wire and the charges blew.

Packed against a solid granite boulder, the massive blast power of twenty kilos of plastic explosive was directed outwards towards the truck just five metres away.

Exposed as they were on the open back the Frelimo troops had no chance.

They were blown off and scattered like leaves in an autumn gale. The truck lifted with the blast, the glass windows shattered and the front passenger door was blown in. The truck rolled over onto its side, landing on top of bodies lying on the roadside.

The explosion blew apart the fuel tank. Diesel dripped everywhere but didn't ignite. A pungent smell of death and hydrocarbons already filled the air as the Renamo rebels opened fire.

With the destruction of the truck, most of the Renamo fire was directed at the VW Combi just twenty metres behind. Rockets and machine-gun fire poured down from above, while Afonso and his assault team riddled the vehicle with gunfire at short range from the roadside. Somebody lobbed a white phosphorous grenade onto the truck and the diesel ignited. Flames and thick black smoke billowed into the air.

It was ruthless and devastating. In the excitement of the moment, the Renamo rebels didn't want to stop. Andy and Afonso had to intervene to stop them using up all their ammunition.

Once the firing stopped, they went onto the road for a close look at the damage.

Inside the VW Combi four bodies were slumped over the blood-spattered seats. The driver and companion in the front were African Frelimo. To our amazement, the two bodies in the back were white European. Both were in military uniforms and we recognized the emblems on the shirtsleeves. They were East German military advisors.

The SAS had taken the Russians out of the game in Zimbabwe with the destruction of the ZAPU armoured advance. The two dead Germans suggested they were now courting Samora Machel, in Mozambique.

Had Machel turned his back on his original supporters from China, we wondered? And if so why?

Afonso and Andy managed to collect a quantity of ammunition from the ambush victims and the odd undamaged weapon. The ammunition was important because several of the Renamo team were down to their last few rounds. This would be a recurring problem with all the Renamo teams. Once they started firing, it was well-nigh impossible to get them to stop.

Afonso had inflicted a stunning blow on Frelimo and their allies, but he hadn't forgotten the wisdom of Mao's doctrine as the group disappeared back into the depths of the Gorongoza National Park: *Best to keep moving. Stretch the enemy resources to breaking point.*

Two days later, Simmo dropped the bridge over the Pungwe River, on the southern approach to the Gorongoza area, and a day after that Rex dropped a bridge over a deep ravine that cut the road coming in from the west.

With these two approaches blocked, Frelimo could only reach the Gorongoza area in two ways. They could either come in on foot or they could use a road from Inhaminga to the east; but by this time Commander Andre and his party had finally reached the outskirts of the settlement and were intent on making that as difficult as possible.

Andre didn't waste any time. On the first night, he sent Horse and a group south to mine the railway where it crossed the road, while he and Pig Dog with three others walked into the settlement to have a look at the Frelimo garrison and the nearby political jail.

Both had barrier arms across the access roads that were each manned by two guards.

The prison consisted of a chain mesh perimeter fence about three metres high with hinged double gates opposite the roadblock. Another two Frelimo sat on wooden stools guarding the entrance.

There was an old brick house in the centre that was obviously the HQ. It was surrounded by numerous low, thatched shelters presumably housing prisoners. Armed guards patrolled the perimeter. They estimated there were ten to twelve guards in all.

The garrison had no perimeter fence, but a sandbagged pillbox with a machine gun protected the entrance to the collection of low, brick buildings with rusting corrugated iron roofing.

A white Isuzu truck was parked at the back and, off to one side, Pig Dog spotted another defensive position with the familiar sight of a 14.5-millimetre KPV gun barrel protruding above the sandbagged wall. It looked like Frelimo had a platoon based there along with a dozen or so others who would run the camp.

Under cover of darkness, Andre and Pig Dog worked out what they would do.

'Andre, we should attack just after dark when they will be having their evening meal,' said Pig Dog. 'In the dark they can't see us and after the attack we will have the whole night to get well away from this place.

'We have brought the two mortar tubes so it makes sense for us to use them against the garrison. To get an accurate range, we'll pace out the distance from the edge of the garrison to a suitable baseplate position about 800 metres away.

'I'll take one radio for the attacking group and we'll leave another with the mortar team so I can control the mortar fire. When you are ready and in place outside the prison, let me know on your radio and I'll tell the mortar group to open fire. As we hear them firing, we'll both start our attacks by killing the guards at the road barriers.'

Andre nodded in agreement.

At 1850 hours the following night, Commander Andre alerted Pig Dog he was in position and ready.

The mortar group commenced proceedings by firing off one bomb from each of the two tubes.

On hearing the mortars, Pig Dog opened fire on the two guards at the roadblock while the rest of his group fired at men they could see walking around the camp.

The pillbox machine gun at the entrance fired wildly in their general direction, but Pig Dog had sent two men off to one side, out of view of the front-facing gun position. He watched as the shadowy forms crept forward and lobbed two grenades into the back of the pillbox then fled in the direction they'd come as they exploded.

The pillbox fell silent.

The first mortar shell landed close to the KPV position and the second ten metres further away. Pig Dog gave the corrections over the radio and another two bombs were fired.

'*Crump! Crump!*' They exploded in the centre of the camp.

'On target. Rapid fire!' shouted Pig Dog, and the mortar group responded with another four bombs from each tube. The Frelimo camp erupted as the high explosive rained down. Two of the buildings were hit. Men were running to escape the bombing and ground fire.

'Hold your fire!' Pig Dog ordered. As the mortars fell silent, he led his attack team into the camp. As they approached a building they lobbed in grenades then sprayed rifle fire through the windows and doors.

A few Frelimo managed to escape but many were stunned and in shock: easy meat for the Renamo men, as they ran through the garrison firing wildly at anything resembling a target.

Pig Dog eventually got them to stop shooting and organized teams to search the garrison.

The KPV had not been fired during the attack and it sat undamaged behind the low wall of sandbags. Better still, the white truck parked at the back of the camp was intact, albeit pockmarked from shrapnel strikes and the windscreen smashed. Pig Dog checked the tyres then climbed into the cab and turned the ignition key. The exhaust belched a cloud of black diesel smoke as the engine burst into life.

Now they could drive back to Gorongoza.

Meanwhile, Commander Andre was poised outside the prison, hidden in a roadside ditch. Two RPD machine-gunners had the front bipods down and lay behind their weapons that pointed at the guards and prison gate.

On his radio Andre heard Pig Dog give the order for the mortar group to fire. As Pig Dog initiated the garrison attack, Andre's gunners opened fire.

Leading the attack, Andre charged past the gate guards, now sprawled on the ground and covered in blood. He pushed open the gates then dropped to the ground as his bazooka team darted past and took aim at the house just twenty metres away.

One rocket went through the open front door and exploded inside the building. Another smashed through the flimsy brickwork leaving a wide hole in the wall.

As they were reloading to fire again, a voice shouted from within the house. 'Stop! We surrender. Do not kill us. We surrender.'

Andre stood up and shouted back. Ordering them to come out of the house slowly with their hands in the air and warning they would be shot if they did not follow his instructions.

Six prison guards slowly appeared and stood in front of them.

'Tell your comrades who are patrolling this prison to drop their weapons and come forward to join you in surrendering to Renamo,' Andre ordered.

One of the men turned and shouted into the camp area. Out of the gloom the patrolling prison guards appeared with their hands held high.

The prisoners were rounded up and assembled in front of the house. Andre addressed them all, telling them of Renamo and how they would now be part of the second war of liberation in Mozambique. And he told them that as Renamo soldiers they would be properly trained, equipped and paid.

Walking in front of the prison guards, he ordered them to stand up and face the prisoners.

'We will take these guards into Renamo, as well, but first I want to know about these men. Did any of these guards standing here treat you badly?' he asked.

The guards hung their heads, staring at the ground and praying they would not be named.

There was murmuring amongst the prisoners then one of them stood up and pointed at one of the bigger guards. 'This man demanded indecent acts. When we refused we were taken away, tied up and beaten.'

Andre didn't say anything. He took the man's arm and led him away. There was a short burst of AK fire.

The men looted the prison then burnt it to the ground.

Pig Dog, meanwhile, had loaded the 14.5-millimetre KPV and a half-full drum of diesel with a handpump onto the back of the white Isuzu, along with arms, ammunition and tinned food they had salvaged from the camp. He ordered the mortar team to stay where they were and on alert, then he radioed Andre that he would meet him outside the prison.

There were forty-two men in Andre's group, and now they had an additional ten prison guards and forty-seven prisoners. With the SAS team there were now over one hundred men to move away and disappear into the bush.

'Andre, we have been lucky to get the Frelimo truck to use to get us well away from this place,' said Pig Dog, 'but now there are too many men for one load. We will have to make two trips.

'About thirty kilometres south there is a road that branches off towards Gorongoza. I will take half the men now and drop them off at a place along that road. I will then come back to collect the others. My suggestion is you stay to look after the situation here until I get back.'

Pig Dog looked at his watch. 'It will take me about two hours to get back here,' he said.

Carrying half of Andre's team and half of the new recruits, the overladen truck lumbered along slowly. On the outskirts of Inhaminga, they picked up Horse and the group that had laid the mines on the railway line.

By midnight, all one hundred men were on the Gorongoza road, some forty-five kilometres away from Inhaminga.

Pig Dog had been considering the situation. 'Andre,' he said. 'With all these new recruits, you will be short of food and you don't have enough weapons for them. My suggestion is you select twenty to go with you now. Horse and I will take the rest in the truck tonight to Rex. They can be trained at Gorongoza. Twenty can then go with Afonso and we will bring ten back to join you.

'Meet us here in ten days' time. We'll also bring you more supplies and ammunition.'

Andre's white teeth flashed in his dark beard as he smiled at Pig Dog.

'We learn much from the SAS,' he said, and patted Pig Dog on the shoulder. 'I'll have twenty men here to meet you in ten days.'

Pig Dog and Horse took the Isuzu east towards Gorongoza while Andre and his merry men disappeared into the bush, heading north towards his base camp, two days' walk away.

The afternoon after the attacks at Inhaminga, an empty freight train en route to Beira detonated the two TMH46 mines Horse and his team had laid on the track. The train was derailed, the weight and momentum of the locomotive carrying it across the road where it came to rest at an angle in a roadside ditch, the carriages concertinaed and twisted mass behind the engine.

The road and rail links to the northern provinces of Mozambique were well and truly blocked.

The Gorongoza antbears had struck with devastating effect and Commander Andre had doubled his forces. Better still, and largely because of the SAS planning, he was yet to suffer a casualty.

And while all this was going on, we were just as busy in the southern Sitatonga area.

First up, I decided we'd do a hit-and-run raid on the heavily defended power station at Chicamba.

It was a long way north of our base area, but with the vehicle we could reach such places without any serious risk of compromising our home location.

We strapped the recoilless rifle and a mortar to the roof rack on the Toyota. Karate did the driving while I tried to do the map reading from the front seat next to him. Orlando and six Renamo squashed into the back amongst the boxes of mortar bombs and shells for the gun.

I gambled that nobody would be on the road after dark – and that proved to be the case. When I reckoned we were within ten kilometres of the target, I picked a spot where we could drive off the road and into cover.

We had had a camo net included in the last resupply drop and had also daubed the white Toyota with blotches of brown and green paint. Paint jobs didn't get any rougher, but that and the net made the vehicle a lot less visible.

We bedded down for the night.

Next morning, I took out a recce party with Karate, Orlando and one of the Renamo team. In daylight I could work out where we were and I wasn't unhappy to find we were just over twelve kilometres away from the target.

Again, I pushed my luck by walking on the road. It was quicker and easier, and we reached the hydro dam without incident just over three hours later.

We moved off the road and climbed a low ridge that would give us cover as we closed in on the target. I picked a spot with a good view when we were still a safe 800 metres away and took out my binoculars.

Immediately below us was the road that wound its way around the western side of the hydro dam, heading north towards the road between Umtali and Chimoio. Across the road the ground was undulating with scattered woodland up to the lake edge.

A finger of land jutted out into the lake, pointing at the switchyard of the hydro station less than 200 metres away across open water. Behind the switchyard and the adjacent dam wall was the Frelimo battalion.

There were five sandbagged heavy machine gun positions on the perimeter around the encampment and power station. Three Russian T54 tanks were positioned in the centre amongst three or four trucks.

Portacom-style accommodation housed most of the troops, and I could see several of them patrolling the grounds and guarding the entrance to the power station.

As formidable as all this was, the metres of open water gave us security. There was no quick and easy way to reach us. By road it would take half a day.

I decided that Karate and four men would take the recoilless rifle out to the lake edge. Their mission was to do as much damage to the switchyard as possible. We couldn't stop them generating electricity but we could prevent it from going anywhere.

I'd told Karate that I wanted him to try and hit one of several transformers attached to the power pylons inside the yard, and then to put a couple of shells into the adjacent switch room. Meanwhile I would get Orlando to take charge of the mortar.

When it was nearly dark, we would drive up the road and stop just below our observation point. Karate would head off to the lake edge with the gun while Orlando set up the mortar tube in the middle of the road.

I would climb back up the hill to control the mortar fire and monitor events. We all had VHF radios. When Karate was ready he'd initiate the attack with the gun, Orlando would start the mortar barrage and I'd control the fire from my hilltop position.

To give Karate a better chance of hitting a transformer, I'd given him two Icarus illuminating rockets. I told him to set himself up for firing then get one of the men to fire off the rockets when he was ready.

I told him I wanted a hit with the first round.

'No problem, Mick,' he said with his crooked-toothed grin. 'I'll get you two transformers.'

From my hilltop observation point I waited tensely, watching with my binoculars. Karate had called to say he would be starting the action in about five minutes.

Whoosh! *Whoosh*! The two illuminating rockets raced into the sky above the power station. Through my binoculars I could see action in the Frelimo camp. Men were running. One of the 14.5-millimetre KPVs then opened fire. I could see the tracer aimed at the parachute flares as they drifted over the power station.

Boom! The deep bass report as Karate fired the recoilless rifle.

There was an explosion and fire as a transformer took a direct hit. It was followed in an instant by an incredible fireworks display. Flashes, bangs and explosions spread through the switchyard as uncontrolled electricity shorted and arced between broken wires.

I heard the mortar fire and waited for the strike. I'd told Orlando to fire just one bomb and await my instructions. It wasn't a bad shot – good direction but it was short and landed in the switchyard where it too did damage.

'Add 100,' I ordered, 'and fire two rounds.'

Boom! Karate fired again and hit a second transformer.

Crump! *Crump*! The mortar was back in action and this time bang on target, the bombs landing in the centre of the Frelimo camp.

We had nine bombs left.

'Fire five bombs, Orlando, then adjust left 100 and fire off the remaining four.' He acknowledged my call and the bombs rained down on the camp.

Karate fired off his remaining rounds and advised he was packing up and returning to the vehicle.

I stayed in position and watched the deadly mortar strike. With the adjustment to the left, Orlando hit one of the KPV positions and it went silent, while the others continued firing at imagined targets somewhere in the sky. Two of the tanks moved away from the mortar strike and fired their main guns in my general direction. The rounds exploded into the hill slope ahead of me. Time to get out of there.

While the Renamo team loaded everything back into the Toyota, Karate and I had one last task. We had brought along two TMH46 landmines and we laid them carefully in the road 100 metres or so away. We brushed the gravel road with branches to hide the mines and our tracks.

Frelimo would undoubtedly investigate at some stage.

The Manica province of Mozambique and the port of Beira was plunged into darkness. Frelimo didn't know what to do and had no idea who was responsible.

And we had only just begun.

Two nights later, we drove north-east and destroyed the road and railway bridge over the Pungwe River, close to the major settlement of Dondo.

The following night, we motored down the Buzi River aboard the vehicle ferry. The ferry operator had willingly participated. We eventually reached open tidal water close to the confluence with the Pungwe. We turned the ferry into the slow current and tied up against a sturdy patch of mangroves.

We were opposite the Port of Beira, most of which was still in darkness. We knew a Frelimo base was located behind the port complex, so we set up the two mortar tubes we had stowed on the deck of the ferry and aimed at what we estimated would be the direction and range of the base.

Hidden behind the clump of mangroves, we fired twenty mortar rounds into the port complex and Frelimo camp. We adjusted the range and bearing slightly as we progressed to ensure a good spread of the mortars and thus, hopefully, do more damage.

To be honest, I wasn't optimistic about the amount of damage we would do, but it didn't really matter.

I remembered the brigadier playing golf with his friend on the course at Umtali when ZANU mortared the town. They didn't do any damage, but psychologically they were big winners. They put the fear of God into Umtali and, as a consequence, the army and police both had to commit to additional patrols in case there was a second strike.

We had done the same to Frelimo.

Stretch the enemy's resources to breaking point, said Chairman Mao.

This was another good way of doing just that.

With our mortar bombs fired, we sailed the ferry boat back up the Buzi to the river crossing point.

As we pulled up alongside the mooring, we thanked the ferry operator. We topped up his diesel tank from our own supply and gave him a big army ration pack and a transistor radio, tuned to the Voice of Free Africa. He was a happy man, who'd been part of an adventure he would never have dreamed of.

We jumped into the Land Cruiser and disappeared back into the bush.

The antbears had struck across a massive expanse of the country. They had done considerable damage and Frelimo were reeling.

While they licked their wounds, Rex and I sent Renamo teams further north and south. We had to spread the revolution we had started.

Rex had Afonso and Andre move up into the Tete province that straddled the Zambezi, while he held the original stronghold in Gorongoza. At the same time, I got Orlando to move south of the Buzi towards the Limpopo and the southern provinces of Mozambique.

Best to keep moving. Stretch the enemy's resources to breaking point.

And that's what we did.

The SAS with Renamo had started a civil war that was to last fourteen long years until a country that was bankrupt, broken and tired of fighting and killing, finally came to its senses and called it quits.

Along the way, Commander Andre Matsangaissa and Frelimo leader Samora Machel were killed.

Our questions about Russian involvement in Mozambique after killing the two East German advisors were soon answered. Machel had indeed been wooed by the Russians, who committed US$550 million in military aid.

That just served to prolong the agony and bring even more misery to the innocent people of Mozambique caught up in this Cold War-motivated struggle.

We pulled out of the conflict in 1980 as our regiment was disbanded, but not before we and the Rhodesian CIO had organized the South Africans to take over looking after Renamo.

With the limited resources we had, it was always going to be better for Renamo to have the backing of the South Africans, and that proved to be the case. They had bigger aircraft, ships and submarines to keep up the resupply missions, and the specially selected men from their Special Forces Recce Commando never allowed the standards Rex and I had set to be lowered.

The final triumph was at the first election in 1994, when Renamo presidential candidate Afonso Dhlakama won thirty-eight per cent of the votes and his party one hundred and twelve of the two hundred and fifty electoral seats.

Afonso warned Frelimo he would have no hesitation in returning to arms if democratic processes were not followed.

Renamo thus became known as the moderating power in the political world of Mozambique, where some looked to emulate the excesses of Mugabe in Zimbabwe.

I met Afonso some years later after visiting my ageing parents who had stayed on in Zimbabwe. It was a special meeting we both enjoyed immensely. Two old comrades reunited after many years.

As I left his office, he called my name. I turned around as he walked towards me, hand uplifted in a high-five gesture.

'*Sambani!*' he shouted as our hands came together.

'*Sambani! Sambani!*' we both cried out.

Epilogue

Californian-born Bob McKenzie joined the US Army and wanted to be a paratrooper. After trials and vigorous physical testing, he was admitted into the 101st Airborne – the famous 'Screaming Eagles'.

The 101st Airborne Division is an elite unit in the United States Army, trained for air assault operations. It is regarded as the most potent and tactically mobile of the US Army's divisions, and became famous in the Second World War for its role in Operation Overlord, launched on 6 June 1944 with the Normandy landings, and then at the Battle of the Bulge in Belgium.

In Bob's time – 1965 to 1967 – they fought in Vietnam, in every area from the northern demilitarized zone all the way down to the central highlands.

They were called the 'Chicken Men' by the North Vietnamese, their interpretation of the 101st insignia, not understanding that it was a bald eagle. They were greatly feared, but they didn't always win the fights.

Bob's patrol walked into a Vietcong ambush. The Vietcong had captured American M16s and used them in the ambush.

A round from the ultra-high velocity carbine hit him in the hip where the bullet disintegrated, as it was designed to do. A big lump of the bullet was deflected vertically up off the hip bone. It flew out of Bob's body and blew off most of the bicep muscle on his right arm. It hit the arm bone and deflected again, travelling through the shoulder before finally lodging against the broad mass of the scapula – the shoulder blade.

A smaller lump of bullet travelled south, bouncing off the pelvis and exiting the body in the upper thigh region.

That's got to be one of the harder ways of earning the Purple Heart.

Bob was choppered out of the combat zone and eventually evacuated back to the United States where he spent the next year in a military hospital.

Once he had recovered, Bob was soon back in training. He may have been badly wounded but there was still plenty of fight left in the man and he was determined to rejoin his famous regiment.

But it wasn't to be.

The medical board believed his right arm had been too badly damaged and reduced for him to be declared fit enough for parachuting and combat. They offered him an open college scholarship. He could do whatever he wanted and it didn't matter how long the studies took – the military would pay for it.

Bob didn't want to go to college. He wanted to get back into the army.

He'd met a girl from Africa whose brother was in C Squadron SAS. He knew the SAS by reputation and hoped his background with 101st Airborne would at least get him a shot at their selection course.

I'd injured my back and after an operation my own recuperation took a full year. Our SAS training officer had been posted to a staff job and we were short of officers, so it suited everyone for me to take over that position while I recovered.

I remember Bob coming into my office and telling me his story.

I liked the guy from the outset. He was about my age and the same sort of size and build; he wasn't carrying an ounce of fat. He was articulate and confident, but polite and respectful with it. Just what you'd expect from a 101st Airborne veteran.

'Bob,' I said, 'we have several men who joined us from the British Parachute Regiment; without exception they have been outstanding. They had no problem adapting to our ways and we have learned things from them as well. You are from the USA equivalent and from what you have told me I have no doubt you too would make your mark here like they have done.

'But there is one issue neither of us can ignore. You took a hell of a knock in Vietnam and it looks like you have recovered well, but you haven't been physically tested since then.'

Bob nodded and I could see apprehension in his eyes.

'Relax, Bob. You have made the effort to come all this way, so I'm not going to turn you away without offering you a chance to physically prove yourself. We have a selection course starting in ten days and I'll put your name down for that.

'The selection course will be your first serious test,' I continued, 'and I have a feeling you will breeze through it. However, you don't get into the SAS until you have passed all our training courses, including parachute training.

'And that's the bit I'm worried about. No issue with the parachuting – you are already a veteran – the big question is whether your damaged right arm